More Prai...

ADDICTION-PROOF YOUR CHILD

"Dr. Peele offers **a smart, readable, commonsense guide for parents** concerned about their children's drug and alcohol use. Persuasively rebutting the alarmist view advanced by the 'experts,' **he shows the importance of reinforcing children's independence, promoting constructive values, and fostering the ability to learn from mistakes.** He also shows how to teach youth to recognize the risks in overusing substances and suggests safeguards for the small minority who are at greatest risk for addiction."

—**AARON T. BECK**, professor of psychiatry, University of Pennsylvania, founder of Cognitive Behavioral Therapy, and winner of the 2006 Lasker Award

"Although you may not agree with every argument in this sure-to-be-controversial book, it should be **required reading for every concerned and thinking parent in America. Packed with practical advice and deep wisdom, it shatters one myth after the next.** Despite what the prevention industry tells us, drugs and alcohol are *not* equal-opportunity destroyers: they are far less likely to ensnare teens who have adopted adult values, discipline, and a sense of purpose. In detail, Peele tells parents how to help their kids develop these strengths. **Jargon-free, intelligent, and humane, this book easily doubles as an excellent primer on parenting.**"

—**SALLY SATEL, M.D.**, coauthor of *One Nation Under Therapy* and author of *PC, M.D.: How Political Correctness Is Corrupting Medicine*

"In this remarkable book, leading addiction expert Stanton Peele writes that much of what we will read in *Addiction-Proof Your Child* is 'common sense—or *would* be common sense if not for the misguided programs and policies that tell us to forsake the wisdom passed down through the ages.' These are words of wisdom, and **each concise chapter is indeed packed with clear, commonsense advice backed up by decades of scientific findings and Dr. Peele's own keen psychotherapeutic know-how. Dr. Peele convincingly dispels myth after alarmist myth about addiction and replaces them with sound strategies to create a 'Non-Addicted America' for our children and ourselves.**"

—**BARBARA S. HELD, Ph.D.**, Barry N. Wish professor of psychology, Bowdoin College, and author of *Stop Smiling, Start Kvetching*

"Dr. Peele presents a succinct, incisive critique of common myths about addiction and treatment. His practical approach to the struggles we all experience emphasizes personal responsibility and a focus on values. Peele's gift for storytelling makes this a highly readable page-turner, and **his examples have a genuineness and warmth that explains why he is a therapist in such high demand.** The book **trains readers to become better, more thoughtful, more empowering role models whether their children use drugs or not.** His anecdotes and explanations show empathy for parents, clients, and teens that no other book on this topic can touch."

—MITCH EARLEYWINE, Ph.D., author of *Understanding Marijuana*

"**A clear and compelling prescription for preventing addictive behaviors through the power of the parent-child relationship.** Dr. Peele begins by asking the obvious but not necessarily politically correct question of what does a child need to know, believe, and experience in order to develop a healthy relationship to alcohol and other psychoactive substances? His answer to this question is both illuminating and controversial. Moreover, it is an answer that is **skillfully reasoned, eminently readable, and solidly consonant with scientific opinion.** *Addiction-Proof Your Child* **will prove to be an invaluable resource to both parents and professionals.**"

—McWELLING TODMAN, Ph.D., director, Mental Health and Substance Abuse Counseling Program at the New School for Social Research

"This book was a page-turner for me. **I'm an addiction psychologist, but I read it as a father.** Fortunately, Dr. Peele is as supportive of parents as he is of children. **If our society shifted to the commonsense approach he so clearly presents, we would have a substantially better place to live:** the serious consequences of addictive behavior would be substantially reduced. Until then, while we advocate for change, at least we can protect our own families."

—TOM HORVATH, Ph.D., ABPP, president, Practical Recovery Services; president, SMART Recovery; past president, American Psychological Association Division on Addictions

"Sure to be controversial, this lucidly written guide is **a must-read for parents** who want honest, research-based information on the best ways to help their children avoid drug and alcohol problems."

—MAIA SZALAVITZ, coauthor, with Bruce Perry, of *The Boy Who Was Raised as a Dog*, and senior fellow at media watchdog group STATS

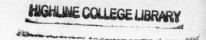

STANTON PEELE, Ph.D., J.D.

ADDICTION-PROOF YOUR CHILD

*A Realistic Approach to Preventing Drug,
Alcohol, and Other Dependencies*

THREE RIVERS PRESS • NEW YORK

www.crownpublishing.com

THREE RIVERS PRESS and the Tugboat design are registered
trademarks of Random House, Inc.

Library of Congress Cataloging-in-Publication Data
Peele, Stanton
Addiction-proof your child : a realistic approach to preventing drug,
alcohol, and other dependencies / Stanton Peele.—1st ed.
p. cm.
Includes bibliographical references and index.
1. Teenagers—Substance use—Prevention. 2. Children—Substance use—
Prevention. 3. Teenagers—Drug use—Prevention. 4. Children—
Drug use—Prevention. 5. Substance abuse—Prevention.
6. Drug abuse—Prevention. 7. Child rearing. 8. Parenting. I. Title.
HV4999.Y68P44 2007 362.29'17—dc22 2006102627

ISBN 978-0-307-23757-6

Printed in the United States of America

Design by M. Kristen Bearse

10 9 8 7 6 5 4 3 2 1
First Edition

To Anna Peele, my addiction-proof child

CONTENTS

ADDICTION-PROOF YOUR CHILD

INTRODUCTION

Although we live in a world where children have unprecedented opportunities and resources, parents are preoccupied with the dangers that can befall them. Suppose you learn that your teenager sometimes goes to drinking parties or, worse, is skipping school to smoke marijuana at a friend's house. What if your college-age youngster was taken to an emergency room after a night of drinking or has incurred large gambling debts? How should you react if children are prescribed powerful psychiatric medications, or if they spend all their time playing video games? How do you prepare adolescents to go off to college, where students engage in massive binge drinking as well as trading pharmaceuticals to help them study, sleep, and party?

I understand these and other concerns you have. But this book is different from any other you will read about adolescent substance use. I believe that the way we talk about drugs in this country is broken and that current approaches will make youthful drinking, drug use, and other dependencies even bigger problems in the years to come. The information I share with you can instead prevent your children from developing substance problems or addictions of any kind. But to accomplish this, you will have to disregard most of what you and your kids are told about substance use.

Despite the very real dangers for your kids in a world where drug use and drinking are commonplace, parents don't need to cower in fear. In place of the standard scare stories, *Addiction-Proof Your*

Child presents the reality of kids' substance use. For example, you will learn that not all youthful drug and alcohol use endangers children's lives and turns them into addicts. You need to be aware of this information in order to actually prevent your kids' substance use—which virtually all adolescents and young adults experience—from harming them.

What makes for successful parenting is old-fashioned and time-tested. In large part it requires you to let children live their own lives and make their own mistakes. You need to rely on your kids' intelligence and judgment as their primary means to handle their lives, even as you assist them by giving them crucial values.

Much of the information I present here is common sense—or *would* be common sense if not for the misguided programs and policies that tell us to forsake the wisdom passed down through the ages. Changing kids' brain chemistry, the experts tell us, will eventually solve addiction, along with the boot-camp treatment programs and just-say-no drug education that prevail now. Trust your gut instincts that this is nonsense. As I show you in the coming pages, a huge body of scientific data shows these policies are useless—and sometimes can be more harmful than doing nothing.

The hysteria over illegal drugs and alcohol often ignores the obvious fact that addiction is not limited to drugs. In fact, there are so many opportunities for children to be addicted—from food to electronics to prescription medications—that we can never eradicate them all. In many ways, typical American childhood experiences predispose children to addiction. Drug czar John Walters declared, based on adolescents' abuse of pharmaceuticals often found at home, "The drug dealer is us."

Your children do face substantial dangers. But if you don't arm your children with a sense of their independence and prepare them to manage their own lives, all the drug education classes and efforts to banish illicit substances will not reduce their risk. *You* are the key to inoculating your children against addictions of all sorts. No educator, physician, or public figure can do that job for you.

MY PERSPECTIVE

I am a sixty-year-old psychologist and the father of three children. More than thirty years ago, my book *Love and Addiction* ushered in a new era in thinking about addiction. In it I explained that addiction was not limited to drugs and alcohol—that it was much more prevalent and mainstream than people thought.

My view that addiction is not limited to opiates, or to drugs at all, is widely accepted today by both experts and ordinary people. Unfortunately, as a result, many people now view a host of other problems in the same mistaken way they think about heroin addiction—as irresistible, irreversible, inevitably deadly.

These ideas are connected to the belief that addiction is a disease. The disease approach, presented by recovering alcoholics and addicts, warns you that adolescents who drink or use marijuana will be unable to control their substance use. In the view of these "experts," any use places young people on their way to becoming addicts like them.

This isn't true. In the first place, adolescent drug use rarely leads to addiction. And addiction itself does not leave people powerless. Most people outgrow substance abuse—even serious addictions. Didn't you or someone close to you stop smoking—the hardest drug addiction of all to quit?

Well-meaning parents are often misled when it comes to deciding if their children's substance use is problematic and, if so, how to help them. In explaining this, I aim to counteract the insanity that says people should hear only the most pessimistic messages. On the contrary, you do the best for your children when you are most optimistic and confident. In line with this, the best way for your children to avoid or overcome addiction is for them to develop fully as human beings.

THREE VIEWS OF ADOLESCENT SUBSTANCE USE

The dominant—alarmist—view in America holds that children's substance use is horribly out of hand and aims for a future where no young people drink or take drugs. Since this state of nirvana has not yet been attained, then a fallback goal from this perspective is that youthful drug use be limited to high-risk children unlike your own—those who live on the wrong side of town.

American drug educators are virtually all of this alarmist school. It is impossible in the United States to acknowledge publicly that ordinary adolescents use drugs or drink and thrive anyhow. Nor is it possible for educators to discuss important research findings such as that moderate drinking reduces heart disease. The relentless message of school drug education, official proclamations about drugs, and statements by public figures is that all drug and alcohol use is bad and should be avoided by young people—that is, "just say no" or "zero tolerance." (Zero tolerance is the policy of suspending or expelling students who are found to use drugs or alcohol.)

The prevailing American view is that adolescents cannot manage—perhaps cannot even survive—using illicit substances. If young people actually use drugs and drink and turn out okay, this dirty secret should never be told. This position is patently absurd: two recent presidents admitted using drugs or drinking heavily, and these admissions do not begin to plumb the depth of public figures' substance use. Nor do they capture your and your friends' drug and alcohol use when you were young. Adolescents, of course, recognize that such drug education is one-sided propaganda, and as a result, they usually turn off to all adult information on drug use and drinking.

At the opposite extreme from the alarmist point of view is what might be called the "benign" school. Since much of adolescent substance use is relatively harmless, since most children outgrow their problem use, since so many adults misuse alcohol and are now using illicit drugs and pharmaceuticals, some well-informed observers believe focusing on adolescent substance abuse is unwarranted.

My view incorporates elements of both of these positions but fundamentally disagrees with both. I believe the alarmist point of view is overstated. At the same time, I believe we need to encourage adolescents to recognize the actual risks of substance abuse and to reject regular intoxication in order to lead richer and fuller lives. Moreover, even though most young people don't develop a drug or alcohol problem, we must deal with reality and safeguard those who periodically misuse substances. This approach, called risk reduction, strives to prevent injuries or other damage that young people who become intoxicated either cause or suffer.

TOOLS THIS BOOK WILL GIVE YOU

The first section of this book examines the wide array of misinformation about drugs and alcohol in the United States and explains how to think about addiction in a more useful way. In place of myths, I relate real information about youthful substance use, both good and bad. In my review of our missteps, I explain what many educators and researchers know: American drug education is a failure.

In the second part of the book, I propose techniques to enable parents to raise children in the modern world so that they can avoid serious substance abuse problems and other addictions. This involves, first, recognizing that you are the most important influence on your children and, second, learning how to use this role to instill values and discipline. But it is only through opportunities to navigate the world on their own that kids learn genuine independence and the skills to handle themselves.

I also describe what we know—which is a considerable amount—about how to teach children to drink moderately and control appetites of all kinds. Much of this information comes from other cultures that do substantially better than the United States in self-regulation of drinking, and also eating. For example, contrary to what you have heard, research actually shows that teaching your children to drink socially at home is the best policy.

The third section addresses either transient or chronic problems your children can have. These problems include a family history of substance abuse, which you *can* avoid passing along to your children. You also want to prevent a childhood or adolescent emotional problem, and certainly the treatment provided for it, from growing into an addiction. It seems hard to believe that therapeutic medications themselves can become addictive, yet pharmaceutical drugs are fast becoming the drugs most commonly abused by young people in America.

You also don't want your children to be harmed by casual drug use or drinking. It is a tall order to safeguard kids in activities they don't want to tell you about. I offer you ways to question your children that elicit honest responses and, more importantly, encourage their ability to protect themselves. I also prompt you to think about ways of reducing their risks if they do drink or use drugs. Should their substance use become seriously harmful, I help you decide when you need to turn to treatment, what your treatment options are, and how to make treatment work for your children.

Lastly, I describe the policies we in the United States must adopt to reverse our tailspin into an increasingly addictive society. If enough concerned parents and citizens get involved in changing drug education and drug policy, we may not always have to row upstream to do what makes sense and actually works.

HOW I DO IT

There is a good deal of information to absorb in the following pages. Along with what research tells us about drugs, alcohol, and child rearing, I include many cases about children and parents. Key facts in these cases are disguised (unless I identify real people whose stories are already public knowledge), while the psychological truths of the stories are preserved.

As a psychologist and therapist, I have examined and conducted addiction research. I have worked with many addicts and their families. I also have spent a good deal of time observing people—it is a habit of mine. And—as I try to teach you to do with examples of scripts and personal exercises you can try—I ask a lot of questions. As much as possible, I try to put you into the real world of dealing with children of all ages so that you are able to help your kids face real, sometimes difficult choices, and so that you can do the same.

PARENTING UNDER STRESS

I am an optimistic and forward-looking person. I don't believe we will, as a society, willingly inundate ourselves with addictions. And my faith that this won't occur is reinforced by my confidence in your good sense. I believe that readers of this book have a great many strengths, strengths I regularly see in people with whom I practice therapy.

Most people avoid or overcome addiction. Perhaps you used to drink quite a bit or take drugs when you were in college. Perhaps you formed obsessive romances when you were an adolescent and young adult. Perhaps you smoked—even beyond your teens and twenties. But most of you have overcome these addictive behaviors.

Likewise, although they may struggle with these same issues, your children have an urge to develop fully into independent adults, as you want them to. Even if *you* have serious problems that you wish to prevent in your kids, you are still likely—with some awareness and planning—to produce productive, happy, non-addicted children.

What kids need to protect them from addiction are the fundamentals of a life: a sense of meaning and involvement, purposeful activity and achievement, caring about themselves and others, and the ability to manage themselves. The importance of these values and skills is not surprising. What's surprising is that we've lost sight of these being the best antidotes to addiction.

Part One

ADDICTION, DRUGS, AND ALCOHOL

One

THE PROBLEM IS ADDICTION, NOT DRUGS

People become addicted to experiences that protect them from life challenges they can't deal with. It is not possible to say that any one thing causes addiction. Most kids who use drugs and alcohol don't become addicted to them. On the other hand, they can get addicted to very typical, common activities—such as eating, the Internet, other media, games, even medications they are prescribed for other problems.

The core of an addiction is that people become enmeshed in an activity that interferes with their functioning and, for children, thwarts their growth. If your children avoid regular involvements and experiences, if they can't cope with their lives, and if you fear that, left to their own devices, they will either collapse or go haywire, your children face addictive problems.

Disagreements about the nature of addiction make for vast differences in how we go about combating it. I do not find it helpful to regard addiction as a disease, which is the prevalent view these days. Although many people, including scientists, now believe that a wide range of things can be addictive, they wrongly persist in seeing addiction as a biological phenomenon beyond people's control.

By contrast, I was one of the first proponents of the view that addiction is not limited to drugs. But its very universality makes it clear that addiction can't be traced to a specific neurological mechanism. If sex or gambling addictions are defined by changes in the brain, why do so many people who find these involvements alluring for a moment, or even enthralling for some time, then simply move on to other activities? As we shall see, the exact same thing is true of "addictive" drugs.

Addiction can be especially debilitating for the young, but young people are more likely than not to outgrow it. The way out of addiction is to develop a range of skills and engage fully in life. The disease mythology is *particularly* unhelpful for young people. Telling adolescents that they have inherited addiction as part of their biological makeup encourages them to get stuck in the problem, rather than motivating them to overcome it.

Although my view of addiction is not the conventional one, my way of thinking has been adopted by many and is gaining influence in the field. My approach includes recognizing that addiction is not limited to drugs, that people overcome addiction when they are motivated and when their lives improve, and that successful therapy for addiction builds on people's own motivation to change while teaching them better ways of coping.

DEFINING ADDICTION

At the same time that not all drug use is addictive, addiction does not have to involve drugs. People can become addicted to powerful experiences such as sex, love, gambling, shopping, food—indeed, any experience that can absorb their feelings and consciousness. Addiction to the Internet is now in the spotlight, and before that came addiction to television and then video games.

Addictions provide quick, sure, easy-to-obtain gratifications, and advances in the electronic age such as the Internet, cell phone, iPod, and BlackBerry bring more addictive possibilities. Two addictions intertwined with the Internet are pornography and gambling. People become enmeshed in these experiences in isolation, rejecting everything else in their lives. A typical Internet pornography addiction case reads like this:

> My son is addicted to pornography. He can't stop looking at porn. He stays up on his computer all night. In the morning he can't stay awake, and he often doesn't go to school. I'm at my wits' end.

Likewise, we frequently hear of people who cannot stop gambling or shopping, often going deeply in debt. Such addicts, as adults, may steal, go to prison, and lose their families as a result.

To come to grips with how widespread addictive experiences can be, consider that love relationships can become addictive. We are all aware of this phenomenon, which is captured in popular song lyrics such as "Why must I be a teenager in love?" But these cases can be remarkably debilitating:

> About a year ago I fell in love with someone I believed was "The One." Ever since then my whole life has been about him—and, as time went by, I've become more and more depressed.
>
> I have always been easily addicted. But before this whole thing started I was a very happy and energetic person with a lot of interests who enjoyed living and loved talking to people. During the time we were together I just threw all of my life away: my friends, my schooling, my dreams. He became the only thing that mattered to me. I continued to feel this way even when I realized that he didn't really accept me.
>
> At some stage we decided it would be best if we stopped dating and tried to be friends, but after a short time I realized I couldn't do that.
>
> Now, I am depressed all the time. I've thought about him every second of my life for the past year. I can hardly sleep, I can hardly get out of bed in the morning. I feel like being alone most of the time. I have no energy, I nearly always feel sick. I find it hard to enjoy anything at all. I can't get him out of my head.

I described addictive love in 1975 in my book *Love and Addiction*. But because this idea is so shocking, it keeps resurfacing as though it were new. A woman wrote in the *New York Times* in 2006: "This is what love addiction did to my life: I dropped out of college, quit my job, stopped talking to my family and friends. There was no booze to blame for my blackouts, vomiting, and bed-wetting."[1]

If we want to understand all kinds of self-destructive behaviors, we need a broader conception of addiction than the simple idea that some drugs are addictive: **Addiction is a way of relating to the world. It is a response to an experience people get from some activity or object. They become absorbed in this experience because it provides them with essential emotional rewards, but it progressively limits and harms their lives.** Six criteria define an addictive experience:

- It is powerful and absorbs people's feelings and thoughts.
- It can be predictably and reliably produced.
- It provides people with essential sensations and emotions (such as feeling good about themselves, or the absence of worry or pain).
- It produces these feelings only temporarily, for the duration of the experience.
- It ultimately degrades other involvements and satisfactions.
- Finally, since they are getting less from their lives when away from the addiction, people are forced increasingly to return to the addictive experience as their only source of satisfaction.

ADDICTIONS VERSUS NORMAL EXPERIENCE

Watching television every night, drinking daily (for an adult), and having an active social life are not necessarily addictions. Broadening the definition of *addiction* does not mean that everybody is addicted to something. The word is now often used casually, even humorously: a friend says he is addicted to crossword puzzles, a baby is addicted to his pacifier, a teenager to her cell phone.

Addictions are harmful, perhaps overwhelmingly so—as in the cases of pornography and love addiction described above. People may joke that they are addicted to exercise or coffee or work, and they can be. But it is only when these things seriously detract from their ability to function that people are genuinely addicted—for example, they can't stop exercising after they have suffered an injury, or they drink coffee throughout the day even though it prevents them from sleeping, or they are so preoccupied with work that they neglect their families.

Here's a case in which being well-balanced saved a man's life:

Peter was in the south tower of the World Trade Center when the north tower was struck. His floor was evacuated down a stairwell. But after going down several flights, a security officer told the evacuees they should return to their offices. A number of people who were in the stairwell with Peter did so.

Peter—who was well paid and worked long hours—thought about returning. The instruction by an official to do so reinforced his conscientiousness and dedication to work.

But Peter also thought about his wife and children, and decided to proceed down the stairs. Soon after he left the building, the second plane hit below the floor on which Peter worked.

After September 11, Peter's wife couldn't stop hugging him. "Every time I see him, I feel such love and gratitude that he was spared," she explained.

Peter was a person who might have been at risk for being caught up in mindless, compulsive working, irrespective of any damage it caused him. Instead, his independent thinking and commitment to his family saved him from addiction. For young people, too, the more connections to life they have, the better able they are to resist addiction. When people give up much of their lives for their addictions, as we saw in the cases of love addiction, it is because their other involvements are superficial or somehow unsatisfactory.

We all rely on fixed elements in our lives, and children especially do. It is essential to your children's security and psychological well-being that you provide them with consistent limits, acceptance, and love. You should also recognize that children and adolescents will often fixate on an object or activity—their stuffed animal or a recording artist, playing with dolls or video games, wearing certain clothes or going to particular places. These fads are normal phases in growing up, and you should accept them as such.

What makes for addiction is when young people cannot extricate themselves from an activity in order to do the things required of them—things that they in some sense would *prefer* to be doing. Instead, they persist in behavior that is consistently harmful, or that is disapproved of by society, or that damages their health, their future, or their relationships with other people.

One of the thorniest problems for parents is deciding whether children are addicted when they use a substance (such as marijuana) regularly but otherwise function successfully. One possibility is that their drug use is normal. A landmark study found that moderate experimentation with drugs characterized the most psychologically healthy adolescents, while heavier use *and* abstinence were both signs of poorer adjustment.[2]

You need to key in on how well your children are coping with the demands made on them to ascertain whether or not they are abusing a substance. But even when they are abusing a substance, it may be wrong to call the problem an addiction or unhelpful to put them in drug treatment. I deal with these dilemmas in Chapter 10.

ADDICTION IN ADOLESCENCE

Some adolescents do become so involved with drugs or alcohol that it completely dominates their lives. Consider these cases:

Alice grew up in a family that had many problems. Her parents repeatedly separated, then got back together. Her father was violent, and screaming and crying were typical in the home.

Alice quickly got used to going out with friends as a way of escaping the turmoil and pain at home. When she was fourteen, she began drinking with these other teenagers, many with backgrounds similar to her own. The first time she drank she became falling-down drunk—"wasted," as she described it. Alice soon became sexually active when she was intoxicated.

Alice would sometimes quit drinking, only to return to it with a vengeance. This became a pattern for her throughout high school. As a junior she attended meetings of Alcoholics Anonymous and entered a six-month period of abstinence. But soon she returned to drinking and began using drugs as well. At first it was marijuana. In her senior year, however, she also used cocaine and took LSD.

Alice was smart and attractive, but her academic performance was lackluster. She decided not to go to college. Instead, she became a waitress at a local restaurant, where other young employees joined her in drinking and using drugs following work.

In adolescence and early adulthood, Alice's life was devoted to intoxication and the activities that surrounded it—which she called "getting rowdy." Since her life centered around drinking and drugs in a way that limited her opportunities, her friends, and her future, Alice was addicted during this phase of her life. But Alice, as typically happens, quit drinking and drugs when she reached her late twenties. Unfortunately, her addictive phase hampered Alice, because of the opportunities she lost, even after she stopped abusing substances.

While Alice's background is common for youthful addicts, hers is certainly not the only path to drug and alcohol excess and addiction.

John's family was stable—his older sister did well in school and went on to become a doctor. His father made an excellent living in the financial industry. His parents got along well together.

But John began abusing drugs early in life. In fact, he had already used heroin by the time he was sixteen. To do so, he associated with other kids who engaged in the most negative behaviors. It was as though—as his father put it—John was "following the loser."

John certainly had ability and enjoyed successes as an adolescent. He was a very good runner, for example, and made the county championships in the quarter mile. His parents devoted themselves to taking him to track meets and getting him additional training—such as a summer track camp—to further this skill.

After he became addicted, John's parents placed him in a series of treatment programs. After each, he returned home seemingly prepared to resume a typical high school existence. But within a matter of weeks or months he was back with his old crowd, abusing drugs and heading to his next treatment episode.

Eventually, John's family felt they had to expel him from the household— he went into treatment, then a halfway house in a different state. His father told him he would continue to help John financially and stay in touch only if John could prove that he was clean.

For a time, John became a pariah to his parents, who felt it was best for their family to expel him from their home. I consulted with John's father and helped him to reach a better resolution with John. Although he didn't quit drinking and continued to use recreational drugs occasionally, John stopped using heroin and started to take his schooling seriously. I describe this harm reduction therapy in Chapter 9.

Both Alice and John began to abuse drugs and alcohol in early adolescence, and the abuse quickly become the focus of their lives. People like Alice—from fragmented, violent, or emotionally disturbed families and from families facing economic hardships—are more likely to abuse drugs and alcohol. But children from stable and prosperous backgrounds also do so. When children from well-off backgrounds abuse substances, they are failing to buy in to their family's values. The pressures placed on them to achieve may then saddle them with emotional problems and bad feelings about themselves.

From an early age John and Alice could not find a positive role for themselves. As a result, both of them developed alternative lifestyles and self-images around drugs and alcohol that locked them out of what society has to offer—at least for a time.

ADOLESCENT ADDICTION IS NOT LIMITED TO DRUGS AND ALCOHOL

Broadening our concept of addiction to include electronic devices, gambling, destructive relationships, and even eating and therapeutically prescribed drugs helps us to understand the troubling behavior of some children and adolescents.

> Alex was a normal, if quiet, child. He didn't have many friends, and from a young age preferred to spend time with electronic gadgets of various sorts. He would sit playing video games or listening to his iPod, making motions in rhythm with the music, for hours at a time.
>
> Alex did well in some school subjects—he got good grades in mathematics—and showed talent in music, which his parents encouraged. Although his father was shy and somewhat withdrawn, his mother was active and verbal and his parents' relationship was stable. Yet Alex never found a group of peers who interested him more than his electronic devices.
>
> When Alex decided not to go to college, his parents were at first shocked. But they came to accept their son's decision—not everyone is suited for college, they thought, and this might be a better path for Alex. Instead of getting out in the world, though, Alex retreated more from it. He spent all of his time alone in his room playing on his computer, listening to music, or watching television.

Alex was addicted to interacting with electronic media and entertainments. Only predictable experiences such as these made him feel safe and in control of his life. Alex was already isolated, and his immersion in the Internet further limited his possibility of developing a social network and outside involvements.

Alex's story suggests something remarkable—that while we are emphasizing the danger of illicit drugs and alcohol, addiction frequently emerges from ordinary aspects of children's lives. In fact, addiction may be encouraged by standard childhood and adolescent experiences—creating questions and concerns for anybody raising children today.

One striking example of how common addiction has become is the meteoric rise in childhood obesity. Overweight in adolescence has tripled in the last three decades while it has almost quintupled for children ages six to eleven.[3] Ironically, one reaction young people can have to their fear of being overweight is to circle all the way around to anorexia or bulimia, another alarming trend among the young. Both obesity and anorexia reflect an all-or-nothing approach people take when they are incapable of controlling an involvement, and both are forms of addictive behavior.

Children are unable to match their appetites with their nutritional needs if they aren't equipped with a sound approach to eating and physical activity. Francine Kaufman, a diabetes specialist at Children's Hospital in Los Angeles, describes the problem as getting "people back in energy balance." She adds, "Yet nothing is fundamentally harder to do" because of a " 'toxic environment' created by modern living, which promotes overeating sugary and fatty junk foods, reinforces inactive lifestyles and focuses on 'disease care' instead of preventative health care."[4]

CAN CHILDREN BE ADDICTED TO PSYCHIATRIC DRUGS?

One important source of addiction is people's emotional problems and bad feelings about themselves, including anxiety, depression, and low self-esteem. Children and adolescents are more likely than ever before to be diagnosed with psychiatric problems such as depression, bipolar (manic-depressive) disorder, and ADHD (attention deficit hyperactivity disorder).

If your children have serious emotional problems, you need to address them. Contemporary psychiatric treatment for young people typically involves giving them drugs. There has been considerable debate about the use of psychiatric medications for childhood emotional problems. Although this book is not a general mental health manual, the potential addictive impact of the drug therapies increasingly administered to children and adolescents is a serious consideration, as we discuss in Chapter 8.

How can drugs prescribed to help children be harmful addictions? Neither I nor the American Psychiatric Association recognizes positive varieties of addiction. When people come to define themselves in terms of substances they use, even if prescribed for them, this dependence on chemicals is in danger of becoming an addiction.

Society has not yet had time to determine the effects of the large-scale psychiatric medication of children, which concerns many experts in childhood development and emotional problems. At the same time, adolescents and college students regularly take pharmaceutical drugs without prescriptions to study, sleep, be calm, stay awake, and party. The recreational use of prescription medications is so widespread among the young nowadays that one anti-drug organization calls them "Generation Rx."

WHAT CAUSES ADDICTION?

Some people are more prone than others to pursue satisfaction through an external fix. "I have always been easily addicted," admitted the young woman we saw earlier who sacrificed her life for a transitory love affair. Some young people turn to addictions because they can't seem to get the satisfaction they crave from their regular lives.

This susceptibility—and its opposite, resistance—to addiction stems from children's lived experiences, including their homes, neighborhoods, and school environments.

Addiction-*proof* children have:

- *Skills* to gain real rewards, and the patience to learn and deploy these skills
- *Values* that sustain moderation and reject addiction
- *Confidence* that they can achieve the goals and gain the rewards they desire

Addiction-*prone* children are saddled with:

- Chronic bad *feelings,* including fear, depression, and anxiety
- *Environments* that deny opportunities for fulfillment and satisfaction
- Histories of *dependence,* including on their parents

These personal assets don't guarantee immunity from addiction, and these deficiencies don't guarantee addiction will occur. But these addiction-preventing and -causing factors are the ones over which you have the most control. In the second part of this book I concentrate on teaching you how to exert your influence to produce non-addicted children.

HOW DO PEOPLE RECOVER FROM ADDICTION?

Although it can be hard work to help your children gain what they need to avoid addiction, there is no alternative. On the other hand, these conditions often change naturally as adolescents mature, develop skills and interests they care about, and become more confident, enabling them to free themselves of youthful addictions. Most people—and particularly young people—leave addiction behind somewhere along their life's path. This process often involves common elements.

Young people overcome addiction when they:

- Develop the skills to gain life rewards
- Reaffirm values they have that oppose addiction
- Resolve emotional problems and become less anxious, depressed, and afraid
- Acquire assets—such as a family, work, status, security—they don't want to lose
- Mature, so that their focus shifts beyond their own needs
- Feel that they control their lives and can get what they want in the world

The easy way to overcome substance abuse is to outgrow it, as most young people do. Koren Zailckas stopped the decade-long dependence on alcohol she described in her memoir *Smashed: Story of a Drunken Girlhood* when she found someone she cared about more than she did about drinking and became serious about developing her skills as a writer. Zailckas' is the typical path out of alcohol and drug abuse.

But Zailckas has been forced to defend her account of her life, since so many experts say that she couldn't do what she says she did—simply outgrow alcoholism.

> I don't identify myself as an alcoholic. That identity didn't feel true to me, so I didn't write it. I also think the brand "alcoholic" prevents a lot of people, especially young people, from seeking help or even reevaluating their relationship with alcohol. In my mind, the whole point of *Smashed* is to say, you don't have to be a quote-unquote alcoholic in order to examine the underlying reasons why you're drinking.[5]

Some of those who have spent their youthful lives getting drunk and stoned suffer from deep-seated deficiencies. Some will have to learn basic skills in order to overcome the life problems that come along with their addiction, making addiction treatment more complicated and difficult.[6] This is the hard (though far from impossible) way to overcome addiction—to build a life, sometimes on top of a pile of rubble.

In the United States, we often attempt to remedy substance abuse by pressing young people into substance abuse (or "chemical dependence") treatment, including Alcoholics Anonymous and similar self-help groups. Does treatment work? It may, but success—as Alice's and John's parents and most of us recognize—is far from guaranteed. And being involved in treatment can have its own drawbacks.

Sadly, unhelpful treatments for substance abuse are the rule. The worst danger is that the treatment can cause people to "take their eyes off the prize"—that is, preoccupy child and parent with tangential issues while overlooking the essential things the young person needs in order to lead a satisfying life. Instead of teaching life skills and engaging young people in regular life activities, the treatment can make addiction the focus of their lives, even after they are abstaining. Thus, even when it "succeeds," this kind of treatment fails to address the underlying causes of addiction in children's lives.

AA and twelve-step treatment are particularly inappropriate for young people, and can be limiting in ways that are themselves addictive. This occurs because such treatment demands that they adopt an identity built around their recovery status, which is everlasting.

Lana was an artist who entered AA as an adolescent; it became the center of her existence for crucial years of her life. Lana's social life revolved around her AA friends. But in her twenties, when the boyfriend she met in the group died of an overdose (Lana didn't know he was using), that world became alien and repulsive to her.

> Finally, I chose to leave AA but continued to stay sober. I didn't know what I believed—I felt continual fear and doubt for the rest of that year. AA, of course, says that you will always be an alcoholic. My ex-AA friends reinforced and encouraged my self-doubt, telling me I would never make it on my own.
>
> It was a slow process integrating into the outside world. I was so used to relating to people with the AA language, I often felt awkward talking to non-AAers.
>
> But I got involved with a martial arts group, reconnected with a loving relative, began working with other artists, and came to feel I was part of that community. In therapy, I learned to accept my feelings and still go out and live.
>
> My life is full now, but it was a long, bumpy road to find the strength to be independent. Now so many things bring me pleasure, fulfillment, and challenge that getting drunk doesn't interest me.

WHERE DO WE TURN?

You're probably concerned about the many ways your children can go wrong, and perhaps this chapter has made you more anxious. The aim of this book is not to scare you but to make you aware of the nature, danger, and signs of addiction, and then provide you with the tools to combat and overcome it with your children. My purpose is to *empower* parents.

Although there is no question that there are more opportunities for addiction than ever, and that more young people enter periods of addiction, I want you to remember that most children don't become addicted permanently.

In the next chapter, we see that the challenges you confront include the likelihood that your children will use drugs at one time or another, just as they are overwhelmingly likely to drink. I didn't say the job of parenting is easy. But you can manage it, just as your parents did.

The skills and experiences you and your children bring to this task are the best antidotes to addiction. You need to learn and teach your children such skills—and feel confident that your children can progress through relying on their own abilities—in order to help your children grow into adulthood.

Two

YOUTHFUL DRUG AND ALCOHOL USE:
WHY IT BECOMES ADDICTIVE OR NOT

Take this quiz, please. If you get four out of five answers right (including being within 5 percentage points for any involving percentages), congratulate yourself that you understand the adolescent substance use landscape. If so, you are in a small minority.

DRUG AND ALCOHOL USE QUIZ

1. What percentage of high school seniors have used an illicit drug?
2. What percentage of high school seniors have ever been drunk?
3. What percentage have drunk alcohol in the last thirty days, and what percentage have been drunk in that period?
4. How many underage college students binge-drink?
5. At what age do Americans binge-drink and use illicit drugs most, and how many develop a substance use problem or addiction at this age?

Answers: (1) More than half (54 percent) of high school seniors have used illicit drugs; (2) well over half (58 percent) have been drunk; (3) almost half (47 percent) have drunk in the past month, while almost a third (30 percent) report having been drunk in that period; (4) 40 percent of underage college students (ages eighteen to twenty) binge-drank in the past month; (5) at age twenty-one, 48 percent of Americans binge-drank in the last month and

22 percent used illicit drugs; a *quarter* of twenty-one-year-olds have a substance abuse problem or addiction.

Does this information worry you? Clearly, efforts to stamp out youthful substance use have not succeeded. Children will very likely be exposed to drugs and alcohol, and an alarming proportion of young Americans abuse these substances, many quite seriously.

Awareness of these facts about youthful substance use is critical for you to confront the challenges you face as a parent. But parents significantly underestimate the chances that their children use or abuse substances. About half of parents are unaware that their adolescent children, ages twelve to seventeen, drink or smoke marijuana. Worse, three-quarters do not realize they have children who get drunk or abuse these substances.[1]

ADOLESCENT USE OF DRUGS AND ALCOHOL

Adolescence and early adulthood are peak periods for drug use and alcohol abuse. With alcohol, young people tend to drink irregularly but intensively, often to intoxication. This style of drinking carries particular dangers (accidents, violence, alcohol poisoning). The good news is that most youths mature out of this type of risky behavior. As adolescents emerge into adulthood, most reduce their drinking and stop using drugs.

Adolescent substance use in the United States is assessed primarily by the Monitoring the Future (MTF) Survey, which has tracked secondary school drug and alcohol use since 1975. Conducted at the University of Michigan on behalf of the U.S. government, MTF surveys about fifty thousand students in around four hundred schools across the country. In 2005, a majority of high school seniors (54 percent) had used an illicit drug—45 percent smoking marijuana and 27 percent using some other illicit substance, including inhalants (many have used more than one drug). Three-quarters of seniors had consumed alcohol and 58 percent said they had been drunk.

HOW ARE WE DOING WITH ADOLESCENT SUBSTANCE USE?

Whenever new high school drug and alcohol statistics come out, officials look for progress. In 1992, drug use by high school seniors was at a relative low of 44 percent, after which it increased sharply. The 2005 figure remained 10 percentage points above that low. Nonetheless, officials announced the good news: "What is significant is that the use of these substances has declined substantially since the recent peak levels reached in the mid-1990s," Lloyd Johnston, the lead researcher, announced.[2] John Walters, the federal government's drug czar, declared: "This survey shows that when we push back against the drug problem, it gets smaller."[3] Still, that more than half of high school seniors used an illicit drug doesn't seem so good. As researcher Johnston put it, "These are not what you would call low rates of drug use by any means."

Drug czar Walters has projected that student use rates will continue to decline, as they did slightly in the mid-2000s. But adolescent drug use rises and falls. It is more accurate to describe youthful substance use as ebbing and flowing, for a variety of reasons, around a persistently high level.

Regular heavy drinking by youngsters in the United States is much more of a problem than drug use. Three-quarters have drunk alcohol, and well over half (58 percent) have been drunk, 30 percent in the past month. As with drug use, these are not the highest drinking rates we have seen over the years. For example, in 1992, 88 percent of high school seniors had consumed alcohol (although drug use was lower). In 2001, 64 percent had been drunk at some point in their lives. But the current figures are bad enough.

YOUTHFUL SUBSTANCE ABUSE GETS WORSE AFTER HIGH SCHOOL

Worse news, for parents and for our society, is that substance use figures increase dramatically following high school.[4] After graduation, 37 percent of those in the eighteen-to-twenty age group binge-drank (five or more drinks at one time) in the last month, the 2004 National Survey on Drug Use and Health found. Among under-age college students, 40 percent binge-drank.[5] As legal drinkers, 44 percent of those ages twenty-one to twenty-five binge-drank in the last month. Americans peak in both drug use and binge drink-ing at age twenty-one.[6] The Center on Addiction and Substance Abuse (CASA) at Columbia University calculated that *half* of all college students regularly binge drink or use drugs illegally.

ARE WE EVER GOING TO ELIMINATE YOUTHFUL DRUG USE AND DRUNKENNESS?

In the mid-1960s, around 5 percent of those ages eighteen to twenty-five had taken an illicit drug. In 2004, ten to twelve times as many, 59 percent, had done so. The genie is out of the bottle. In all likelihood, these figures will not decline dramatically, or may not decline at all. Perhaps they will even increase. Even the most opti-mistic estimates leave us with a large proportion of young people who use drugs illicitly and binge-drink—by any measure, a signifi-cant and ever-present problem.

LET'S TALK ABOUT SUBSTANCE *ABUSE*

In the last chapter, we focused on addiction. But the American Psy-chiatric Association's diagnostic manual identifies two degrees of substance use problems—abuse and dependence.[7] Abuse is prob-lematic drug use and drinking; dependence is equivalent to addiction or alcoholism. Abuse is measured by repeated problems—social, job-related, psychological, medical, or legal—a person has due to drug or alcohol use. Dependence involves physical problems such as withdrawal or extreme psychological difficulties such as repeatedly trying unsuccessfully to reduce or quit use or being preoccupied with obtaining, using, and recovering from a substance.

In some countries, many accept that young people drink or take drugs. Americans are uncomfortable about youthful substance use—including even the adolescents and young adults who themselves drink and take drugs. Americans are more likely than people in other countries to decide they are addicted to drugs or that they are alcoholics.[8] Although they are afraid of dependence, this apparently doesn't stop American young people from drinking and taking drugs. Then, taking seriously all of the warnings they've heard, they seem to conclude, "I'm using drugs and drinking—I must be addicted!"

The National Survey on Drug Use and Health measures how many people are clinically diagnosable as abusing, or being dependent on, alcohol or drugs. The figures are quite startling: more than a fifth (21 percent) of those ages eighteen to twenty-five abuse or are dependent on alcohol or drugs. As we saw at the beginning of the chapter, a quarter of twenty-one-year-olds abuse or are dependent on a substance. Alcohol is the worse culprit—twice as many young people have an alcohol problem as have a drug problem (although some have both). CASA found nearly a quarter of *all* college students abuse or depend on alcohol or drugs.

On the other hand, only 7 percent of those twenty-six years of age or older abuse alcohol or drugs. That this figure drops by two-thirds (from 21 percent to 7 percent) for those above the age of twenty-five is important and supports our thesis that addiction most often is self-curing. As true as this is, however, research over the last two decades also indicates that many young people have been slower to achieve sobriety than they once were.[9] Although drinking and drug use are actually on the decline, more young people are continuing their problematic use until later in their lives. As a result, between 1992 and 2002, the overall alcohol abuse rate in the United States increased over 50 percent.[10]

The paradox of why young people currently are so likely to become dependent on substances and, more often than in the past, to extend their problems later into life says much about the nature of childhood, adolescence, and young adulthood today, and the issues you face as a parent.

WHO ABUSES DRUGS AND ALCOHOL?

Do better-educated people abuse drugs and alcohol more or less than those who are less educated?

Attending college doesn't make young people less likely to binge—to say the least.[11] However, for adults, education works against alcohol abuse. The National Survey on Drug Use and Health finds that the higher an adult's education level, the more likely a person is to drink but the less likely to binge-drink.[12] Education seemingly encourages people to drink, but *to control their drinking.*

PAST MONTH DRINKING BY ADULT AMERICANS
ACCORDING TO LEVEL OF EDUCATION

	Percentage who drank in the past month	Percentage of drinkers who binge-drank in the last month
No high school degree	36	63
High school graduate	49	52
Some college	59	44
College graduate	66	32

Many people assume, mistakenly, that better-educated people are equally or even more likely to abuse drugs and alcohol. Don't feel bad if you make this mistake—you probably have been misled by lectures and television programs telling you that alcohol and drugs are equal-opportunity destroyers. The distinction between use and abuse, with drugs as well as alcohol, is an important one. Those with a zero-tolerance mentality by definition fail to make that distinction; instead, they categorize *all* use as *problem* use.

Everything you know about life should lead you to recognize that being better educated, having a good job, and doing well in life are antidotes to substance abuse. The reason most young people are able eventually to quit drugs and problem drinking is that they acquire jobs and families.

This Case Is so Typical It's a Nonstory

Bill was an active teenager in high school—playing in the band, dating and attending parties, and maintaining a B+ average. He also smoked marijuana and drank, sometimes becoming intoxicated. A friend of Bill's was suspended when marijuana was found in his locker. Bill quit using drugs for a while, but then started again.

Bill got into the state university, where he majored in business. He continued to use marijuana and to drink, and he sampled cocaine. He studied accounting, making use of his strong computer skills. He was hired in the comptroller's office of a large electronics firm. Bill got married and had two kids. Over the course of time he quit using marijuana and getting drunk, switching instead to a glass of wine with dinner.

DRUG AND ALCOHOL LIFE PATHWAYS

The drug and alcohol use data are startling and understandably alarming to parents. Most children, adolescents, and young adults do in fact take illicit drugs and drink. Yet in most cases, your worst fears—the ones spread by the alarmist, zero-tolerance educators and officials—are not going to be realized. A minority of these young people, although still a large number in absolute terms, have a substance problem, and many fewer do as adults.

In this sense, information about youthful substance use is reassuring. However, nobody wants their children *ever* to fall into the group that has a problem, or even to face this risk. Since this risk exists, it is important to understand how most adolescents and young adults avoid substance abuse in the first place, and how so many in the minority who do abuse substances quit as they mature.

Following are the variety of drug and alcohol trajectories young people's lives take, for better and worse.

INITIAL PERSONALITY/PARENTING PROFILES

Anti-drug speakers who come to your children's school to lecture kids are often recovering addicts or alcoholics themselves. They tell students that drug users' problems stem solely from their drug use: "If it weren't for this one unaccountable problem that took control of my life, I'd be just like you!" The speakers are striving for a powerful impact, but this message doesn't fool the young people who hear and rightly reject it.

In fact, adolescents who have problems with drugs typically have a range of other problems. These are the kids who are prone to get into trouble, who can't seem to find themselves, who lack focus and confidence. They are the most likely to sneak cigarettes, impulsively steal, or vandalize property. They more often suffer from parental neglect and emotional problems such as depression.[13]

Emotionally vulnerable children comprise a somewhat separate group of substance abusers (some kids have both characteristics). The first group, *anti-social* addicts or substance abusers, seek pleasure without restraint and enjoy flouting regulations. The second, *psychological* substance abusers, seek relief for their emotional pain.

Getting Off on the Wrong Foot

Josh never did well at school. When his teachers tried to engage his parents in a discussion of Josh's lack of motivation, Josh's father responded with outrage: "*You're* responsible for giving him an education."

Josh was targeted for special programs for high-risk children. When a high-profile anti-drug spokesperson came to the school, Josh and a group of his friends rushed up to congratulate the speaker—as they were encouraged to do by their counselor. But Josh had been smoking marijuana and drinking with many of the other kids who were part of the drug counseling program.

Whenever Josh got in a fight, cursed a teacher, or had some other trouble (which was not uncommon), his parents were summoned by the vice principal. The parents' reactions were the same each time. His father was irate toward both Josh and the school authorities, while his mother was withdrawn and depressed.

Eventually, Josh was referred to a psychologist. The psychologist's assessment was chilling: "Josh does not see any possibility of achieving what he wants in life through his own efforts. He does not believe that activity A on his part will lead to reward B. Thus he sees no point in trying to accomplish anything. Instead, he grabs for whatever gratification he can conveniently find, usually illicit. I have found this outlook to be true of two groups of people in my professional experience—drug abusers and criminals."

REINFORCING SETTINGS AND NEGATIVE LIFE TRAJECTORIES

Of course, children are not isolated agents in life—they grow up in families, with friends, in neighborhoods. These can either ameliorate or exacerbate their problems. Josh's parents were not likely to curb his anti-social tendencies—they played a major role in creating them. His peers were equally high-risk kids—in part because his school grouped them together. Neither his peers, his parents, nor the neighborhood in which Josh lived offered him attitudes, values, and opportunities to counteract his anti-social, criminal, and addictive tendencies.

Robert Zucker, a University of Michigan psychologist, has traced worsening substance abuse life paths.[14] Children who grow into adolescent substance abusers and whose problems persist into adulthood often combine many risk factors. These include family histories of alcoholism and anti-social behavior, a weak family structure and family discord, associations with other kids who have similar outlooks and problems, and school and social failures that isolate them further.[15] Emotional distress often feeds into this process, since such children are also often depressed and anxious.

Remember this clear picture presented by the data—drugs and alcohol are *not* equal-opportunity destroyers. They're not mysterious goblins that suddenly appear to destroy the lives of happy, well-adjusted young people. Instead, you need to be alert to the risk factors in your children—identified in this chapter—that make them susceptible to substance abuse.

WHY DO KIDS USE AND ABUSE DRUGS AND ALCOHOL?

What exactly do adolescents with these problems get from abusing substances? And why do otherwise normal kids also take drugs and drink? In the first place, young people typically seek adventure and risky experiences, which have always come with the territory of childhood and adolescence. To a large extent, however, this adventurousness and abandon are now denied children (as we will see in Chapter 6). One alternative way for them to gain such experiences is through drugs and alcohol. Furthermore, this kind of experimentation offers them an artificial sense of being grown up and independent of their parents.

Along with making them feel alive and adult, drug and alcohol use brings adolescents acceptance and approval from their peers. Not only do their peers want them to share drug and drinking experiences, but many young people are more relaxed and feel better about themselves when they're intoxicated. Drugs and alcohol relieve social anxieties, which are at a peak during adolescence, and help to reassure them that other kids like them.

Many young people are insecure because of their uncertainties about themselves and what they will become. Along with their capacity for fun and exuberance, they tend to doubt themselves. After all, they haven't had enough experience to allow them to develop the confidence that they can handle adult challenges. Drug and alcohol use diverts young people from the uncertainty and anxiety in their lives by offering a shortcut to a sense of self-worth.

Of course, heavy substance use is likely to backfire and result in more negative consequences for such kids, thereby exacerbating their bad feelings about themselves.

Partying Hardy or Burying Consciousness?

Sally was known as the hardest partier in her sorority. She planned all week for weekend binges that extended from Thursday until Sunday. She would drink and take drugs throughout the weekend, urging others to join her in keeping the party going when less hardy souls went to bed—or fell unconscious. She slept only as long as necessary to replenish her batteries to drink and drug some more. Sometimes Sally's partying simply continued from one weekend through to the next.

Sally often seemed to be enjoying herself, engaging in casual sex or antics she would never attempt while sober. It was typical for her to find herself wearing a different set of clothes from those she started the evening in without being able to recall why or how she had changed.

Just as often, however, she felt anxious and depressed while she was sober during the week. Going back to school on Monday was always a terrific downer for Sally, and she would stop drinking Sunday night only when her friends insisted that they had to get to bed in order to go to class the next morning.

Remarkably, as smart and energetic as she was, Sally was able to maintain a decent grade point average at a good university. But as she approached graduation, Sally was filled with dread. What had she actually learned in college? How would she bear up under a full-time job? What would become of her?

Sally's sorority sisters found Sally unconscious at midday—which was unlike her. They noticed a bottle of pills next to her and rushed her to the university hospital, where her stomach was pumped and she recovered. No one knew whether Sally had been partying or had attempted suicide. Sally herself could not explain what had happened. Was it an excess of partying, or a deathly fear of being alive?

We will follow Sally through her drug treatment in Chapter 10.

HOW YOUNG PEOPLE OUTGROW SUBSTANCE ABUSE: "MATURING OUT" TRAJECTORIES

Most adolescents don't extend their substance abuse into adult life (as Bill, earlier in this chapter, did not). Unless your child's life is fraught with risk factors, youthful substance use, even when problematic, is not "a crystallized trait or disease, but rather . . . a dynamic, evolving, by-product" of shifting life factors.[16]

Young people's situations change rapidly. Many abuse drugs and alcohol during the customary youthful period—but no longer. A few become dependent on these substances extending into early adulthood but nonetheless pull themselves back from long-term abuse and addiction. Some young people do not finally leave substance abuse behind until they become fully adult, when life *demands* that they grow up, due to "marriage, pregnancy (for both women and, to a lesser degree, their spouses), and full-time employment and homemaker status."[17]

A critical factor for achieving sobriety is psychological stability. Kids' drinking and drug problems "are more likely to be temporary" so long as they don't have "prolonged bouts of psychological problems in earlier stages of the life span."[18]

Of course, emotional problems can be addressed—and, along with them, the person's substance abuse.

A Good—but Troubled—Girl Recovers from Addiction

Sybil grew up in a prosperous suburb, where her father was a doctor. But Sybil was psychologically vulnerable. She was overweight and wasn't socially successful. For these and other reasons she felt she disappointed her parents.

Sybil did not take drugs or drink in high school, where she did well academically. But when she graduated from high school, she began abusing substances with a vengeance. At college, she found a group of outsiders who accepted her. She started dating a boy in the group who was a heavy drug user.

Years later, after Sybil entered therapy, she felt that she had been depressed since childhood. Drinking or smoking marijuana relieved her bad feelings about herself. She felt free when intoxicated to embark on long, funny monologues that amused her friends. It was at these times that Sybil finally felt that she was valued.

When Sybil was twenty-one, she overdosed on painkillers and her family hospitalized her at a well-known drug treatment program. Sybil embraced her treatment and quit drugging and drinking. But she still felt emotionally fragile, and continued in psychotherapy after she left treatment.

Always a hard worker, Sybil embarked on a successful career by becoming a therapist herself. She finally settled down with a man who had never been involved with drugs. In her late thirties, she had a daughter.

Although Sybil apparently recovered in an orthodox treatment program, she ultimately rejected the philosophy she was taught there. She began having wine during dinner with her husband. When asked how she overcame her drug addiction, she answers, "I addressed my emotional problems—and continue to."

Sybil quit her addiction following treatment, no matter how she feels about that experience now. In the first chapter, we noted Koren Zailckas' memoir *Smashed*. Zailckas often drank around the clock, frequently blacking out and sometimes requiring emergency care. Yet she recovered without treatment when she settled into a job and a relationship after college. Zailckas also committed herself to figuring out what caused her drinking problems.

Zailckas' self-cure approach is common, even typical. In a massive study conducted by the National Institute on Alcohol Abuse and Alcoholism, forty-three thousand Americans were interviewed about their drinking over their lifetimes. More than 10 percent were alcohol-dependent at some point. Of this group, about a quarter had been treated—including attending AA, receiving care for the consequences of their alcohol abuse in a hospital emergency room, or entering a substance abuse program.

This leaves three in four American alcoholics who are never treated for their alcoholism. Amazingly, that group fared marginally better than the minority that did get treatment. A little less than a quarter (24 percent) of untreated alcoholics were still alcohol-dependent when interviewed for the study. Of those who had been treated, 28 percent were still alcoholic.[19]

Even factoring in the likelihood that treated alcoholics often, but not always, have more severe drinking problems than those who aren't treated, it is startling to learn that the large majority of alcoholics are never treated and that the large majority of these recover anyhow. Of course, you shouldn't ignore a serious drinking problem your child has. But keep in mind that anyone who labels your child a lifetime alcoholic can't know that and is probably mistaken.

WHAT STOPS KIDS AND ADULTS FROM ABUSING SUBSTANCES?

Personality and disposition don't lead to substance abuse in isolation. Just because people are impulsive or depressed doesn't mean that they will turn to drugs or alcohol. Individual, family, or social forces very often prevent them from doing so. Or they may just resist the impulse to take or abuse substances because they think it is wrong to do so or they have other things they want to do more.

To put it simply, many people who feel like doing something that is harmful don't do it. It's called self-restraint. The more stable and supportive their social situation, the more likely people are to exercise restraint. But adolescents and young adults may control themselves even when surrounded by excess. For example, one study found four types of reasons college students had for limiting their drinking in that heavy-drinking environment:

1. *Preference for self-control*
   "I've seen the negative effects of someone else's drinking."
   "Drinking heavily is a sign of personal weakness."
   "It's bad for my health."
   "I'm concerned about what people might think."
2. *Influence of upbringing and respect for authority*
   "I was brought up not to drink (too much)."
   "My religion discourages or is against drinking (too much)."
   "I'm part of a group that doesn't drink much."
3. *Attempts at self-reform*
   "I've become concerned with how much I've been drinking."
   "Someone suggested that I drink less."
   "I was embarrassed by something I said or did when drinking."
4. *Performance aspirations*
   "Drinking reduces my performance in sports."

"Drinking interferes with my studies."

"I wouldn't want to disappoint my parents."[20]

All of these reasons are based on kids' values—a topic we deal with in the next section.

WHAT THESE FINDINGS TELL YOU ABOUT PREVENTING YOUR KID FROM ABUSING DRUGS

Research on drug abuse reminds you of important issues for raising your children. These things won't really surprise you—they represent commonsense principles that we will deal with in greater detail in the next section. But you need to realize that ordinary good parenting techniques make it unlikely that your child will become addicted.

1. ADDRESS POTENTIAL EMOTIONAL PROBLEMS. Although your children's problems do not mean they have a lifetime disease, you still need to help them overcome emotional difficulties. If your children don't develop—or if they overcome—a psychological disorder, they are unlikely to abuse substances over the long term.

2. ENGAGE CHILDREN IN POSITIVE ACTIVITIES. Get your children involved in activities and off the couch. Excessive TV viewing and video game playing often precede and accompany excessive adolescent drinking.[21] Be sensitive to whatever your children like and are good at. To a large extent, the key to children's success at growing up is for them to discover what they do well and enjoy and to pursue those activities.

3. REWARD POSITIVE BEHAVIOR; DO NOT ACCEPT MISBEHAVIOR. In the next section we see that successful parenting requires you to set limits for children. This includes rewarding their positive behavior (such as willingly shoveling snow or mowing the lawn, helping others, doing something—athletic, academic, artistic—well) or calling them to task when they do the wrong thing (breaking other kids' toys, degrading other kids, ignoring your rules). This differs from permissiveness or, at the other extreme, immersing yourself in every detail of their lives. Children raised in this way (called

authoritative parenting), even disadvantaged youths, have fewer behavioral and substance problems.[22]

4. DEMAND CHILDREN BE RESPONSIBLE. Expect children to follow through on their promises and obligations: to complete scheduled projects, fulfill what is asked of them in your home and at school, work seriously at jobs, take care of themselves and their siblings and their property. Likewise, you must hold your children accountable for—by owning up to and making good on—any harm they do to others and to society.

5. PAY ATTENTION. Of course, you need to show your children that you love them. But beyond loving them, you need to be aware of what they are doing so that you can be in tune with their lives and help them when they need it—when they encounter problems they can't handle or have prolonged dips in their moods. Just because your child is unlikely to grow into an adult addict or alcoholic doesn't mean you shouldn't be engaged with him or her—up to a point.

PUNISHING KIDS' DRINKING AND DRUG USE

Many of you who are now parents used drugs or drank when you were younger, and some of you still smoke a joint on occasion. (We know you are out there: the National Survey on Drug Use and Health found in 2005 that more than 5 percent of those ages fifty to fifty-four were currently using illicit drugs, a percentage that has been rising for middle-aged Americans.) So, in many cases, you are asking your children not to do what you yourself did, or do. This can cause you conflict—are you a hypocrite to disapprove of and punish their behavior?

Do as I Say (Not as I Have Done)

Len was conflicted after he smoked marijuana with some old friends at a college reunion, then returned home to deal with his son Arthur, who spent his days at friends' houses taking drugs. How could Len justify penalizing Arthur for what he himself did?

Len was in a different situation than his son was. There's a difference between drug use that's secondary to a productive school or work life, as Len's had been and still was, and drug use that is part of adolescent bad behavior and perhaps more serious delinquency, as unfortunately it was for Arthur. Arthur wasn't developing skills and progressing in life the way his father had at his age, and Len was right to try to turn around Arthur's behavior to put him on a positive path.

A FEW WORDS ABOUT SMOKING

First, the relatively good news about one substance we worry about kids using—cigarettes. According to the 2005 MTF survey, half of high school seniors have ever smoked, 23 percent in the last month. Although this remains a troubling figure, it is much reduced from the three-quarters who had ever smoked in the late seventies and the two-thirds who had in 1999; 35 percent had smoked in the last month in 1999.

How did this reduction in such a harmful and powerfully addictive habit come about? We convinced many young people that using cigarettes isn't good for them. We succeeded by providing accurate information that made adolescents decide it was best for their own life goals not to smoke—because it made them less attractive and gave them bad breath, detracted from athletic and sexual performance, and would make their lives less enjoyable not only in the long run but currently. Accuracy and relevance are critical elements of successful drug education.

At the same time as youthful smoking has decisively declined, it remains by far the most prevalent harmful drug habit young people have. In addition to about a quarter of high school seniors, according to the National Survey on Drug Use and Health (NSDUH), 37 percent of those ages eighteen to twenty, and more than four in ten (41 percent) of those ages twenty-one to twenty-five, currently smoke, often while they're out drinking.

Of course, along with regular (addicted) smokers, many young people have experimented with this drug. Adolescents and college students will be exposed to cigarettes just as with other substances. So, even with smoking, relying solely on the message of total, life-long abstinence doesn't make for effective prevention.

Young people who smoke are also more likely to use or abuse other substances. As a group, according to NSDUH, 20 percent of current cigarette smokers use illicit drugs, compared with 4 percent of non-smokers; 44 percent of current cigarette users binge-drink, compared with 16 percent of non-smokers; 17 percent are heavy (regular binge) drinkers, compared with 4 percent of non-smokers.

Like other substance abusers, smokers are lower down the social totem pole. Among those ages eighteen to twenty-two, 30 percent of full-time college students smoke cigarettes, compared with 45 percent in that age group who don't attend college. Unemployment encourages smoking: 44 percent of jobless adults smoke, compared with only 29 percent of those with jobs. Among adults, 35 percent of those who haven't completed high school smoke cigarettes, while only 14 percent of college graduates do—even though college grads are much more likely to drink.

Thus, the same things that prevent substance abuse of all types apply to nicotine, too. Since smoking is far more common among the less well educated and less affluent, this is one more reason to encourage kids to pursue educations and careers and families. These, and other responsible and satisfying pursuits, are the best protection against smoking, as they are against all addictions.

The success we have had in educating adolescents about cigarettes, based on speaking to them in terms of their own interests in ways that make sense to them, are the ones we should adopt in educating them about drugs and alcohol. Unfortunately, as the next chapter shows, we can't seem to do this.

Three

WHY OUR DRUG EDUCATION DOESN'T WORK

Selden Bacon, a pioneering alcoholism researcher, likened the American approach to alcohol education to what driver education would be like if "knowledge about automobiles and their use . . . [was] limited to facts and theories about accidents and crashes."[1] Although most older adolescents drink—and most who do so drink regularly—prevention efforts concentrate on abstinence, while education dwells solely on the dangers of alcohol. This is a good part of what makes American drug and alcohol education an exercise in delusion and futility. Yet parents are so intimidated by this indoctrination that they passively accept it.

While writing this book, I attended a high school drug and alcohol prevention program for parents in a nearby community. Six panelists who had firsthand knowledge about teenage drinking and drug use spoke, with the chief of police moderating. The night consisted of a series of scare stories. The school counselor reported that binge drinking at parties was common and that typically when she asked a class if anyone had never been drunk, only one or two hands would go up. Marijuana use has become common among even very young kids, the prosecutor told us. She added that assaults, date rapes, and accidents in our community were frequent results of teenage binge drinking. The judge talked about the many adolescent drunk drivers in his court—whom he penalized severely, as well as forcing them to watch films about people killed and maimed due to drunk driving.

Presumably assuming that, like audiences at a slasher film playing at the nearby multiplex, our appetite for carnage could not be slaked, panelists piled more on. The DARE detective described how a young man in an unnamed town nearby had died after using drugs. The psychiatrist from the treatment center explained how the drug use and drinking that kids engaged in attacked the adolescent brain and led directly to drug dependence.

After the speakers finished, I rose to voice my reservations about the messages being presented: "Clearly, panelists believe the situation is bad, has gotten worse, and continues to deteriorate. Does anything that has been said here tonight differ in any way from anything parents have heard for the last ten years?" I paused. "If not, then why will we get any better results from repeating them? In fact, the research shows that these kinds of messages—like the DARE curriculum in our schools—are ineffective, even counterproductive."

The police chief cut me off. "This is not a debate. As for those so-called DARE statistics, you cannot prove a negative. The situation might be much worse without DARE."

WE ARE LOST, AND EVERYONE KNOWS IT

The United States spends more money on advertising and education programs warning kids about the dangers of substance use than any other country. This money is wasted, and everyone knows we are failing. The evidence of our failure, in the form of abundant teenage drug use and drinking, is inescapable. But just as children are not discouraged from drinking and using drugs by our programs, Americans are not discouraged from redoubling failed prevention efforts.

Oddly, parents' nights such as the one I attended *prove* that what we're doing doesn't work, as those best informed about the situation are most acutely aware. When I contacted some of the panelists privately, even they expressed frustration. "I know what we're doing is not working," the school's student assistance counselor told me. Most importantly, this brand of drug and alcohol education does nothing at all to prepare adolescents for the dangers that the majority who will use drugs or drink are actually likely to encounter.

The most frustrating aspect of this is that there *are* numerous, effective alternatives to DARE and its ilk, but politics and bureaucratic inertia prevent us from changing course and adopting them. In Chapter 11, I give an idea of what such sensible drug education policies would look like; in Appendix A, I provide resources for accessing these alternative education techniques.

HOW BADLY ARE WE DOING?

Let's quickly recap the facts showing that our prevention efforts are failing.

ILLICIT DRUG USE

By the time they are high school seniors, more than half of American youths have taken an illicit drug.[2] In the past month more than a fifth (22 percent) of twenty-one-year-old Americans did so. Overall, our nation's drug consumption has undergone a revolution in the last half century. Going back to the mid-1960s, only 5 percent of young Americans in the eighteen-to-twenty-five age bracket had taken an illicit substance—less than one-tenth of the figure today. Drug use is expanding worldwide to some extent. Still, the United States does poorly by international standards—for instance, ranking fifth highest among thirty-five nations in the rate of marijuana use by fifteen-year-olds.[3]

America is pioneering a new kind of drug abuse in the twenty-first century, as we witness the steady growth of illicit use of prescription drugs. Most new drug users now take prescription medications illicitly, rather than marijuana.[4] This has prompted the Partnership for a Drug-Free America to call today's adolescents "Generation Rx."[5]

ALCOHOL USE AND ABUSE

To start with, we are not discouraging underage drinking by a long shot. In 2004, half of fifteen-year-olds, three-quarters of eighteen-year-olds, and 85 percent of twenty-year-olds had consumed alcohol while all of them were underage. Well over half (56 percent) of twenty-year-olds had drunk alcohol in the previous month.[6] The truly alarming statistics, however, are the ones showing *how* young people drink. If drinking sensibly can be considered a skill, American education does even worse at teaching that than at promoting abstinence.

Drinking by American youth is notable for its extremity—consisting almost totally of intense binges of intoxication. Not only don't they drink moderately, they don't even believe in the concept of moderation. American high school seniors are more likely to disapprove of drinking one or two drinks nightly than of having five or more drinks once or twice each weekend.[7] Yet such binge drinking at early ages is especially disturbing because it is a long-term health hazard.[8]

DRINKING AMONG AMERICAN YOUTH

Age	Ever Drank	Drank Last Month	Binged Last Month
18	76%	46%	33%
20	85%	56%	40%
21	90%	70%	48%

Early binge drinking is all the more distressing because it marks young people's drinking throughout early adulthood. Kids don't stop bingeing when they can drink legally. Almost half of twenty-one-year-olds (48 percent–70 percent of those who drink) binge-drank in the past month. Fully 41 percent of Americans in the eighteen-to-twenty-five age bracket drank to excess at least once a month in 2004; in 1997, the figure was only 27 percent.[9]

Despite the efforts of the College Alcohol Study at Harvard University, which has highlighted and targeted the problem, binge drinking is getting worse on college campuses.[10] Forty percent of underage college students binge-drink.[11] Increasingly, female college students are binge drinkers, and many students are what is termed "extreme" bingers—drinking two or three times the amount that comprises a binge—beginning when they are freshmen.[12] CASA reports that half (49 percent) of all college students binge or use drugs at least monthly.

PATHOLOGICAL DRINKING AND DRUG USE

A large number of young Americans have a serious drinking or drug problem. Among those eighteen to twenty-five, 21 percent abuse or are dependent on a substance (mostly this involves alcohol, although problem drinking may be combined with drug abuse).[13] At the age of twenty-one, when they may legally drink, 25 percent display a significant clinical drinking or drug problem (again, for most their problem is, or includes, drinking).

YOUNG PEOPLE ARE DOING MORE DANGEROUS THINGS

In just a three-year period (between 1998 and 2001) the proportion of eighteen-to-twenty-four-year-old college students who reported driving drunk rose from 26 to 31 percent.[14] Of course, young people begin this behavior in high school, when a fifth of teens drive under the influence of alcohol (and 15 percent drive while high on marijuana).[15]

FOLLOW THE LOSERS

"Would you get financial advice from someone who went bankrupt?" asks drug policy reformer Ethan Nadelmann. In any other type of education it doesn't make sense to present as experts people who have endangered or ruined their lives due to the behavior they are teaching others about. Yet school drug education programs invariably turn to former substance abusers as models for students.

Listen to Us—We're Addicts!

At a special assembly, men and women in recovery from drug addiction and alcoholism lectured tenth graders. A speaker, glaring ominously, intoned, "One in ten of you kids is already addicted or alcoholic. By the twelfth grade, it is one in four. Unless you enter recovery, many of you will die from drug or alcohol use."

The speakers claimed the greatest danger was for those students "who feel that they can drink moderately, or control their drug use." As one put it, "The kids we feel sorry for are those who don't think that what happened to us will happen to them. No one comes out on top of drugs and alcohol!" He fixed his gaze on several well-scrubbed kids: "You're the ones I mean."

Rather than just hearing from recovered addicts, schools might invite Americans who have used drugs *without* harming themselves. Or one of the majority of adults who drink moderately—including the parents of many students—might tell how they do it. American drug education never presents people who have used drugs and gone on to make a positive contribution, such as President Bill Clinton. Kids also won't hear from those, including President George W. Bush, who overcame a drinking problem without the benefit of an organized program such as Alcoholics Anonymous.

Such hypocrisy is de rigueur. Public figures who tell the truth about their drug use risk damaging their careers. When Kareem Abdul-Jabbar described his collegiate drug use in his 1983 autobiography, *Giant Steps,* he was roundly criticized for presenting an irresponsible role model to American youth. The fact that Abdul-Jabbar had gone on to quit drugs and lead a disciplined life as a Muslim, a father, and a professional athlete did nothing to defuse the controversy. Obviously chastened by the public outcry, Abdul-Jabbar later rewrote his life story to eliminate any mention of his drug use (*Kareem,* published in 1990).

In another example, then New York City schools chancellor Joseph A. Fernandez wrote an autobiography in 1992 that revealed his heroin use as a young man. In *Tales Out of School,* Fernandez boldly described how, after surviving a drug overdose, although he didn't quit drugs completely and immediately, he went on to join the Navy, get a college degree, and then obtain a doctorate. He hoped his example would inspire the children under his charge, but

Fernandez had violated a taboo. Admitting he used drugs in the first place and continued to do so while in the service, finally quitting without going into rehab, amounted to heresy. Soon after the book was published he was forced to resign, his distinguished career in school administration over. So much for his idea of allowing adolescents to see models of people who progress beyond serious drug abuse to become productive citizens.

In his bestselling memoir, *Dreams from My Father*, Barack Obama described his youthful drinking and drug use. However, he blamed this use on his deep-seated angst about his racial identity. Thus he still implies that it's a very wrong thing to do rather than just saying it was a normal coming-of-age experience.

Showing kids only examples of people who *can't* control their use may convince young people that they are indeed powerless over drugs. The message to kids is that when a person does stray from the path of total abstinence, their doom is inevitable. Furthermore, this tells them they have no control over or responsibility for the consequences of their drug use.

WHEN DRUG PROGRAMS FACILITATE DRUG ABUSE

As we saw in the last chapter, children are least likely to become substance abusers when they become engaged in school life. School programs designed to combat drug abuse themselves often prevent this from happening.

I Wanted Brad to Excel at Shop. Was I Wrong?

Brad was an awkward, overweight teen. His ungainly physical appearance reflected deeper problems. He shuttled between his divorced parents' homes, and he didn't feel welcome in either.

Brad was good at woodworking, and his shop teacher, Joe, encouraged Brad. Brad often headed to the wood shop after his classes, where he worked with the teacher. Brad made a mirrored hall stand of which he was terribly proud. Joe had it displayed in the school lobby.

Joe knew that Brad took drugs. "I thought if I could get him working with his hands, he'd quit that drug stuff. He needed something to take him away from his home situation and the other misfit kids."

In the middle of his freshman year, however, Brad became a protégé of Celia, the school's drug counselor. Instead of going to the shop in free moments, Brad joined a group she organized for drug users. With a pass from Celia, he often skipped classes to hang out in the counselor's office with other high-risk kids. At a drug awareness assembly, Brad and the other group members sat onstage behind Celia. She introduced them as students who were in "early recovery." The other kids in the auditorium applauded.

Joe questioned this role for Brad. "I thought the other students pitied the kids onstage. I wondered if they even mocked Brad and the others. He still dressed like a sad sack. I felt sorry for him up there.

"He never did come back to work in the shop after that," Joe recalls sadly. "Naturally, I never said anything. People seemed to feel that this was a good thing for Brad to do. I only wanted him to develop a useful skill and feel proud of something he did well."

In fact, Joe's approach of helping Brad to develop his skills and interests rather than focus on his weaknesses *was* better for the boy. This should be the goal of drug education and treatment for high-risk kids, rather than persuading them that they are addicts. Students who decide they are addicts or alcoholics and who attend college may also try to isolate themselves from other students, and universities have created "recovery" dormitories (also sometimes called "substance-free" or "wellness" dormitories) for them. Although residents of these dorms are somewhat less likely to drink, most still find abstinence difficult to maintain on campus.[16]

SO FAR, DRUG EDUCATION HAS FAILED—LET'S DO MORE OF IT!

A *Los Angeles Times* article entitled "Anti-Drug Overdose?" reported that scientists find popular school programs don't help, and "some researchers even suggest that school drug-prevention programs could do harm, particularly to younger students."[17] The article described a ninth grader, Mariana Kouloumian. Introduced to moderate drinking at home, Mariana was "taught in elementary school not to drink or use drugs ever." But this message "didn't square with what she saw in the real world." As a result, "at 14, the Los Angeles girl dismisses much of what she learned in the drug-education program."

The article discusses DARE (Drug Abuse Resistance Education). Founded in Los Angeles in 1983 by that city's police chief Daryl Gates, DARE dominates American drug education—three-quarters of American school districts use DARE.[18] For all its good intentions, there is no evidence that DARE actually works. Instead, research has consistently found that students who attended DARE training in elementary school go on to use as many drugs as those who didn't participate[19]—sometimes they use more.[20] Public health researchers have repeatedly declared unambiguously that "DARE is ineffective."[21] As a result, DARE is not included among the U.S. government's list of effective prevention programs.[22]

Under pressure as an organization to change its methods, DARE revamped its curriculum to offer instruction in decision making and social skills to older kids. The new program is marketed as "high-tech, interactive, and decision-model-based." But the fundamentals of DARE remain the same: police officers lecture children never to use drugs or alcohol.

Giving schoolchildren "positive exposure to the police" is often offered as the rationale for using police as drug educators. Though that is a laudable ideal, it doesn't serve the purpose of drug education. Police officers are not known for their skills at communicating with young people, nor are they typically very knowledgeable about drug and alcohol use—at least that which does not lead to criminal activity. The brief instructor training and DARE tools that police officers are furnished don't change what makes DARE fail.

School drug education is just one part of the American policy of saturating young people with negative information about drug use. In 1998, Congress appropriated more than $1 billion for anti-drug advertisements aimed at youngsters ages nine to eighteen. In 2006, a government study found that the ads did not reduce children's drug use. In fact, the research discovered that some groups of young people who were exposed to the ads were more likely to begin using marijuana. Drug czar John Walters simply rejected the evaluation the government had paid more than $40 million for, and said his agency would continue to produce the ads. (See Appendix B.)

HERE'S AN IDEA: LET'S SCARE KIDS ABOUT USING DRUGS

A favorite prevention technique in DARE is the tale of drug horror. No drug-use-disaster story is too gory or implausible.

Don't Rub Your Eyes with Spicy Chicken when You're Stoned!

Like many high school students all over the country, Amy and her friends immediately perceive stories they get from DARE officers as insults to their intelligence. One story in particular got them going.

According to the police instructor: "A teen in a town near here smoked marijuana with his girlfriend. The marijuana was laced with some other drug. The two of them took a walk, like people high on pot often do. When his girlfriend started freaking out the kid panicked and ran to a neighboring house to call for help. Since no one was home, he broke the glass on a sliding door, cut an artery in his arm, and bled to death."

Amy and her friends could barely suppress their laughter. Afterward, they circulated a series of jokes mocking the oblivious DARE officer: "A kid got stoned, then got the really spicy chicken at the Chicken Wing. He started rubbing his eyes and went blind! That's why you should never use drugs!"

Certainly, young people can be hurt by using drugs, but how often do they bleed to death because they break into strange houses seeking emergency care? The sheer unlikelihood of such a tale seems almost calculated to make sure students ignore it, along with more plausible dangers.

The formula of telling a horror story involving death or permanent injury is a hoary one. Even reputable news outlets seem to throw their journalistic standards out the window when it comes to tall tales about drug use. The granddaddy of these urban myths is the story about LSD users being blinded.

The hoax that college students had been blinded while on LSD appeared in newspapers and magazines nationwide twice in the space of a year. The first time, on May 18, 1967, the *Los Angeles Times* reported that four Santa Barbara college students had damaged their eyes by staring at the sun while they were under the influence of LSD. Although the article gave no names, it provided such medical details as "a pinhead-size hole was burned into the retina of each eye of the students." The story was repeated in the *New York Times* and *Time* magazine before it was discredited.

Less than eight months later, on January 13, 1968, a *Los Angeles Times* headline declared, "6 College Men Take LSD, Blinded by Sun." This time, the victims "suffered total and permanent blindness by staring at the sun while under the influence of the drug LSD . . . all lay on their backs in the grass and were not consciously looking at the sun." Again, the story spread throughout the national media before it was revealed to have been fabricated by a misguided public official.

By promoting these myths—and buying in to them ourselves— we lose the opportunity to see things as they are, and to urge kids to take realistic precautions. Our society's way of combating drug use actually contributes to the problems we dread.

LET'S HEAR FROM THE AUDIENCE— BUT NOT ADDRESS THEIR CONCERNS

Bad things do sometimes happen to people who use alcohol and drugs, as everyone knows, including your children. You and your children can prevent accidents like these by having the forethought to take needed precautions and the self-regard to remedy problems when they do occur. But how to do this is not information you and your kids can obtain in school prevention programs.

At the evening about substance abuse I attended with parents of high school students, the message that the three hundred of us in the auditorium heard loud and clear was that despite all kinds of effort put out by the community, adolescent substance abuse had spiraled out of control. The parents of these teenagers, it was implied, were in large part responsible for this failure. Although the parents' attendance showed their interest, one after another of the speakers told us we were oblivious to the problem.

Parents responded with concern and fear for their children, and with trepidation about upsetting the group mind-set. Several audience members spoke about their own children who had been in drug treatment (one of whom subsequently died). These parents agreed with the speakers about how devastating drugs and alcohol were to adolescents.

A couple of people besides me questioned the apparent consensus at the meeting. A young man from a neighboring private school spoke up: "Why should those in your generation have had the chance to take and enjoy drugs, while my friends and I shouldn't have that chance?" The school counselor replied, "Yes, but all of those people I knew who took drugs back then have become severely addicted, or died, or went into treatment." The majority of parents in the audience who themselves had taken drugs could have testified that this was ridiculous. None did, however.

The main part of the audience that night, the silent majority, were average parents who were trying to figure out what to do should their children drink or use drugs. They had been bombarded with claims that adolescent substance abuse pervaded their community. They had been instructed to be vigilant about their kids' drug use and drinking. If they discovered that their kids were using, the single solution offered was to seek treatment.

A few parents did ask about serving their kids alcohol. The pediatrician on the panel said that he had grown up in an ethnic group where drinking was a regular and positive experience. But the topic of social drinking was quickly passed over and there was no discussion of how parents could provide a positive home drinking environment.

Of course, parents cannot be satisfied with events where their stupidity and the failure of the entire system are the featured themes. Many have the appropriate reaction: like their kids, they question and resent the nonsense they are being taught. Sometimes they have the wherewithal to take matters into their own hands—as you may have to.

Parents Question Authority

At her school's drug and alcohol awareness night, Ann listened to scary talks about the damage children in the school had suffered. She was particularly struck by the stories a counselor told about frequent incidents of alcohol poisoning among teens.

When Ann asked whether it was all right to give children wine occasionally, the counselor was adamant: "That is the biggest mistake that you can make. The earlier children drink, the more likely they are to continue to drink and to become alcoholics. The kids who overdose on alcohol are ones whose parents let them drink." (On the contrary, in Chapter 7 we will find that research shows that children who drink with their parents are one-third as likely to binge as those who don't do so.)[23]

It struck Ann that many of the parents in the auditorium she knew took the same approach she did—but not one of them spoke up to support her. She felt isolated and foolish. Although no kids she knew had suffered alcohol poisoning, she now questioned her own approach.

Sylvia was a Turkish immigrant who had come to the United States to study and now taught at a university here. She sent her son to a Quaker school. Sylvia loved both the Quakers' educational program and their social consciousness.

One thing bothered Sylvia: the school's anti-alcohol attitudes. Teachers solicited students' opinions on most matters. But when it came to their opposition to drinking they were intransigent.

Sylvia was resolute in her own approach to drinking. Turkey is a wine-drinking culture where children are given alcohol. In the European School Survey Project on Alcohol and Other Drugs (ESPAD), a study of fifteen- and sixteen-year-olds conducted in thirty-five Western countries, Turkish adolescents had the lowest rate of drunkenness.[24] (Another study that did not include Turkey, the World Health Organization's Health Behavior in School-Aged Children, identified Macedonia, another culture that teaches young people how to drink, as the country with the lowest rate of drunkenness among the thirty-five countries included in that survey.)

Sylvia's father had given her wine mixed with water when she was a small child—and she did the same for her own son. For his part, her son marveled at what he regarded as the crazy drinking of adolescents at his school. "They act as though they'll never have another chance to drink."

Sylvia requested that her son be excused from alcohol education classes. She simply stated, "My culture has a different approach toward alcohol."

Eleven-year-old Monique told her mother, Mary, that the DARE officer told her class: "Look around: one in four of you will die from drugs!"

Mary called the school, outraged. "What do you mean, scaring small children about taking drugs and dying? It will just make drugs a big deal for them. And where did this cop get that 'one in four' bullshit?

"Another thing; my daughter was promised an ice cream and skating party when she graduated from DARE if she signed a pledge not to use drugs or drink until she was twenty-one. Don't send that pledge home with her. It's none of your business what I teach my child about drinking."

Ann intuited that her school's program was nonsensical, but she wasn't armed to confront its irrationality and to argue for what she felt was right. Sylvia was firm about her positive cultural heritage, one she wanted to pass along to her son. Mary confronted and resisted the entire spectrum of drug education poltergeists. She believed she should teach her children drinking in the home and that institutions should stay out of people's personal lives. Although few people are firebrands like Mary, in your own way you need to transcend the anti-drug and anti-alcohol propaganda that dominates the current debate.

CRITICAL THINKING 101

Remember in school how you were told to question received wisdom and to make your own intellectual connections so that the material made sense to you? You surely ought to do no less when contemplating drug education, which is a lot more important to you than a literature course. For example, when you hear one of those strange stories about death and destruction resulting from drug use, use your critical faculties and request the following information:

- Can you give us more exact details?
- How frequently do such events occur in this school district?
- What can we learn from this story to protect our children?

The last, of course, is the most important, crucial question. If the answer is, "Tell kids not to take drugs," then your follow-up questions are: "Didn't anyone tell those kids not to take drugs?" and "What about the majority of high school seniors who still take drugs? Are we just going to let them go blind or die? Or is there something we can do to help and protect them?"

The sad fact is that the people we hope will guide us through the thickets of adolescent substance abuse will not help you. In the absence of useful information, you are left to your own devices. For example, the school counselor described to me how students in our community had previously organized their own safe-rides program. With no school support, she said, it petered out. "I have told my own children to call me if they found themselves in that situation," she added. But this professional didn't initiate any discussion of such a crucial, potentially life-preserving technique during the parents' information evening.

For his part, the DARE officer boasted to me privately: "I don't go in there telling them, 'Don't do it, don't do it.' They're not going to listen to me." At the same time, he contradicted himself by saying, "I want kids to know they can't use drugs without harming themselves."

How can you and others help your children, who are more likely than not to use drugs and drink to excess, to protect themselves? This is the subject of Part III, where I review techniques you can use with your kids (in Chapter 9) and drug education that actually works (in Chapter 11).

KIDS KNOW A THING OR TWO

It *is* true that you probably don't know the full extent of your own children's drinking and drug use. Most parents don't recognize when their kids are seriously involved with—or even have problems around—drugs and alcohol.[25] Being out of touch with what your children are doing means that you cannot help them deal with these experiences. On the other hand, if you *don't* learn that your children are using drugs and drinking in high school, this is usually a sign that your kids are managing their use. They may actually know a good deal about how to avoid damaging themselves when they take these substances.

Amy and her friends—who ridiculed the DARE officer's story—are going to good colleges where they plan to prepare themselves for solid careers. Perhaps we feel they'd be better off if they didn't use drugs and drink. Maybe they will decide that themselves at some point. But in the meantime, they are not self-destructive people. When they use substances, they take precautions that no adult has advised them to, but which they know make sense. They deride other kids' recklessness, indicating that they are not so foolish or self-abasing.

Carla Is a Slut

"Did you see what Carla did at that party?" Amy asked Bill. "She got wasted on her first date with Tom, and then went into a bedroom and hooked up with him. She's such a slut!"

It is unkind of Amy to mock a girl who has so little self-respect that she engages in risky drinking and sex. But it describes her and her friends' attitudes—that they need to keep their heads when they drink, not risk physical danger (as by driving drunk) or put themselves in the hands of people who would harm or take advantage of them. They can curtail their drinking when necessary, even if they do become tipsy. They know how to select safe environments, to rely on friends, and to place limits on their behavior.

We rarely hear about students who do well and use drugs and drink. But as we saw in the last chapter, kids who succeed at school are just as likely (or perhaps even more likely) to use substances as kids who are less academically successful. At the same time, they are less likely to harm themselves. *The Notebook Girls,* a joint diary by four girls at an elite New York high school, described how kids accomplish this.[26]

Interview with *The Notebook Girls*

Why would you want to publish your diary?
LINDSEY: A lot of people—parents and adults—are interested in knowing about kids' lives, not specifically ours. . . .
How'd you guys get such good grades?. . .
LINDSEY: It's not hard to, like, smoke pot and also get good grades. We're not unique. . . .
COURTNEY: It's about making choices, like "I went out on Friday, so I'm not going to go out on Saturday" or "I am going to smoke right after school and, like, by late evening I can do schoolwork." None of us went to school high.
SOPHIE: I did, once.
COURTNEY: But it wasn't, like, a regular thing. You would never blow schoolwork to have fun.
SOPHIE: I didn't smoke before school. Or before a test. Those were stupid mistakes other kids made.[27]

The girls had values and activities that took precedence over their drug use. This is the key to all controlled use of substances, by young people or adults. And convincing children they cannot exercise such choices is a road map to abuse.

Very few of us could tolerate knowing everything our children are up to, just as there are many things we never wanted our parents to discover about us (and thank God they didn't). When we get a glimpse of the inner lives of even the most responsible and successful high school and college students, we are sometimes shocked. In Part III, we will encounter good kids who do experience problems. Even so, rest assured that virtually all young people have a natural urge not to hurt themselves.

DRUG EDUCATION THAT WORKS

Successful education of any kind fully engages children. An effective instructor elicits and builds on students' knowledge and viewpoints, encouraging an honest exchange. Instead of distorting and burying the truth, such learning explores ways kids may change dangerous behaviors, or at least how they can protect themselves against excess and danger. In the last section of this book, along with effective treatment and risk prevention techniques, I suggest a blueprint for meaningful drug education. At the same time, you can overcome the monumental stupidity we have observed in this chapter to protect your kids from the real dangers young people face.

Part Two

RAISING A
NON-ADDICTED CHILD

Four

YOU CAN RAISE A NON-ADDICTED CHILD

You now know what addiction is, the facts about youthful drug use and drinking, and how substance use and abuse are mistaught in our schools. Armed with this information, you can consider your role as a parent in raising a non-addicted child.

First, you need to accept the importance of your parental role. Ironically, much of what you hear about children's development will discourage you from believing that. The perceived disempowerment of parents is itself a central part of the problem.

Judith Rich Harris struck a chord in America with her book *The Nurture Assumption: Why Children Turn Out the Way They Do*. Harris claims that peer groups or genetically inherited traits, but not parenting, determine how people turn out: "How the parents rear the child has no long-term effects on the child's personality, intelligence, or mental health."[1]

In a sense, this message is terrifically reassuring, because it takes the pressure off you as a parent. It presents a comforting antidote to the Freudian view that how you handle each childhood hiccup and burp impacts children's personalities in ways that will only be apparent when they end up on a therapist's couch.

Harvard psychologist Jerome Kagan takes an intermediate position between these extremes. Kagan has found that children can modify their inbred temperaments in response to their changing worlds.[2] On one hand, this means that children can overcome—or at least augment—distinctive dispositions in order to become the kinds of people they want to be. On the other, Kagan's perspective indicates that you can be a very caring, concerned, hands-on parent who doesn't abuse your children and *still* have a child with drug, alcohol, or other addiction problems. But you certainly influence the likelihood that this will occur.

If your child becomes addicted to drugs, you can't help worrying—was it something you did that made your child go wrong? At the least, parenting an addicted child is humbling. In Chapter 1, we saw the case of John, who came from a well-heeled and successful family. Whenever his parents described their son's drug problems, they immediately stressed how much they had been involved in his life—how they took him to his athletic events, sent him to special camps, and, after he was addicted, enrolled him repeatedly in the best treatment programs available.

The National Alliance for the Mentally Ill (NAMI), a support group for the parents of mentally ill children, contests the view that parents are responsible for their children's emotional problems. We can sympathize with NAMI's goal of protecting these parents from a further burden of guilt. But the most effective parents accept the responsibilities of parenting and believe and act as though they matter.

This book will not be endorsed by the Web site maintained by the National Youth Anti-Drug Media Campaign (www.TheAnti Drug.com), which recommends methods for monitoring your children's behavior to make sure they never take drugs.[3] The Web site and I agree, however, that, as the site puts it, "You matter. You can influence your child's behavior."

PARENTS *DO* INFLUENCE THEIR CHILDREN

You indisputably influence your children by the values you convey to them. How else do children learn what is right or wrong? What are their political attitudes? What are their religious beliefs? Of course, children don't necessarily adopt their parents' values, religion, and political attitudes wholesale. But very often, even when children seem to be reacting against their parents, they express points of view and values very close to those of at least one parent.

Who Knew She Was Paying Attention?

Lily was a hardworking lawyer who often spent weekends at the office and traveled extensively, which her two daughters resented. Their resentment grew when, after the younger daughter graduated from high school, Lily and her husband were divorced.

Lily was also a loving and committed mother. She prepared breakfast and saw her two daughters off to school every day she was at home. Lily wanted to be a part of her children's lives in every way she could. Her children were very successful in school and never had emotional or substance abuse problems.

So Lily was anguished when her older daughter, Laura, criticized her for breaking up the family. Laura had already consciously adopted a different style from her mother, emphasizing in her dress and demeanor that she wasn't as "uptight" as Lily.

But when Lily visited Laura at her elite college and asked her what she planned to study, Laura answered, "Law." "What kind?" Lily queried. Laura told her, "Litigation, like you."

Lily discovered that Laura regularly donated blood. Lily had always donated blood as a commitment she made to her community. Laura told her, "It's something I feel strongly that I should do, Mom."

So beware: your children might be like you! They learn basic values at home. It seems safe to assume that all concerned parents accept that they help to shape their children in these ways. (I bet even Judith Rich Harris feels this way.) Good parents, no matter what they believe about children's inherited traits, spend time deciding the best places for their kids to go to school. They worry about whether they are giving their children enough—and the right kind of—attention. And they discipline their children when they feel the kids have done something seriously wrong.

From the other direction, we are all aware that parents are capable of traumatizing their children. Belittling children, ignoring their emotional needs, or abusing them will have a serious negative impact. Even Nora Volkow, director of the National Institute on Drug Abuse, who predicts we will solve the problem of addiction through neurochemical research, says that "addicts are more likely to have been unnecessarily stressed during childhood (from neglect, emotional, physical or sexual abuse, or poverty) and they're less able to deal with stress as adults."[4]

ARE CHILDREN FORMED IN HEAVEN?

Some religions believe that people's lives are foreordained by God even before they're born. And many believe that science today endorses a similarly fatalistic view. As such ideas about genetic predisposition enter the mainstream, parents can feel that there is really no point to fighting children's biological destinies. This view has become especially prevalent around adolescent substance abuse and addiction.

It's true that children often have distinctive temperaments from birth. One often cited example is the disposition to be shy. There is strong evidence that children have innately different reactions to stimulation. Some withdraw from external stimuli, which manifests itself as shyness.

But genetic inheritance is not destiny with shy children. Jerome Kagan points us toward our best understanding of the interaction between nature and nurture here. His research shows that about 20 percent of kids are born hypersensitive to outside stimuli. Such children feel tense and inhibited in the presence of other people.

But, Kagan found, these kids are no more likely to grow up to be shy than other children.[5] If you have children like this, you can gradually expose them to stimulating environments and to other people so that they can accommodate to the world in their own ways.

Warren, Let's Count Your Friends

Warren was an extremely shy and passive child. For instance, he refused to interact with any adults other than his mother and father.

Warren's parents, Stu and Grace, recognized this was a problem, and they thought carefully about how to help Warren emerge from the protective shell he built for himself. They arranged for Warren to be with other kids by taking friends of Warren's with them on weekend excursions.

By kindergarten, Warren had a small group of pals. But when they came to his house, he was very finicky about his possessions—for example, he sulked when they didn't put away his toys. He fought with several of his friends over this.

Stu sat down with Warren one day. "How many friends do you have, Warren?" Stu asked. Warren named four. Stu then asked Warren, who was already very good at math, "How many of your friends did you fight with in the last two weeks?" "Two." "What percentage of all your friends is that?" "Half," Warren answered. Stu concluded, "What will the percentage be if you fight with one or both of your other friends?"

Warren considered his answer for a moment, then asked to excuse himself. He was more tolerant of his friends' shortcomings the next time one visited.

Grace found it difficult at first to see where her husband was going with his intervention. When Warren said he had four friends, she chimed in, "No, you have more." She wanted to boost Warren's self-esteem.

Stu was aiming for something else. He was using Warren's own values and inclinations to help Warren develop his skills and motivation for dealing with other children. Stu was practicing a technique we will learn in the following chapters, *motivational interviewing*. Most important, both parents didn't take for granted that Warren would be a reclusive teenager or adult.

A trait at the opposite extreme from shyness and withdrawal is labeled *impulsiveness, thrill-seeking,* or *aggressiveness*. Some theories hold that children who seek excitement while ignoring social constraints and the feelings of others are predisposed to crime and addiction. On the other hand, business entrepreneurs often display such traits. Both types of people tend to take risks and ignore others' warnings.

Ivan the Conqueror

Ivan drove his parents to distraction with his impulsiveness. As a teenager, Ivan rarely considered the consequences of his actions. Once he rolled his bowling ball down the alley before the automatic pin setter had risen, just missing it. As his friends tried to imagine the consequences, Ivan laughed uproariously.

Ivan was not successful in school and was often disciplined. After graduating from high school, Ivan joined the army. Where many others found the experience of battle frightening and disorienting, Ivan enjoyed his military stint. He came home viewing himself as someone who could be a valued member of society.

Ivan became a trader in the extremely volatile commodities market. He had the ability to shrug off losing many thousands of dollars. After Ivan's clients had taken deep losses, they were taken aback when Ivan nonchalantly told them, "We're going to make a killing tomorrow." Ivan was well suited to a risky occupation that earned him a sizable income.

You can always help children with distinctive personalities to find fulfillment. It just takes a little creativity on your part. A study of children of alcoholics found that thrill-seeking children of alcoholic parents more often become alcoholics themselves. Yet many do not develop alcoholism. "One of the take-home messages of the study is that those thrill-seeking tendencies can go in a variety of directions, and are not necessarily predestined to seek out alcohol or drugs," said researcher Richard Grucza. Grucza suggested that parents of such children direct them toward sports.[6]

These cases—and the best research—make the essential point that although people differ at birth in temperament and in other ways, parents aren't powerless against these tendencies. As another way of looking at it, consider that people adopt addictions, such as smoking, that are in line with their personalities (for example, smokers may be anxious people). Yet although they don't change their personalities, they often do quit smoking.

WHAT DOES THE GENOME TELL US?

The answer to the question "Have they found the gene for alcoholism and addiction?" is, "Yes, so far they've found fifty-one of them." This is the number of regions on the genome associated with alcohol dependence in one study.[7] More sites will undoubtedly be connected to addiction in future research.

Genetic investigators have been mapping the genome— identifying sections of DNA (genes) on human chromosomes and relating them to individual traits. It seems to some observers that this process will produce a map of human nature and behavior, where every action is directly connected to a section of DNA.

But the results of the genome research are much more complicated than this. Scientists who actually relate genetic material to human characteristics are among those most modest about identifying genes that determine mental illnesses and behavior. Even if they were inclined to make such connections, premature and erroneous claims of having found "the" genes for bipolar disorder and schizophrenia have deflated such optimism.

One surprising result of studying the genome is the discovery of just how little we can tell based on particular genes. Most of the DNA on human chromosomes is not organized into specific genes. Much of this genetic material directs the pace at which other genes express themselves. Moreover, environmental experiences (including those in utero) influence the expression of genes. For these reasons and others, simple relationships between individual genes—or even groups of genes—and specific traits are rare.

How much room the genome leaves for parental influence and (for want of a better word) choice is especially evident in the area of addiction. Genes could certainly impact human reactions to alcohol, drugs, sugar, or excitement and stimulation in general. For example, alcohol may make some people feel tremendously relaxed. But what makes them regularly drink until intoxication, which is required to be an alcoholic, when their drunkenness hurts their lives, people they love, or activities they are deeply involved in? Genes simply cannot explain this.

The scientific reaction to the study that found fifty-one genes related to alcohol dependence was to note how complicated tracing the path of alcoholism has become. Including drug addicts and those addicted to cigarettes, sex, food, gambling, shopping, and the Internet in the research would certainly expand the number of genes implicated in addiction. When a large and shifting number of genes are associated with a condition, it is as though everyone is susceptible. Nora Volkow has said: "Some people may be naturally better protected against addiction than others, but that's not enough to keep someone from becoming addicted."[8]

I INHERITED IT FROM MY DADDY

The complexity of genetic relationships doesn't translate well into popular culture. Therapists, people in addiction support groups, and just plain Joes and Janes—understandably wishing things to be as simple and straightforward as possible—have run wild with the idea of inheritance of addiction.

What Have You Done to My Son?

Rafael and Christine had a difficult marriage. They approached life in very different ways. Rafe was a relaxed, laissez-faire father, Christine a meticulous, demanding mother. Rafe also drank much more than Christine, who rarely imbibed. She wanted Rafe to quit drinking and attend AA meetings.

The couple often disagreed about their teenage son, Gary. When Gary became fascinated with pornography and racked up charges for calls to 900 numbers and pay-per-view sites, Rafe decided to buy Gary his own porn videos. "It'll save us a fortune," he told his wife.

Christine, meanwhile, took Gary to a sex addiction specialist. Afterward, she confronted Rafe angrily: "He said Gary is a sex addict and that he inherited it from you and your alcoholism."

When couples are at loggerheads, it is difficult for them to make crucial decisions about their children. Obviously, Christine and Rafe need help in parental decision making, setting consistent limits and deciding what behavior is acceptable and what isn't—the subject of the next chapters.

In this case, the couple needs to decide whether Gary is addicted or going through an ordinary phase (on top of which are their differences of opinion about whether Rafe has a drinking problem). But there is certainly no scientific justification for the therapist's conclusion that Gary inherited his behavior from Rafe—Christine simply adopted this position as part of her power struggle with her husband. This glib genetic explanation for their child's and their family's problems is not at all helpful.

People often prefer to view their habits as genetic inheritances, since this lessens their responsibility for their behavior. Famous drug abuser and rocker Ozzy Osbourne produced two drug-dependent children. Osbourne's daughter, Kelly Osbourne, explained that she and her brother, Jack, "became inclined towards drugs because of the faulty genes that we were born with." But her nineteen-year-old brother viewed things differently. On the TV program *Entertainment Tonight,* Jack said that "as a child he thought his rock star dad was 'cool' for partying and taking drugs and alcohol. 'In a really sick, dark way I wanted to be a druggie.' "[9]

Drew Barrymore is another celebrity addiction story. At thirteen, she was described in *People* magazine as America's youngest addict. At fourteen, she wrote an autobiography, *Little Girl Lost.* Experts pointed out that Barrymore's father, mother, and grandfather had all been alcoholics or addicts, so her propensity for addiction was a family trait. But when she became a successful actress as an adult, Barrymore stopped seeing herself as an addict and, as a result of this change in her self-image, people no longer think of her as one.

We'll never know whether the children's addictions in these cases were inherited or acquired. The question is whether these young people could have avoided addiction, and how their parents could have helped them to do so. In one scene on their reality TV series,

The Osbournes, Ozzy told his children never to drink or take drugs, using himself as the negative case. This parenting tack obviously proved unsuccessful. For reasons we will explore in Chapter 7, preaching abstinence can actually increase the likelihood of excess.

Yet most people manage to avoid repeating their parents' addictions, and in Chapter 8 we discuss how you can prevent this inheritance from occurring. More to the point, most people—like Drew Barrymore—overcome their own addictions. If people inherit their addiction to cigarettes, how have fifty million Americans quit smoking? Is there a separate gene for quitting addiction?

Genetics are never destiny, outside of eye color and some rare inherited diseases. Whatever you hear elsewhere, addiction is not about faulty genes. In this area, we have free will, and with it responsibility. The important message for you and your children is that their lives—and drug use and drinking—are theirs to determine.

THEORIES THAT SAY YOU DON'T GET OVER ADDICTION

Another spate of scientific theories strives to explain why people cannot escape addiction. Like the law of inertia in physics, these theories purport to show that drinking and taking drugs set forces into motion that are impossible to reverse. R. Andrew Chambers of the Yale School of Medicine and his colleagues claim that drugs stimulate parts of the adolescent brain critical to the children's development—particularly their tendency toward impulsive and risky behavior. This action of the drugs on their brains, in the researchers' view, causes children to continue taking drugs.[10]

Young people's natural tendency to explore their identities encourages them to experiment with drugs and alcohol. At the same time, according to Chambers, drug experiences affect neurological development. Drug use and drinking make young people more likely to take risks, to suppress good judgment, and to have sex.

To explain why this behavior perpetuates itself, Chambers and other drug researchers point out that drugs increase levels of dopamine, the chemical in the brain underlying pleasure. In this model of addiction, young people need to take drugs to maintain their habitual dopamine levels. Perhaps adolescents who cannot produce sufficient dopamine (or whose brain receptors don't permit enough to enter their nervous systems) are those who then become addicted. Since eating, gambling, pornography, and other experiences elevate dopamine levels, this theory offers the chance to explain all addiction in one fell swoop.

But the very universality of dopamine as a mediating chemical in our brains makes us wonder how people come to be addicted to drugs or alcohol, or anything else, if so many people try any or all of these things without becoming addicted. That some are predisposed to addiction due to deficient dopamine in their brains is likewise unconvincing, among other reasons because so many addicts do outgrow addiction as they mature.

Another theory was tested with rats by Aaron White and his colleagues at Duke University Medical Center. When adolescent rats were administered alcohol, the researchers found, the rats became less sensitive to its effects, and thus had better balance when intoxicated. Tested as adult rats, these adolescent "inebriates" did not show the kind of impairment of motor skills mature rats typically display from drinking.[11] Desensitized to alcohol's effects, adolescent drinkers are prone to continue drinking heavily and to become alcoholics when they mature, according to White.

As interesting as they are, these theories don't explain why adolescents continue to devote themselves to drug and alcohol intoxication. Because people can tolerate alcohol and function more readily doesn't mean they will always prefer getting drunk over pursuing other options in their lives. In order to binge-drink or to drink alcoholically, kids still must be motivated to imbibe large quantities of alcohol. This motivation isn't due to brain insensitivity to alcohol. Rather, those few adolescents whose binge drinking evolves into permanent alcoholism lack the motivation, ability, and opportunity to move beyond adolescent problems and traps.

White's and Chambers' theories are examples of the standard research sponsored by the National Institute on Drug Abuse (NIDA) and the National Institute on Alcohol Abuse and Alcoholism (NIAAA). The goal of these agencies is to explain why alcohol and drug use, especially by the young, is bad. But politics sets the agendas of these supposedly scientific organizations and undercuts the validity of their work. Funded researchers must support the institutes' predetermined point of view instead of openly exploring scientific questions.

A *Scientific American Mind* article about research on the effects of alcohol asserted that "an encounter with the familiar stimuli will make the feeling of need for the substance almost irresistible"; "routine alcohol consumption changes circuitry in the brain in ways that lead to addiction"; "simple willpower may be insufficient to break the grip"; "victims can no longer free themselves from the bottle."[12] Rather than science, such verbiage resembles the anti-alcohol temperance rhetoric of earlier centuries. And although presentations and theories like these can sound convincing in isolation, they ignore the essential finding that excessive drinking does not lock people into alcoholism. The scientific data show that most people outgrow their early substance abuse.

IT IS NORMAL FOR PEOPLE TO ESCAPE DRUGS AND ADDICTION

The NIDA's and NIAAA's own research shows people typically quit drug use, addiction, and alcoholism, as we saw in Chapter 2. The National Survey on Drug Use and Health measures how many people have used drugs in their lifetimes versus how many have done so in the past month. According to this NIDA research, most Americans who experimented with powerful drugs when they were younger no longer use them: of all Americans who have ever used heroin, crack, or cocaine, fewer than 10 percent used each substance in the past month.

Moreover, adolescents and young adults who abuse alcohol and drugs, even to the point of becoming dependent on them, overwhelmingly outgrow this state. The NSDUH found that 21 percent of Americans between the ages of eighteen and twenty-five either abused or depended on alcohol and drugs. Yet only 7 percent of Americans twenty-six or older did so, and this percentage declines steadily with age. This drop-off is not caused because many substance-abusing young people die. In 2002, 17,944 youths aged ten to twenty died out of 40,000,000 Americans that age, or .4 percent (according to the Centers for Disease Control's National Center for Health Statistics). And, of course, only a portion of these have died as a result of substance use.

The massive National Epidemiologic Survey on Alcohol and Related Conditions likewise found that of all Americans who have ever been alcoholic, about a quarter are currently alcohol-dependent. This is so even though only a quarter underwent treatment—but no more treated alcoholics achieved remission than untreated alcoholics. Moreover, the large majority of subjects in the study continued to drink, but in a moderate or non-alcoholic way.[13]

As we have seen, Koren Zailckas' book *Smashed* described a life dominated by drinking from early adolescence through college. But after her decade-long dependence on alcohol, Zailckas quit getting drunk. Instead, Zailckas took up opportunities to work, to communicate, and to form an intimate relationship. Her ability to do so resulted from values and strengths she had suppressed but which ultimately won out. Zailckas also placed a strong value on self-reliance, which is why she refused—and continues to refuse—to label herself an alcoholic.[14] We consider how you teach your children such values and skills in the next chapters.

CAN YOU MAKE YOUR CHILD TALENTED?

Along with theories about how genes make children turn into adult addicts and alcoholics is the parallel view that gifted people are born that way. Yet my approach to drugs and alcohol suggests that you also hold the key to whether your children accomplish something of value.

Whether genius and creativity are inherited is frequently debated. Some look to brain research to tell us exactly what talents children will have. But recent neurological research actually reveals the opposite. "It is increasingly clear that cognitive functioning cannot be pinned to spots on the brain like towns on a map. . . . [The brain's parts act] not like parts of a machine, but like instruments in a symphony orchestra."[15]

Special talents have not been located in brain circuitry. Says Alice Flaherty, a neurologist at Massachusetts General Hospital, "To be a truly creative chess player, probably just loving the game and playing it ten hours a day may be more important than having some special pattern recognition ability in your brain."[16] The *Cambridge Handbook of Expertise and Expert Performance* shows that inborn talent is "highly overrated" and that skill and expertise are invariably the result of practice.[17] "Expert performers—whether in memory or surgery, ballet or computer programming—are nearly always made, not born."[18]

So we will work on the principle that what you and your children do is more important for what they become than how their brains were formed by genes or in the womb. There are thus few limits to what most children can accomplish—other than self-imposed ones. This is important to note because the single best way for your children to protect themselves from addiction is to become deeply engaged in positive activities.

Michael the Musician

Michael's father, Alan, had wanted to be a musician—but settled for becoming a Web graphics designer. He introduced his son to the joys of music, which Michael took to with a passion. At the age of seven, he began playing a kind of jazz piano that amazed his parents and other adults. Michael could do a reasonable rendition of McCoy Tyner when he was twelve years old!

Michael was also a cheerful and social child. From his teens on, he played in a variety of jazz ensembles, often rubbing shoulders with older musicians. His parents worried whether this would expose him to the drugs for which musicians were infamous. Indeed, a close friend of Alan's who *had* become a professional musician had died a heroin addict.

Thus, they were deeply concerned when they discovered marijuana in Michael's room—although Michael continued to do well in school and to have friends outside the music world. Should they insist he give up playing jazz piano in order to guarantee his sobriety?

I wouldn't tell Michael to quit music (if that were even a possibility). His resentments would be a far greater motive for mischief than any peer pressure he faced to use drugs. Moreover, Michael's commitment to his art is his most steadying resource. The ability to concentrate on accomplishing something of value is *protection* against addiction, especially if accompanied by other positive values. Michael's parents should be confident that they taught their son values that will sustain him in a healthy, productive lifestyle.

The doubts Michael's parents felt represent their uncertainty about whether Michael was capable of making sensible decisions on his own. That he had been practicing piano, joining bands, and going to rehearsals and performances could give them confidence he was. They had solid evidence that the independence and self-management they had allowed Michael had paid off. We explore how to encourage such self-discipline and autonomy in the following chapters.

WHAT YOU AND YOUR KIDS
BELIEVE ABOUT GENETICS MATTERS

In Chapter 7, we will see that some groups do better than others at encouraging achievement and discouraging alcoholism and addiction. Chinese and other Asian Americans are one such group—students from these backgrounds often excel in American schools by dint of their hard work, which in turn is encouraged and rewarded by their parents. They also have the lowest rates of youthful substance abuse of any group.[19] University of Michigan psychologist Harold Stevenson notes: "Asian-Americans work harder largely because they share a greater belief than do other Americans in the efficacy of hard work and the malleability of human nature."[20] That is, they believe that effort, not inherited intelligence, makes a person smart and leads to success.

Just as Chinese Americans succeed at inspiring greater effort by regarding intelligence as something that comes with work, Stanford psychologist Carol Dweck has found that children are motivated best when they are praised for their efforts, rather than for being "smart." Some young people view their intelligence as a set trait (an "entity"). They then avoid challenges, because if they failed, this would show they aren't intelligent. Students who view their intelligence as something they can change by exerting themselves, on the other hand, willingly take on challenges and persist in their efforts to overcome failures.[21]

In other words, it pays to convince your children—and for you yourself to believe—that they hold their destinies in their own hands. This view is called *self-efficacy,* and it plays a critical role in addiction. In a study of which patients succeeded in alcoholism treatment, psychologist William Miller and his colleagues found that those who sustained remission were marked by their coping skills and their rejection of the idea that their alcoholism is a disease.[22] These patients showed that believing in their ability to fight alcoholism—their sense of self-efficacy—is the critical element in actually winning the battle.

How do you give your children self-efficacy? Through your treatment of them (by praising their efforts, for example, rather than their ability) and the values you convey. We turn now to the challenge of teaching children these values.

Five

DISCIPLINE AND VALUES

I Can Do as I Please

Jennifer's parents catered to her needs. They shrugged as she dashed around the house with a wagon or on roller skates. They said nothing when she acted up in public or at friends' houses. When she was thwarted, Jennifer immediately began wailing until her parents gave her what she wanted.

Eventually, Jennifer learned enough self-control to do reasonably well in school. But when she was out from under adult supervision, all hell broke loose. By adolescence Jennifer had acquired a taste for drugs and her pleasure seeking had begun to get her in trouble. She wasn't able to set limits on her substance use—including damaging other people's homes and violating the trust of people she cared about—all of which made it difficult to maintain relationships.

Jennifer joined an ever-changing cast of characters in her revelries. When the drugs and fun were exhausted at one party, they would move on to the next.

As a college freshman Jennifer was snorting cocaine with some friends in her dorm room when she began to feel dizzy. Her "friends," seeing that she was having problems, quickly left. Fortunately, before she passed out Jennifer was able to call her parents. They in turn reached college staff, who rushed Jennifer to the hospital.

The incident could have seriously hurt Jennifer, but thanks to the timely intervention, she recovered after a few days of bed rest.

Jennifer still badly needed to find limits and values that would sustain her—an important part of growing up which she had so far avoided. The children most at risk for abusing substances are those least likely to assume adult values, discipline, and maturity. This is a deficiency many children now seem to have.

DO OUR CHILDREN LACK BOUNDARIES?

Jennifer's inability to set limits for herself may be more common in her generation than earlier ones. But we should look carefully before joining the familiar refrain that modern youth lack discipline. What objective signs point to changes between the generations? How do your children's experiences differ from your own?

One sign that parents are demanding less discipline from children is the "I can't get my child to go to bed" syndrome that pervades middle-class American families. How many parents do you know who are up until all hours of the night because they can't get their kids to sleep? I often talk to therapists or professionals in child development who struggle with this problem with their own children—a problem nobody recalls previous generations agonizing about.

Somehow, kids have managed to go to sleep on their own for centuries. Now we require experts such as Dr. Marc Weissbluth[1] and Dr. Richard Ferber,[2] whose books and videos help parents gather the courage not to rush to their children whenever they cry. Our reluctance to insist that children sleep according to a reasonable and healthy schedule is part of a new cultural view that children are fragile and easily hurt. Knowing that the adults are unable or unwilling to reject their demands, today's children come to feel that they rule the roost—as indeed they often do.

OVERREACTING TO THE ABSENCE OF DISCIPLINE

Desperate to find someone to impose discipline on kids since they can't, many parents and other Americans welcome institutions that seem to systematically abuse adolescents. One program of this type that achieved notoriety was organized by the Lifer's Group at Rahway State Prison in New Jersey. Called Scared Straight, it exposed adolescents to hardened criminals who, screaming, confronted the kids jaw to jaw. A documentary film (which won an Academy Award in 1978) claimed that over 90 percent of the kids who participated in the program cleaned up their acts.

But impartial research tells a different story. One investigator compared the incidence of delinquent behavior in children before and after attending Scared Straight against similar measurements for kids not attending the program. He found that the program had the *opposite* of its intended effect: after participating, kids *increased* their level of anti-social and criminal behavior. This increase didn't occur for non-participants.[3]

A multimillion-dollar industry has arisen to straighten out wayward adolescents in boot camps or through other "tough love" methods similar to Scared Straight. Some parents swear that these programs saved their children's lives. But research here too—cited in Maia Szalavitz's book *Help at Any Cost*—finds their overall impact is negative. In addition, a number of teens have been injured or died in boot camps and other treatment programs. In one remarkable story brought out by a court case, Szalavitz describes how Lulu Corter was held involuntarily by KIDS of New Jersey—a drug and mental health treatment center—for thirteen years, from the age of thirteen until she was twenty-six.

Abusing children is not right *or* effective. This reality doesn't change when the abusers are lifers or counselors. The absurd premise of programs such as Scared Straight—that entrusting young people to criminals is beneficial for them—underlines how desperate we are as a society to remedy adolescent misbehavior. How could we endorse counseling that takes the form of adults sticking their faces into young people's and shouting threats at them? Your own experience should validate the research showing that adolescents subjected to this kind of treatment are in fact *more* likely to misbehave.

SETTING BOUNDARIES

Learning boundaries is a normal part of growing up. Parental failure to provide this essential training has created an audience for television programs such as *Nanny 911* and *Supernanny*. Episodes of these shows begin with small children who are completely out of control—screaming, cursing, and hitting siblings and even parents. Then the nanny arrives. The television nanny teaches parents how to modify their ineffective reactions to their children. She helps them set boundaries and enforce time-outs when children act out, then allow the kids back into the family fold when they apologize. Parents learn that their actions have consequences and that they must be consistent in enforcing rules.

Frequently, the nanny makes parents aware that they are favoring one child or failing to give attention to their children at the right times while overreacting at others. Parents are also reminded to express care and affection to their children even as they insist on good behavior. These shows point to important parenting principles that are now often missing in our culture:

SETTING LIMITS AT HOME

- Discuss with your spouse your respective roles in family problems.
- Agree with your spouse on limits and resolve to enforce them.
- Insist, firmly but gently, that your children follow the rules you establish.
- When children violate your rules, create an appropriate mild punishment.
- Readmit the children to the family circle with enthusiasm and love.
- Express love and caring frequently to your children.
- Be patient and remain calm—you are the parent, the one in charge.
- Repeat as necessary.

Steps resembling these are used in treatments for the most uncontrolled children and adolescents, therapies we review in Chapter 10. Ways to access these therapies and other resources for your children are listed in Appendix A.

DELAYING GRATIFICATION

The ability to delay gratification underlies self-control and discipline. This trait develops early in childhood, according to research conducted by psychologist Walter Mischel: "To function effectively, individuals must voluntarily postpone immediate gratification and persist in goal-directed behavior for the sake of later outcomes."[4] That is, if children learn to put off tempting short-term rewards, they will get more benefits in the end. Mischel found that children who were able to delay gratification are more socially adept and cope better with frustration and stress as adolescents. It also should come as no surprise that, since they completed their work before seeking entertainment or other diversions, they also got better grades. In fact, this ability predicted school success better than IQ did.

The inability to wait for gratification is central to addiction. We saw in Chapter 1 that addictive experiences are marked by their immediacy, which addicts crave because they are incapable of achieving more permanent rewards through sustained effort. This deficiency now appears to be affecting many children in our culture. According to Dr. Mel Levine, for the current generation of children "everything has to be immediate, like a video game . . . they have a lot of trouble doing things in a stepwise fashion, delaying gratification."[5] It is disturbing to think we may be creating an entire generation of children who are prone to addiction.

You help your children avoid addiction, on the other hand, by teaching them how to work for long-term rewards. To do so, you will have to combat the dominant contemporary "can't-wait" philosophy. Limit electronic entertainments and encourage hobbies that train skills, such as music lessons and tennis practice; insist that your children do their homework *before* watching TV; ask them to wait until they leave a supermarket to have a treat; require that they work to earn clothes and other things they want. Having your children join you in performing household tasks also offers them a model for postponing fun until necessary work is done.

Children and adolescents are by nature impatient and want things immediately. So you have many opportunities to teach this life skill.

> EXERCISE. Have you told your children they can't have something they want until they've completed a task? Don't make up a task in order to justify giving them a reward, and don't compensate every effort they make. Rather, allow children to complete important projects they are—or should be—engaged in before giving them a reward.

It is hard to take a stand in a culture where kids may actually be right when they complain that "no one else's parents" behave this way. But you're going to have to ask yourself, "If those other parents jumped off a bridge, would I jump with them?"

Okay, We're Different

Donald and Libby insisted that their three children have dinner with them on Friday nights, when family members discussed current events, schoolwork, and movies. The children got used to telling their friends, "We can't go out on Fridays—that's family night." And, of course, studying came before partying in this home.

Don and Libby also insisted that the children do chores, and everyone in the family helped on larger jobs, such as painting. The parents got involved in projects with their kids. At one point, their youngest daughter, Angela, made purses from discarded jeans, which she sold to her friends. Libby showed Angela how to use a sewing machine, as Libby's mother had shown her.

Without being told to, the children called their parents when they were going to get home late. The kids' friends often commented on how much like adults the children were: "They're so responsible." Although they didn't tell their parents, the children were proud of how their family dif-fered from the norm.

TWELVE VALUES THAT PREVENT ADDICTION

Perhaps you thought I was permissive when I indicated that I expect many young people will drink or take drugs. However, I am any-thing but permissive when it comes to discipline, setting boundaries, and teaching children to pursue long-term goals. The fundamental values you teach your children will persist throughout their lives and determine how they react when they encounter drugs, alcohol, and other challenges.

Here are twelve basic values that will help insulate your children against addiction:

1. A SENSE OF PURPOSE. Children, like adults, are less likely to act destructively when they feel their lives mean something. This sense of purpose gives children an attachment to life that sustains them and allows them to overcome setbacks and challenges.

2. ACHIEVEMENT AND ACCOMPLISHMENT. Children need to feel that it is right and worthwhile for them to do things well. It can even be valuable for them to believe that they are special, that it is okay to be exceptional and stand out. Achievement also requires the ability to delay gratification—because real accomplishment involves effort, trial and error, and sometimes even failure and pain. Aiming only to be a part of the group—to strive for the lowest com-mon denominator—is dangerous. It may cause children to reject gifts they have or make them unwilling to excel.

The Humble Shall Inherit the Earth—Not Likely

As a child Lester excelled at soccer and was selected for the county all-star team. He was talented academically and musically as well.

Lester was also taught humility as a virtue. He felt it was wrong to stand out or believe that he was better than others. In his early teens, he started acting out in school, as though he wanted to renounce his gifts. One of the ways he did this was by joining the drinking and drug-taking crowd.

Whenever Lester accomplished something significant—in school or athletics—he was struck with guilt. He worried that he thought too much of himself. He would then go on a bender with the crowd as proof that he didn't really think he was superior to his friends.

Lester's life would be plagued by his difficulty in coming to grips with his talents. He would constantly come up against the dilemma of whether to develop his special gifts or to blend in with the group.

3. CARING ABOUT ONESELF (SELF-ESTEEM). Adolescents avoid damaging themselves when they value and know how to take care of themselves. Believing that they deserve good things in life, that they should be healthy, and that others respect them makes it unlikely children will be trapped by an addiction. Children who recoil at the idea of hurting themselves instinctively reject excessive drinking and drug use.

You can't buoy children's self-esteem by heaping unconditional praise on them—as appealing as this can seem. Although you love your children unconditionally, you need to affirm their real accomplishments. Kids need to learn they have the power to gain praise and esteem from others through their own actions. Addicts often believe they "should" have love and recognition without understanding how to earn these things. They may seek approval and affection through drug use and drinking.

4. CARING ABOUT OTHERS. Not caring about others is a central component of the addictive outlook—it is both a cause and effect of addiction. Substance abusers form relationships solely to gratify their own needs, often leading to the kind of destructive relationships that are themselves addictions. Your children should want to enhance their friends' lives by helping others, enjoying their company, and relishing the appreciation and respect of other people. They make the effort to do these things when they connect caring *for* others with being cared *about*.

5. RESPONSIBILITY. Responsible people accept the consequences of their actions—which makes it less likely they will act out in the first place. Responsible people do what they say they

will, show up when they promise, and carry their weight in any endeavor—as you should insist that your children do.

6. MANAGING MONEY AND OTHER ASSETS. One special area of responsibility is money, along with other assets (such as time, energy, and the goodwill of others). Every addiction—to drugs, alcohol, gambling, shopping, love relationships—wastes money and other resources. Addicts sacrifice everything they have for one destructive activity. Remember the love addict in Chapter 1: "During the time we were together I just threw all of my life away: my friends, my schooling, my dreams." If your children learn to value their own and their family's resources, they will be less likely to squander them on addictions.

Save Your Pennies

Shelly's parents earned modest incomes, yet they prided themselves on their nice home and the comfortable life they provided for their children. They emphasized to Shelly the importance of being careful with money. When Shelly was eight, her parents started a savings account for her.

In college, Shelly started attending fraternity parties, where she drank a good deal. She began seeing one boy, and their dates usually ended up in a bar. Her boyfriend was well off, and he paid for their drinks. One night, however, he became so intoxicated that Shelly had to pay the bill. Her eyes widened as she tallied the cost of their night's drinking.

Shelly stopped dating this young man and going to drinking parties. She just couldn't help calculating what the booze she and others drank was costing, and what better use that money could be put to.

7. AWARENESS OF ONESELF AND ONE'S ENVIRONMENT. Children who value being awake and aware dislike the unconsciousness that drugs, alcohol, and other addictions entail. You should therefore welcome your children's expanding awareness of the world. Encourage them to ask questions and to think for themselves. We will see in Chapter 10 that AA and treatment programs teach the opposite—that patients must suppress their critical thinking. Indeed, by ignoring

research and continuing inane policies, as we saw in Chapter 3, the drug czar, drug educators, and proponents of boot camps are actually *endorsing* an addictive value.

I Think, Therefore I Am

Denise was part of an intellectual and artsy crowd in high school. They enjoyed getting together to talk and listen to music, go to movies, and create their own entertainment—one night they wrote and acted out their abridged version of *Gone With the Wind*. Sometimes, they smoked marijuana, which made them laugh and talk animatedly.

Denise went to a party one weekend night with a boy in her class who had asked her out. Bottles of alcohol were quickly produced and passed around. At first, Denise found the conversation and antics amusing. But after a while people began babbling, some of the kids passed out, and everyone was rowdy.

This was simply not Denise's idea of a good time. She called her father, who came to take her home.

8. ADVENTURE AND EXCITEMENT. A full life involves taking reasonable risks, and sometimes indulging in outright adventure. The emphasis in addiction theories on the danger of risk taking can be misleading: childhood, adolescence, and early adulthood are important times for exploration and excitement. When you accept this sense of adventure in your children you can help them find constructive outlets for their youthful daring, such as camping, sports, trips with friends, and other novel and exciting experiences.

9. PLEASURE AND FUN. One problem with conservative formulas for sobriety is that they sound so dull. In order to "just say no," kids need things to say yes to. And particularly as children turn the corner into adolescence, pleasure often involves indulging appetites with sex, food, and alcohol. The ability to enjoy sensual experiences without addiction requires that children also appreciate the deeper pleasures to be found in relationships, work, and community. We discuss how to teach children to enjoy sensual pleasures reasonably in Chapter 7.

10. SOCIAL, POLITICAL, RELIGIOUS, OR OTHER COMMIT-
MENTS. A critical element in avoiding addiction is that children are
able to focus beyond themselves—raising their eyes from liquor
bottles or drug packets to be concerned about the community and
the world. Substance abusers have no value that prohibits littering,
acting out, and offending the senses of those they bump into when
intoxicated or stoned. Drug- and alcohol-abusing adolescents do
not volunteer for community cleanups. They don't read the news-
paper and concern themselves with world events. They usually
don't even bother to help around the home.

Having deeper social, political, or religious values, on the other
hand, helps to rule out destructive involvements.

I Won't Go There

Jeff smoked marijuana and occasionally snorted cocaine. He was also a
committed environmentalist.

A magazine article Jeff read that described the tremendous toll that
coca production took on South American forests made a big impression
on him. He couldn't get a photograph out of his mind that showed how a
coca processing plant stripped the surrounding forest of foliage and pol-
luted nearby water.

The next time he was offered cocaine, Jeff refused it, and soon he gave
up all drugs. He could no longer rationalize his continuing to use substances that hurt what he cared about.

11. EFFICACY. Children are prone to addiction when they don't feel
competent or able to get what they want. Instead, they attempt to get
these things magically—through drugs, alcohol, cheating, or fantasy.
Recall the psychological evaluation of Josh in the previous chapter:

Josh does not see any possibility of achieving what he wants in life through
his own efforts. He does not believe that activity A on his part will lead to
reward B. Thus he sees no point in trying to accomplish anything. Instead,
he grabs for whatever gratification he can conveniently find.

Children need to know how to navigate their environment and overcome problems without being beset with anxiety. They need to believe that their efforts will produce rewards. Together, these experiences give children the sense that they control themselves and their worlds. This sense of empowerment makes children less likely to turn to drugs to provide a false sense of control. It also enables them to manage their involvements with drugs or alcohol, including quitting them.

Mind over Matter

Fred started taking painkillers in college, using his friends' prescriptions on weekends. He enjoyed the sensation of restfulness, almost oblivion, that came over him after taking a Vicodin or similar drug.

Friends warned Fred that he could become dependent on Vicodin and that it was a particularly difficult drug to quit. But Fred continued his use. At some point he realized he was taking the drug—which he was now buying from a dealer—daily, even several times a day.

One night Fred ran out of Vicodin, but his supplier was out of town. He frantically began calling around to friends who had previously shared their prescribed painkillers. But it was already past midnight, and he couldn't reach any of them.

Finally, Fred looked at himself in disgust. "I don't need these drugs. I'm going to quit tonight." His roommate, who had been observing Fred's panic, quickly told him that wasn't possible—"You need to get professional help, or go to the doctor."

"I'll see a doctor in the morning. But once I wake up, I'm going to be an ex-user."

Fred couldn't fall sleep for what seemed like all night. The next thing he knew, however, his roommate was shaking him awake. "Are you all right, man?" he asked Fred.

"Not bad," said Fred. Actually, although he did feel lousy and slept fitfully for some time, he was secure in his resolve never to use the drug again.

Of course, people should seek medical supervision if they need it to withdraw from powerful drugs. On the other hand, a sense of controlling oneself and one's universe is a tremendous aid to resisting and overcoming addiction. When people quit after decades of smoking, everyone admires them for their incredible strength. Of course, they were weak enough to be enslaved by their unhealthy habit up to that moment. Efficacy, along with other values, can remain dormant until people seemingly out of nowhere activate this feeling.

What's a Three-Decade Addiction Compared with One's Values?

Oscar began smoking as a teenager and continued his habit for thirty years. At his peak, he smoked four packs of unfiltered cigarettes a day. Oscar quit smoking in 1963, the year before the surgeon general's 1964 report on the cancer-causing nature of cigarettes gave many people a reason to want to. Oscar's reasons for quitting were more personal.

While eating lunch with a group of fellow employees, Oscar went to the cigarette machine to purchase a pack. On that day, the price of a pack of cigarettes had risen from 30 to 35 cents. A co-worker said, "Look at Oscar—if they raised the price of smokes to a dollar, he'd pay it. He's a sucker for the tobacco companies!"

Oscar was a union activist and shop steward. He lived his pro-labor beliefs—it was Oscar's job to stand up when called on by workers who felt the company was wronging them. Suddenly, he looked at himself as someone the tobacco companies had in their hip pocket.

So Oscar's co-worker's comment hit him where he lived. "You're right— I'm going to quit," Oscar said, and after he smoked all the cigarettes he had just bought, he never smoked again. Oscar is now ninety-two.

Oscar's resolve to quit was based on a value that was central to his life. Your children will resist and overcome addictions when their lives are grounded in strong principles. Sometimes people sacrifice even strong values they hold to an addiction. Therapy that helps them realize, or rediscover, critical values is one of the best routes to recovery, as described in the last section of this book.

12. MATURITY. An ability to delay gratification, an awareness of others, and a concern for the wider world are the hallmarks of a mature person. Kids are not born with these qualities; rather, they need their parents' help to acquire them. By planting the seeds of such important values, you allow your children to develop as full human beings, and to be best able to resist addiction.

HOW DO YOU TEACH CHILDREN TO FEEL EFFICACIOUS?

Self-efficacy and maturity are fundamental anti-addiction values. Yet it is a mark of our contemporary society that we want to hold our children's hands, protecting them from growing up as well as from all possible danger. You have to let go; independence and self-efficacy can come only from kids' own experience, as we see in the next chapter.

Six

INDEPENDENCE AND CONTROL

The "secret" to avoiding addiction is to raise children capable of managing themselves and leading their lives independently.

You may anticipate hoped-for scientific advances, such as a vaccine to prevent drug addiction. You can learn methods for monitoring your children's behavior, including drug testing and spying. And, of course, if you need it, the United States has the most elaborate treatment system in the world for childhood and adolescent misbehavior, substance abuse, and emotional problems. Then there's the pill National Institute on Drug Abuse researchers pray they will someday develop to cure addictions.

These techniques express a broad American desire to protect and help our children. But they do not reduce addiction. Not only are we failing to curb addiction, but somehow childhood is encouraging it. For example, youthful drug and alcohol abuse and dependence are actually increasing.[1] How shocking this is, given our aversion to illicit drugs.

Because we worry more than ever about the dangers our children face, we have accelerated our attempts to scour the risks from their lives. But in the effort to do so, we seemingly have become our own worst enemy.

WE CAN'T CONTROL OUR CHILDREN'S WEIGHT

The clearest indication that our children can't manage themselves is their weight. Although we as a society are preoccupied with good nutrition, exercise, and the dangers of overweight, children have never been fatter, or worried more about being fat. Over the last three decades, obesity has more than tripled for adolescents and almost quintupled for children ages six through eleven.[2] Other societies are also facing weight problems with their young, but none is as bad as the United States. An international comparison of fifteen-year-olds among thirty-five Western nations found Americans were the most overweight: they had *five times* the average international obesity rate. At the same time, American youths were second in terms of their dieting and weight control efforts.[3]

You know that your children should limit their intake of fat and sugar; that's why you feed them low-fat, unsweetened foods. You know that physical activity is essential; that's why you drive them to so many soccer matches and got them tennis lessons. But your children are more likely than you were to become heavy anyway—although you fear pointing this out because you are afraid to make them anorexic.

Growing Up Obese

Julia had never had a weight problem (although now, in her fifties, she certainly worried about putting on some pounds). Nor was her husband overweight. So she was mystified that her daughter Annette had gained thirty pounds in college.

Julia's concern was aggravated because, fearing anorexia, she had taken her daughter to a specialist when she became very thin in high school. The doctor had cautioned Julia to keep her eye on her daughter and make sure Annette had complete, healthy meals.

Thus Julia was perplexed when she confronted an obviously heavier daughter coming home from college. Somehow, she herself had known when and what to eat to maintain her weight through her pre-motherhood years. Yet her very smart and aware daughter failed to accomplish this.

Why did her daughter—who knew so much more about nutrition and exercise than Julia had at her age—have so much trouble with her weight? It was as though Julia had some secret knowledge that her daughter had never learned. Or else there was something in the air that was making her daughter—and so many other young people in America—fat.

When Julia gently broached the subject of her weight gain with Annette, she bristled. "Mother, you of all people should know not to talk to me about that—are you trying to make me anorexic?"

Annette is a young woman who does well in college and has a great deal of self-respect. But her fight so early in life against misusing food and overweight is striking. Our inability to prevent obesity for young Americans is also the most concrete and obvious example that young people's entire worlds work to create dependencies and problems. You may have to rethink our society's—and your own— style of dealing with your children if the status quo is creating so many problems.

ARE WE LESS HEALTHY THAN OTHER SOCIETIES?

Our society's health problems include not just obesity, and they concern more than the young. Americans, young and old, are much less healthy than those in comparable countries that spend less money on health care, have fewer gyms, and obsess less over fatty foods than we do. In its survey of the health of fifteen-year-olds in thirty-five Western nations, the World Health Organization found that American teens ranked twenty-eighth in terms of the percentage saying their health was good or excellent.[4]

At the other end of the age spectrum, a team of American and British researchers compared the health of Americans and Brits in late middle age (fifty-five to sixty-four). Americans had more of every disease than the English, including diabetes, hypertension, heart disease, stroke, lung disease, and cancer. Although poorer people were less healthy in both countries, those at the top of the social scale in the United States had disease rates comparable to those in the lowest English social rung.[5]

The English are healthier even though Americans spend twice as much per person on health care as the British. Smoking rates were comparable between the two countries. We certainly worry more about drinking and alcoholism than the British, but this doesn't make us healthier. The English were more likely to be heavy drinkers, while Americans were more likely to be obese. While 23 percent of English adults are obese, 31 percent of Americans are. (Frighteningly for us, the English are the fattest Europeans!)[6]

Why are English people healthier than we are? For the researchers, "the considerable differences in adult health between England and the United States could well have their origins in differential childhood experience of disease in the two countries." Of course, this begs the question "How come American children are fatter and more diseased than British children?"

ARE AMERICAN CHILDREN OVERPROTECTED?

One of the hallmarks of American society is that we treat children well. We are the model of a child-oriented society. Our children are the best protected—with baseball helmets, infant car seats and seat belts, immunizations and drug education, and on and on—in history. Why, for all of our care and concern, aren't our children healthier?

We need to question our protectiveness. One of the most perplexing aspects of being a good parent is that you can do *too* much parenting. You want your children to grow up successfully, and as a result, you try to guide and protect them. But such efforts are self-limiting—controlling children too much has as many dangers as some kinds of neglect.

You know that children can be "spoiled"—that is, given things without earning them. You also understand the idea of children being overprotected—when parents are too afraid to allow children to explore the world and be independent. There are real consequences to such missteps by parents. In our society, where many parents in similar situations take comparable approaches to child rearing, we see the same problems writ large in a whole generation.

My Neighbors Think I'm a Neglectful Parent

Janet had grown up in England but went to college, got married, and reared a family in the United States.

As an outsider, she was constantly struck by differences in her upbringing and how her friends were raised. Janet thought Americans lived in a bubble. They seemed to feel that without all their luxuries, life was dangerous. These differences struck her doubly when she had her own children.

For example, Janet—who lived in a very safe neighborhood—would let her two kids out to play at an age when none of the neighboring parents would consider doing so. Janet laughed when her kids picked up something harmless but dirty to put in their mouths. But the other parents thought she was courting major diseases.

Later in life, as a present for graduating from an elite high school, Janet and her husband sent their daughter to Europe with a friend. They had a general idea of the girls' itinerary, but the two of them were largely on their own. The kids had a Eurail pass and were going to stay at youth hostels.

Since the friend's family was less well-off, Janet didn't purchase a cell phone for her daughter that could be used in Europe or give her a credit card. That way, she thought, the other girl would not feel disadvantaged.

But Janet discovered that the friend's parents got *their* daughter such a cell phone and a credit card. Janet decided to let her daughter go without these conveniences anyway. She *wanted* her to travel without an ever-present safety net. But Janet was roundly criticized by other parents who thought she was taking unnecessary risks—they considered a cell phone and credit card obligatory for youthful travel. "You should have seen the shit I got!" she said.

The trip was largely uneventful, and the girls felt tremendously independent and had a lot of fun. At one point, Janet's daughter almost ran out of money. Without a cell phone, and unable to brandish a credit card, she had to really scrimp until she could get in touch with Janet.

Janet observed, "Did she suffer? A little. Is she better off for the experience? Definitely. She learned to cope on her own like she never did before. What she learned, including about herself, was priceless."

Perhaps Janet strikes *you* as extremely daring, more so than you would be. Nevertheless, her example is valuable. You need to be, like Janet, a critical consumer of parenting advice. And sometimes this means resisting pressures and trends that seemingly everyone endorses. You may need to resist peer pressure in the same way that you wish your children would!

The overprotection of American children begins in infancy. The CBS newsmagazine program *60 Minutes* aired a special on the "echo boomers" (the offspring of the baby boom generation).[7] Experts interviewed for the program noted:

Echo boomers are the most watched-over generation in history. Most have never ridden a bike without a helmet, ridden in a car without a seat belt, or eaten in a cafeteria that serves peanut butter.

"Sometimes, they don't know what to do if they're just left outside and you say, 'Well, just do something by yourself for a while,'" says Howe [social historian Neil Howe]. "They'll look around stunned. You know, 'What are we supposed to do now?'"

Dr. Mel Levine, an expert on childhood learning, said: "Parents feel as if they're holding on to a piece of Baccarat crystal or something that could somehow shatter at any point."

In addition to the increased dependence of children and adolescents, there is more dependency at the other end of childhood. Colleges note that parents now often contact administrators and instructors to ask about their children's courses, complain about grades, and otherwise intervene in their offsprings' lives. And many young adults rely on their parents after they graduate from college, often returning to live in their parents' home, sometimes into their thirties. Even when young adults live on their own, their parents often help support them. Childhood dependence is becoming for many a semi-permanent feature of life.

If young people don't have opportunities to manage their own lives and take responsibility for themselves, if (as we saw in the last chapter) they don't know how to delay gratification, what results might we expect? We have seen that these are the characteristics of addicts. Somehow, we have gotten into the position where our style of caring for our children increases their susceptibility to addiction.

WHAT DO CHILDREN DO LESS OF ALL THE TIME?

The single most noticeable difference in children's experience today versus past generations is that children spend less time unsupervised. They rarely go outside on their own to play by themselves or with other children. This is a chief cause of the meteoric rise in childhood obesity.

But the impact of this change in childhood experience extends beyond weight gain. Children now have less practice at managing time on their own, at overcoming problems and dealing with others without adult intervention, and at simply "gathering wool"—letting their minds roam in timeless contemplation.

Self-directed activity contributes to virtually all of the values and abilities that combat addiction, such as:

- Independence—the belief and value that they can take care of themselves
- Competence—the actual ability to deal with life
- Overcoming obstacles—solving problems on their own
- Involvement—children invest more in activities they select themselves
- Using imagination and creativity
- Learning to daydream and have an empty mind
- Learning to deal with people
- Responsibility
  - Planning and conducting activities
  - Handling consequences

Do you remember (or, if you're an echo boomer yourself, can you imagine) as a middle schooler taking long bike rides or riding a bus and being with friends for an entire Saturday? Perhaps you went to the local swimming pool, or maybe to the movies. No adults were involved—it was your own idea of fun. You had nothing else scheduled. You were supposed to be home for dinner. Maybe you had a disagreement and got angry at your friends. Maybe you were late and your parents got worried. But your parents never thought to prohibit you from taking such jaunts in the future. After all, that was what adolescence was about. Such outings involved a remarkable amount of independence, something today we wouldn't permit preteen children, children in their early teens, or maybe even high school students to do.

WHY INDEPENDENCE SEEMS SO DIFFICULT

Among the reasons children no longer play on their own is the perception that they are in danger from child molesters and kidnappers. But all indications are that the level of this kind of child abuse hasn't increased, and that most such abuse occurs within the home. Stranger kidnappings of children remain extremely rare. What's changed is that you are much more likely to hear about such events today, since they are a primary feature of cable news. But, as a parent, you are just as obligated to assess the real likelihood of harm for children as to protect them from every conceivable danger.

What, Me Worry!

Bill always wondered about the popular view that children shouldn't play outside by themselves. He went to his town's police station to ask how many kidnappings had occurred in his community. The captain he spoke with seemed surprised by the question and asked Bill, "Why, do you know of any?" When Bill said no, the cop said, "I've been here twelve years, and I haven't heard of any."

In fact, children are most likely to harm themselves, or else be harmed by friends or other adolescents. The leading causes of death for youths ages eighteen to twenty-five are accidents, murder, and suicide. However, violence by teenagers itself dropped 71 *percent* between 1993 and 2000.[8] Death from all causes for teens and young adults dropped by almost 40 percent between 1950 and 2000.[9] In 2002, according to the Centers for Disease Control, the death rate for Americans between twelve and twenty was 1 in 10,000 annually.[10]

While we often externalize our fears, imagining kidnappings and harm from other outside sources, the greatest dangers are right under your nose. Your children are most likely to damage themselves either by an accident or by their own hand, or through unwise relationships with people their own age. The best guarantee against these dangers is that your children know how to make good decisions and take care of themselves.

Take Me, I'm Yours

Wanda's parents cared for her very much—they always wanted her life to be great. They even went to new movies they knew Wanda would want to see to make sure they weren't scary or otherwise inappropriate.

Wanda's parents sent her to a private girls' school that extended from kindergarten through middle school. They then decided it would be best for Wanda to go to a public high school.

Feeling socially out of it, Wanda was extremely suggestible. She would do nearly anything to fit in. This soon involved going to parties where adolescents drank and made out.

Wanda didn't know the appropriate level of sexual contact. So she did everything but have intercourse, which she knew was wrong. She drank to become intoxicated in order to suppress her discomfort and uncertainty in these sexual situations.

Wanda disguised her new social life from her parents. She looked forward to going away to college, when it wouldn't be necessary to conceal her alcohol and drug use and her sexuality. Together, she and her parents decided she would attend a college a few states away, but still near enough to drive home for holidays.

It became apparent at college that Wanda did not have well-developed self-protective mechanisms. Although it violated her own values, she became drunk and slept with whomever she dated.

Still, she kept her grades up. At one point, a campus drug dealer found Wanda's combination of good-girl image and complete pliability useful, and he camped out in her dorm room to deal drugs.

When the campus police broke up their drug ring, Wanda was suspended. She returned home crestfallen and disgraced. Her parents, protective as ever, immediately enrolled Wanda in a drug treatment program.

This story, of course, is what you are frightened about. But fear about what could befall her made Wanda's parents unwilling to give her a chance to learn how to take care of herself. And so, when no longer under their supervision, she self-destructed. The remedy for Wanda's disastrous lifestyle was for her to know her own mind and to follow it. We will see in Chapter 10 whether treatment enabled Wanda to do this.

HOW INDEPENDENT CAN YOUR CHILD BE?

Opportunities for independence occur at every stage of your children's lives, even as infants and toddlers. Children are always striving to do things—feed themselves, explore their environments, hold conversations, use machines. There are many things you don't want to let them do. But think carefully about what you permit or don't permit. When there is no real danger of harm, always try to let your children extend their horizons and competencies. To do so, you have to learn to control your anxieties.

There is no more essential task in combating addiction than to strike a balance between protectiveness and fostering independence. While there is no easy formula for navigating between these shoals, there are some general rules to keep in mind:

RULES FOR CHILDHOOD ADVENTURES

1. Don't assume that your child can't do something; rather, explore the possibility.
2. Remember daring experiences you had, and consider allowing your child to do the same.
3. Rehearse with your child difficult outings or demanding activities, teaching them how to take over for themselves.
4. Constantly reevaluate the limits you set based on your child's growing maturity and demonstrations of competence.
5. Don't overreact to failures—they are merely signs that you may need to slow down or simply try again.

Take the Bus

Phyllis was raised in an Eastern European immigrant family. There was no extra money and everyone in the family pitched in and helped out. The family valued education and Phyllis was very smart; she became a doctor. Her husband was a lawyer, and their children attended a private secondary school.

Phyllis found that she was much less protective of her children than other parents. Since Phyllis had herself taken public transportation as a young teenager, she taught her daughter to do the same. Phyllis began taking Sara on trains and buses when Sara was thirteen, examining maps as they went. Sara was traveling on her own at fourteen.

Other children viewed Sara as an expert in getting around the city and went with her downtown. Parents who would never let their children take the subway by themselves readily let them go with Sara. But if Phyllis hadn't given Sara the freedom to travel by herself, then Sara wouldn't have been a person other children and parents relied on.

Sara asked to spend a year in China when she turned sixteen. Phyllis researched the program and found it was safe and supportive. Sara thus lived with a Chinese family for nine months—taking buses around the country and learning Chinese.

Phyllis is a careful parent, perhaps a little more daring and with more resources than average. She also placed a high value on independence. She permitted Sara to rehearse in a protected way a critical activity, travel, that both opened the world for her and set a pattern of self-command that carried over to everything she did.

THE SPECTRUM OF CHILD-REARING STYLES

There are some basics of raising children that you undoubtedly recognize. You know that displaying love and acceptance is critical. You also know that a disturbed family life creates risks—one of the major factors in children's substance abuse is being raised in a family with conflict and violence, emotional instability, or parents who themselves have mental and substance abuse problems. (I deal with this danger in Chapter 8.)

Clearly, ignoring or neglecting (or rejecting) your children is wrong and harmful. But as we've seen, there are dangers in the opposite direction: of overprotection, overinvolvement, overindulgence, overdirection. For people reading this book, these are probably the more likely mistakes. And such errors are fostered by the zeitgeist—the current trends in parenting behavior.

Research in child development has identified four types of parental child-rearing styles: permissive, neglectful, authoritarian, and authoritative.[11] In the permissive style, parents allow children to do pretty much what they want—the children lead the parents. Discipline is little evident.

Neglectful parenting is a variation of permissiveness in which parents are not even aware of their children's activities. When we think of neglectful parents, we often envision extremely busy professionals who are so involved in their careers that they don't pay attention to their kids. But this is rare. The myth of the absent parent is the most common wrong answer given for why kids have more emotional problems than previous generations. Research in fact shows that parents today, even single ones, spend *more* time with their children than their parents did with them.[12] The more likely kind of neglect is when parents' own lives are out of control and disorganized because of substance abuse or emotional problems.

Authoritarian parents are overinvolved and overdirective in their children's lives. They tell their children how to think and how to react. Children of such parents are unable to develop their own ways of dealing with the challenges of life. When their parents are absent, the kids have no mechanisms to regulate themselves. Ironically, this style is possible even with—and may actually result from—parents working more. When such parents do interact with their children, they overprotect and overindulge them to compensate for their infrequent contact. In between, they turn their kids over to professional caregivers whose full-time job is watching the children.

Be Careful, Don't Think

On even such simple things as what—or who—she liked, Jasmine's parents would immediately intervene with their opinions: "Susan is very nice. You should be friends with her." "We think that you need to take gymnastics—you'll like it." Jasmine became incapable of even telling how she felt about things. She was in the habit of hearing first from her parents before deciding.

Finally, the authoritative (note this is different from authoritarian) child-rearing parents establish clear boundaries for children but allow the children independence of thought and action. These children develop the ability to regulate themselves. For example, one study examined whether children referred to their parents' standards or their peers' in decision making (children who refer to their peers are of course more likely to abuse substances). Adolescents with authoritative parents were more likely to use their parents as reference points in their decision making, while those raised by authoritarian, permissive, or neglectful-rejecting parents more often looked to their peers for standards.[13]

Thus, the answer to the question "How can I guard my child against the influence of unhealthy peers?" is to let them exercise their judgment as much as possible at home. Children whose parents gently guide them to independence will be unlikely to follow others blindly when they leave home.

> EXERCISE. List the decisions your children have made for themselves in the last week. You can ask yourself this question even about a three-year-old: Did he choose his cereal? Even posing this question should make clear to you that you need to explore and expand the possibilities children have for regulating themselves, as appropriate for their age.

These issues play out in terms of drug and alcohol use. The permissive style is to allow your children great latitude in making life choices, but to do so carelessly. The neglectful style is to allow children to roam freely, with little or no knowledge of their whereabouts. Sometimes parents combine the permissive-neglectful and the authoritarian styles of child rearing. For example, when they pay attention to children, they completely dominate kids' thinking and actions. Yet most of the time they are preoccupied with their own lives and ignore their children. They may allow the children to wander the neighborhood on their own, or have no knowledge of their school activities and participation. The children have no obligation to account for their time.

THE DIFFERENCE BETWEEN INDEPENDENCE AND NEGLECT: MEANING AND PURPOSE

Remember, your ultimate goal is that your children find meaning in life and seek positive activity and accomplishment. How do you indicate to your children that you wish and expect them to lead useful lives—that is, that their time and life have meaning—without programming their every movement? You engage in constructive activities yourself and insist that your children do likewise. Encouragement of self-directed engagement is the critical element distinguishing the authoritative parenting style from neglect, on one hand, and dominance, on the other. Phyllis, who taught her daughter Sara to take the bus, was neither a neglectful parent nor an authoritarian one.

Yet sometimes children develop positive connections with a minimum of parental direction. We imagine that our children can barely survive without our constant, direct intervention. We feel sorry for families where parents don't exercise such supervision. Neglect and abuse are certainly not antidotes to overprotectiveness. But children sometimes thrive even when they are left totally to their own devices.

Can Neglected Children Become Independent?

In her remarkable memoir *The Glass Castle,* writer Jeanette Walls described her hardscrabble existence with two wayward parents (her father, Rex, was alcoholic). Traveling from town to town, often going hungry, humiliated by schoolmates, Jeanette and her three siblings not only survived but for the most part prospered. They developed into talented, responsible, mutually supportive, and self-reliant children. And they were tough. Eventually, the four children moved themselves to New York City when barely out of high school, leaving their parents behind!

The youngest of the four Walls kids developed emotional problems. But what can we make of the success of the older Walls children in the almost total absence of parental supervision? In the first place, Rex and Rose Mary, Jeanette's mother, were talented people who encouraged their children to engage in constructive activities. Jeanette's parents taught her to shoot a gun and a bow and arrow. Jeanette made her own braces because her family couldn't afford orthodontia. Rex marveled, "Those braces are a goddamn feat of engineering genius. And I think they're by God working."

Whenever Jeanette asked Rex the meaning of a word when she was doing her homework—in the one large room they all shared—he told her to consult a dictionary, then engaged her in elaborate discussions of the definition's accuracy. Jeanette and her older sister graded assignments for their hapless mother when she got a job as a teacher. It wasn't surprising that Jeanette became a talented writer in school and then chose writing as a career, while her sister became an illustrator (their brother became a police officer).

The Walls family was an extreme experiment that none of us would want to try. Yet they do illustrate that a nondirective and participatory education through lived experience—a kind of "world as laboratory" approach—gives children beneficial experiences. Although Rex and Rose Mary could be abusive and neglectful parents (Rex stole money from his children, and the kids had to scavenge for food in school trash cans), they still remind us that children can exercise remarkable independence and competence, often more than you can imagine.

I Didn't Know She Could Do That!

When Abby, at age twelve, neglected to bring home her valuable wristwatch after a weekend visit to a camp friend's house several towns away, her mother, Evelyn, was extremely upset. The next Sunday, Evelyn found a note, along with Abby's wristwatch: *I'm sorry, Mommy. I won't do it again.*

Evelyn asked Abby how she got the watch back. "I took two buses to my friend's house on Saturday, and picked it up." Evelyn was stunned—she had driven Evelyn to her friend's house and the route was extremely complicated. "Abby, don't ever take a trip like that again without telling me." Inwardly, Evelyn marveled at her daughter's competence.

WHAT'S THE FIRST EXAMPLE OF CHILDREN REGULATING THEIR APPETITES?

You begin affecting what your children put in their bodies from birth, when you feed them. Of course, human beings and animals have been feeding their offspring since the beginning of time, so you know it can be done. Only now, with the abundance of food all around, it seems so much harder. Aside from its importance in sustaining life and health, how children eat is their first and most enduring exercise in managing their appetites. It may preview how they will deal with drugs and alcohol. It will certainly impact their health over their lives.

How does your behavior affect your children's eating? Obviously, it is better if you eat well—moderately and healthfully. At the same time, however good or bad your diet is, you can give your children good nutritional information and advice. You can do so in a way that isn't strident, educating children about food and a proper diet, the need for fruits and vegetables, limiting sugar intake (such as in sweet drinks), and so on. When you exercise, whether through walking, aerobics, or sports, involve your children if you can.

Children are more likely to accept your advice when you are genuine and are trying as best you can to practice it yourself. And they will continue to accept the advice when they see in you the benefits they will get—such as being active and healthy in adulthood. They are more likely to accept messages that are put in positive terms, not as put-downs or dire warnings—"You are looking so healthy—there's a glow in your cheeks that makes you so pretty" as opposed to "I don't know *how* I'm going to get you to eat properly."

EXERCISE. Think how to encourage your children to eat better. How do you present healthy foods positively to your children? Do you forbid treats and ban them from your home? Do you scare your children about the dangers of sweets, telling them they will become fat (or that they are fat)?

Answers to these questions are to allow your children some sweets under appropriate conditions, emphasize positive messages, lead by doing, and so on. We will see in the next chapter that the same rules, values, and cultural guidelines can apply to both food and alcohol.

Can Children Learn a Positive Lifestyle and Use It Later?

Anna's parents taught her the value of a good diet and exercise, but Anna would have little of it. She rejected fish, vegetables, and all but a few fruits.

She thought it an affront to her dignity to have to walk anywhere. In short, she was a card-carrying member of the echo boomer generation.

At the same time, Anna aspired to be an actress and starred in several school plays. At one rehearsal, a schoolmate noted indelicately that Anna, despite being thin, was developing "cottage cheese thighs." This hit Anna hard, since she was thinking about making acting a career.

It was as though Anna had been storing up all the information she had heard from her parents and read in teen magazines for this moment, and then she went beyond it. She became vegetarian, eating soy and beans for protein. Broccoli became her snack of choice. She went to the gym with her father and took walks with both her parents. She dated boys who liked to exercise, which they did together.

After she made these changes, Anna's fellow cast members admiringly noted her improved figure. More importantly, she had taken ownership of her own diet and health. She was now prepared to go off to college without adding the fifteen pounds freshmen seem almost inevitably to put on. She was also unlikely to abuse her body with drugs or alcohol or to form destructive relationships.

CHECKING ON YOUR CHILDREN:
MOTIVATIONAL INTERVIEWING 101

Most efforts to control teen drug use (such as those detailed on the Web site TheAntiDrug.com) focus on monitoring children. This involves checking their clothes, examining the pupils of their eyes, listening to their phone calls, searching their rooms, and—at home and in school—testing them for drugs. After reading this chapter, you have reason to be uneasy about such a top-down approach to discipline. It is unlikely to prove effective in the long run. Spying conveys a lack of trust and sets up an adversarial relationship with your children. It also contradicts the goal of creating autonomy and independence. And it can be difficult to beat your children at this game.

Of course, you need to know what your children are doing outside the home—up to a point. But children have their own lives, and you need to respect that. This is part of your job of encouraging independence and their job of growing up. And this part of their lives should grow larger. Sometimes this will mean that your children will do things you prefer they not do when they are out from under your scrutiny. But practicing independence also means you can't control all of these things. Learn to live with it.

Consider sex. You hope you have conveyed your values successfully to your children. But by the time they enter their late teens, you are going to have a hard time changing their minds about what level of sexual activity is right for them. On the other hand, you continue to be their parent, and you can help them to sharpen and to adhere to their values. Likewise with drugs and alcohol.

How do you do this? You ask them questions.

EXERCISE. Do you know how your children feel about important aspects of their lives? Start a conversation with them about something critical to them (school, their futures, diet, their families, you) and ask them to describe their feelings. *Do not react until they are finished* except to ask for clarifications. When you do react, use only a neutral tone of voice. Do not indicate disappointment or hint that you feel their answers are inadequate or should take a different direction.

Of all the skills you need to develop, asking questions is the most important. Communicating through exploratory questions is called *values clarification* or *motivational interviewing*. Such questioning is intended to solidify your children's values in their own minds as a guide to their behavior. In order to really ask questions, which in some cases means you will hear things you don't like, you need tolerance.

You should also practice harm (or risk) reduction. This means helping children limit the damage of negative behaviors, keeping them safe so they have the chance to outgrow those behaviors, the way that Anna did with her unhealthy diet and lack of exercise. Children usually stop using drugs and alcohol. But a frightening prospect is that, through accidents or other missteps, some of them will not survive adolescence, or else will irreparably hurt themselves. These are preventable tragedies.

Risk Reduction in the Home

Betsy was a devout Christian who consulted with me about her daughter Leslie's troublesome sexual activity and drinking. She had come to me because Leslie had recently attended a concert at a large arena and become so drunk that security ejected her—leaving her to stagger around alone in the parking lot.

I asked Betsy what her daughter thought about their family and home. She told me that Leslie, typically for a teenager, had many complaints, including that they weren't as rich as her friends. Leslie predicted that she would do much better financially than her parents.

Leslie was expressing her own values and goals. The task for Betsy was to connect her daughter's behavior with her aspirations. We worked on questions Betsy could ask her daughter about attaining her goals. One such question was, "How do you think the people who make as much money as you want to performed when they were in school? How did they spend their spare time?"

I was teaching Betsy how to conduct a motivational interview. That is, she was learning how to ask questions—some neutral, some leading or even provocative—so that her daughter could understand that her self-destructive behavior undermined what she really wanted. You will learn more about motivational interviewing and risk reduction in Chapter 9.

HOME AND AWAY

The point of teaching children independence is that it best guarantees that they will be able to manage their own lives. Children with authoritative (rather than authoritarian) parents remain truest to their parents' values as opposed to peers' values. Fostering independence gives children the best chance at succeeding away from home—for example, when they go to college.

You may impose all kinds of restrictions on your kids. But children, no matter how insulated from danger and damaging behavior at home, at some point must face the challenge of meeting the outside world. It is evident that many kids today have not been adequately prepared for this challenge and as a result cannot handle the stress of being away from home and making their own decisions for the first time. This makes them both unhappy and terrifically susceptible to peer pressure—for example, in the areas of sex and substance use. Such deficiency at self-management is disturbingly widespread.[14]

Recall Phyllis, who accompanied her daughter on buses and subways, reviewing transit maps and locations with her as they went. Phyllis was preparing her daughter for her own independent forays. You can use this as a model in all areas of children's lives, including alcohol and even drugs. The key is to allow your child as much free rein—while still under your supervision—as possible. In order to do this, you will need to trust your judgment above the advice of experts, and often in the face of your own anxieties. The next chapter, for example, tells you that you should disregard what you have been told about teaching your children how to drink alcohol.

Seven

THE MODERATING HOUSEHOLD

The media beamed across the country a research finding that adolescents whose parents allowed them to drink at home were twice as likely to binge-drink as kids whose parents did not permit this. The study seemed to say that the best policy is for parents to forbid drinking at home.

Except that is not what the study actually found. Although kids who attended drinking parties in their or other kids' homes were twice as likely to binge, the study found that children who drank at home *with* their parents were *one-third* as likely to binge.[1] So, actually, *not* drinking at home with your children is a risk factor for binge drinking.

Although drinking overall by young people has decreased in recent years, drunkenness hasn't. High school seniors drink less than they did in 1991, but just as many get drunk. This paradox exists because in the United States, kids' typical style of drinking is to binge. More high school seniors think it is wrong for people eighteen years and older to "take one or two drinks nearly every day" than think it is wrong to have five or more drinks once or twice each weekend.[2]

Somehow high school students have learned to drink in the unhealthiest way. Public health specialists warn that binge drinking is the worst pattern for young people, particularly for their cognitive functioning: "repeated, abrupt increases of alcohol levels in the brain, followed by abstinence, induces more damage in the brain than the same amount of alcohol taken uninterrupted in the same length of time."[3] On the other hand, the U.S. government's 2005 *Dietary Guidelines for Americans* recommends one or two drinks daily for adults who drink, because this amount reduces heart disease.

Most adolescents drink, most college students do so regularly, and most in both groups who drink will binge. Can we reduce young people's binge drinking? Can you give your children a better message about drinking, one that stresses health, fun, moderation, balance, and responsibility? What relevance does this message have for drug use by your children? Can they learn habits of moderation across the board, for example, in their diets and spending habits?

LEARNING DRINKING AT HOME

The study of parental permission to drink and children's bingeing involved more than six thousand teens ages sixteen to twenty in 242 communities. About one in four teens had attended a party where alcohol was supplied by a parent. These adolescents were twice as likely as average to have drunk alcohol, and to have binged, within a thirty-day period.

The researchers concluded that hosting drinking parties conveys to children that adolescent drinking is okay, so children go out and drink excessively on their own. Apparently, parents who felt they were helping their children to avoid driving drunk and other high-risk drinking behaviors by permitting them to drink at home were making a big mistake.

But the adolescents in the study who actually drank *with* their parents were about half as likely as average to have drunk alcohol at all in the prior thirty days and were one-third as likely to binge. Drinking with children in a family setting substantially reduces excessive drinking by children, even when they go out on their own.

These differences in parental behavior and adolescent drinking recall the distinction among permissive, authoritarian, and authoritative styles of child rearing from the last chapter. Simply giving children a license to go ahead and drink is permissive child rearing.

Modeling appropriate and responsible drinking, and expecting your children to behave the same way, embodies the authoritative style. Authoritative child rearing respects children's ability to exercise control and responsibility and prepares them to do so. "It appears that parents who model responsible drinking behaviors have the potential to teach their children the same," the study's lead researcher announced.[4]

ALCOHOL IS THE DEVIL—NEVER DRINK!

The most important determinant of how people drink is where and among whom they live. Cultural and social groups convey a message about alcohol that leads people to expect certain experiences from drinking. One cultural recipe for drinking is to forbid it. Such cultures demonize alcohol as an evil and uncontrollable force. This is a cultural variation of the authoritarian approach to youthful drinking. Some cultures, on the other hand, have few guidelines for drinking, which represents a permissive style.

Yet another group of cultures portrays drinking as one of life's ordinary pleasures. In these cultures, children are taught how to enjoy alcohol while keeping its use within reasonable bounds so that it does not become destructive—a version of authoritative parenting.

We saw in the case of parenting styles that the authoritarian style encourages rebellion. Once children are outside their authoritarian parents' control, they have a tendency to go wild. There is a cultural equivalent. That is, if most people in a group abstain because of religious beliefs, then those in these groups who *do* drink tend to go overboard.

Groups in which children learn social drinking as a norm, on the other hand, are less likely to binge. Two researchers studied the impact of religious views on drinking by adolescents of various Protestant affiliations.[5] One group of Protestant sects was categorized as proscriptive—they disapproved of or forbade drinking. Proscriptive denominations produced more abstinent youths, although still a minority—two-thirds drank nonetheless, compared with 90 percent in nonproscriptive sects. But at the same time, more youths in proscriptive sects binged, and binged frequently—22 percent overall had binged five or more times, which was three times as many as binged in nonproscriptive sects (7 percent).

When alcohol is presented as impossibly dangerous, it becomes alluring as a "forbidden fruit." An Israeli researcher observed, "Forbidding drinking and conveying negative attitudes toward alcohol may prevent some members [of a cultural group] from experimenting with alcohol, but when members violate that prohibition by using alcohol, they have no guidelines by which to control their behavior and are at increased risk of heavy use."[6]

Praise the Lord and Pass the Booze

Saul was raised by strict Southern Baptist parents. The idea of original sin was driven home to Saul—that he was a sinner whose sexual and other urges were evil, and that his only route to salvation was through accepting Jesus and suppressing his urges.

Neither his parents nor his grandparents drank (although he later learned one grandfather had been a heavy drinker and hell-raiser himself). The drinkers he occasionally saw—for example, in country bars—were often drunk and rowdy. Saul thus associated drinking with acting out. He was intrigued by drinkers—why would they sin this way at the cost of everlasting damnation?

Saul became fascinated by sex, alcohol, and drugs. Their very sinfulness was an allure for him. Saul was also lonely. His family was poor and they were outsiders in the community. So he was glad to be accepted by some other adolescents in middle school.

But these kids were outsiders themselves. And they partied. Saul began drinking and taking drugs with a vengeance. He said to himself, "If I'm going to sin, it's all or nothing." Even so, he was terrifically guilty about his drinking and drug taking—and the sex he engaged in while intoxicated. He escaped his sense of sinfulness only when he got drunk.

Saul never drank without becoming intoxicated. To drink, he had to sneak out of his house, obtain booze illegally, and find someone's unsupervised house or go into the woods. All this meant that he would drink until the supply of booze was all gone and he was falling-down drunk.

As Saul matured, his drinking and drug use worried him. He still found his greatest pleasure was a rousing night out. But the negatives of his drinking were becoming clear to him. He often felt physically depleted and depressed.

Saul's only choice seemed to be to quit entirely—which he was loath to do. Would he become a lonely outcast again? Or, on the other hand, would he enter middle age as one of those barflies his parents sneered at? But becoming a relaxed social drinker did not seem to be an option for Saul.

This choice between abstinence and excess is not a good one to force on children. (Strangely, as we saw in Chapter 3, this is what American alcohol education strives for.) If a child is thinking, "If I drink, that means getting drunk," then the battle is already lost.

The first major cross-European survey of drinking styles found drinkers in two countries, Italy and Ireland, at opposite extremes: 2 percent of Irish men drank daily, compared with 42 percent of Italian men. But 48 percent of Irish men binge-drank at least once a week, while only 11 percent of Italian men did.[7] These adult styles of drinking carried over to teen drinkers: 27 percent of Irish fifteen- and sixteen-year-olds were drunk at least ten times in the prior year, while only 2 percent of Italian teens were.[8]

In the United States, Harvard psychiatrist George Vaillant found that Irish American youths were seven times as likely to become alcoholics as Italian American youths—even though Irish men in the study were also more likely to abstain. Vaillant observed:

It is consistent with Irish culture to see the use of alcohol in terms of black or white, good or evil, drunkenness or complete absti- nence, while in Italian culture it is the distinction between moder- ate drinking and drunkenness that is most important.[9]

Italian, but not Irish, culture supports teaching children to drink.

Jewish youths are also given alcohol at an early age at home. A survey by the World Health Organization found 10 percent of female and 21 percent of male fifteen-year-olds in Israel had been drunk two or more times, compared to 23 percent and 30 percent in the United States. Northern European countries, which also have strong prohibitionist traditions, had the highest teen drunkenness rates—the figures for Denmark were 65 percent of girls and 68 percent of boys.[10]

While American alcoholism experts focus on genetics and an individual's disposition to drink, these data show that cultural drinking styles often lead to colossal differences in drinking behavior. Such major cultural variations in drinking are even more evidence that children can be taught to drink moderately at home, and that your modeling of social drinking is hugely important. If alcohol was demonized for you, you should consider the risks of passing this attitude along to your children and how to reverse it in your own family.

YOUR SOCIAL STATUS AFFECTS YOUR DRINKING

Political correctness makes it hard for people to accept that one culture's views on alcohol work better than another's. The same is true of Americans' views of differences between social classes. While Americans love to believe that all groups are equal, social class is an important determinant of getting ahead educationally and economically in America, and it is becoming more so. Fewer Americans in recent decades have escaped their social origins.[11] My father sold shoes and my mother didn't graduate from high school, but I got a Ph.D. and became a psychologist and author. However, when I attended college forty years ago, it cost a fraction of what it does today.

Children in higher socioeconomic groups have advantages in education and training: their parents have more money to send them to school, and parents can teach them more and prepare them better for college and good careers. And some social groups also assist children to drink moderately. According to the 2004 National Survey on Drug Use and Health, among those eighteen and older, only 36 percent of Americans who didn't graduate from high school drink—but more than six in ten of these (63 percent) binge-drink. On the other hand, 49 percent of high school grads drink, among whom 52 percent binge. For college graduates, 66 percent drink, 32 percent of whom binge.[12]

The key is to understand the factors that help some social and ethnic groups do better at creating moderate habits in children. One take-away message is that, all other things being equal, your children will be healthier if they get more education and do better financially. However, you don't have to be well-off to take good care of yourself—you and your children can adopt what works best no matter where you stand on the socioeconomic scale.

THE JEWISH AND CHINESE MODERATION RECIPES

Moderate drinking is also evident among certain American ethnic groups. Jews invented moderate drinking in the Western world. They distinguished themselves from their tribal neighbors who used alcohol as part of orgiastic celebrations. The Jewish tradition of moderate drinking is very much tied in with religious and family rituals. According to the Virtual Jerusalem Web site, in Judaism

> alcohol is a sober pleasure. . . . We appreciate the fact that it gladdens the heart, and include it in all our festive occasions. What would *Pesach* [Passover] be without the four cups? Or *Shabbat* [Sabbath celebration] without *Kiddush* [a glass of wine]? Every holiday, and personal occasions like weddings and *Britot* (circumcisions) include a *Kiddush*.[13]

Children participate in these ceremonies—yes, they drink wine four times during Passover. And wine is put on the lips of the newborn infant during the *bris* (ceremonial circumcision).

Two researchers wanted to see if traditional Jewish values still encouraged moderation among modern Jews. After confirming other research finding that Jews had a far lower rate of alcoholism than other ethnic groups, they identified a set of precepts Jews used to reinforce moderate drinking:

1. LEARNING MODERATE DRINKING IN CHILDHOOD. Jews in the study usually had their first drink as children, "in the home as a part of religious ceremonies . . . only about 5 percent of the sample recalled their first drinks as [occurring] outside the family and later than childhood."

2. INSULATION BY PEERS. As adults they associated almost exclusively with moderate drinkers, often other Jews. When they observed others drinking badly, they rejected those people. As one subject described: "This one guy was making a real ass of himself. He'd had too much to drink and it made everyone uncomfortable. I guess our friends just are not heavy drinkers. . . . I think he eventually got the message, because he was one of the first to leave."

3. REFUSAL SKILLS. Jewish interviewees were "generally unafraid to offer an assertive 'no' when they are encouraged to drink more than they wish." A typical respondent declared, "If everybody is drinking and I feel like having a drink I'll have a drink. If everybody is drinking and I don't want a drink, I don't drink."

4. VIEWING ALCOHOLICS AS OUTSIDERS. Jewish respondents associated heavy drinking and alcoholism with non-Jews. The authors noted that Jews commonly use the Yiddish expression "*shikker vie a goy*" (drunk as a Gentile). As one respondent claimed, "It sounds like a stupid generalization, but non-Jewish people drink more heavily than Jewish people. That's a generalization I've been brought up with . . . and I still think it's true."[14]

The WHO survey of thirty-five Western countries found Israeli fifteen-year-olds ranked thirty-fourth in frequency of teen drunkenness. The same differences are found on U.S. college campuses: Jewish students get drunk less often and have fewer alcohol problems than other college students.[15] Of course, as with all cultural distinctions, fewer people in one group having a problem doesn't mean none.

The Smell of Wine on His Lips

Seth remembers the rituals of his childhood with great fondness. "Every Friday we lit the Shabbat candles, said a prayer, and drank wine. Later that night, my father would tuck me in and kiss me, and I smelled the wine on his lips. I can never forget that aroma and that sensation of being loved and protected by my family. Now I think of it when I light the candles with my son, say a prayer, drink the wine, and then tuck him in."

The Chinese are very similar to the Jews in this regard. Far back in their history, the Chinese were noted as moderate drinkers. The same has been true in the United States. One investigator examined police records to discover the incidence of drunkenness in New York's Chinatown. Of 15,515 arrests over a seventeen-year period, *not one* mentioned drunkenness. The investigator noted how Chinese children learned to drink:

> The children drank, and they soon learned a set of attitudes that attended the practice. While drinking was socially sanctioned, becoming drunk was not. The individual who lost control of himself under the influence of liquor was ridiculed and, if he persisted in his defection, ostracized. His lack of continued moderation was regarded not only as a personal shortcoming, but as a deficiency of the family as a whole.[16]

If you attend a Chinese wedding or other celebration on either coast or in Hawaii—or elsewhere in the world—although alcohol is freely available, you won't see anyone drunk.

THIS IS NOT PERMISSIVE

Since Jewish and Chinese families serve very young children alcohol, their attitudes toward drinking might seem permissive. But they are not. Acting out under the influence of alcohol—drunkenness in general—is strongly censured in both cultures. Staggering drunks are pointed out to young people and ridiculed. The Jews who were studied were contemptuous of groups in which heavy drinking was the norm.

Likewise, for the Chinese, drunkenness invites ostracism. This seems to be true as well for other Asian groups in the United States.[17] The National Survey on Drug Use and Health found one exception to the coincidence of high abstinence and high bingeing in ethnic groups: a lower percentage of Asians drink than other groups, *and* the smallest proportion of Asian drinkers binge. In college, "rates of drinking and heavy drinking have been found to be lower among Asian-American . . . college students than among other ethnic groups."[18]

IS ALCOHOL A GOOD THING?

Many people around the world find drinking extremely pleasurable. It caps off their day, cements relationships, commemorates special events. Don't you know many responsible people who enjoy drinking wine (or Scotch, vodka tonics, or beer)? These people are doing more than controlling their drinking—they are having fun. Surveys find that a large majority of people drink in order to have a good time and that they enjoy the experience.[19]

Such ordinary drinkers differ from problem drinkers, whose purposes in drinking we examined when we defined addiction in Chapter 1. Those who abuse and depend on alcohol and other drugs consume them in order to feel okay about themselves—to gain essential feelings of self-esteem, of being accepted by others, and of calmness and control. This difference between types of drinkers is described by the idea that "normal drinkers drink to feel good, while problem drinkers drink to feel better." Of course, drinking excessively makes unhappy, anxious, and desperate drinkers feel worse.

But most drinkers are of the happy, moderate type. One study that gives a flavor of the positive feelings that most drinkers experience is the English Mass-Observation (M-O) Archive. This study periodically surveys people about their ordinary activities. One survey asked respondents to write about pleasure.[20] A typical response was from a forty-two-year-old man:

> I am sitting outside a cottage in the evening somewhere in France on a warm evening. It's a rural area—there is no traffic noise, no dogs barking, nobody asking me to do things for them. I have a good novel and a glass of red wine. In the background the crickets are chirping. Perhaps I am sitting with my wife who is reading a book as well, or perhaps I am with a group of 6 male friends who I go cycling with every other year and we have been for a meal and some drinks in the local bar. This for me is probably the ultimate pleasure![21]

Geoff Lowe, an English psychologist, notes in distinguishing youthful drinking and imbibing by middle-aged subjects in the M-O Archive study: "Among those older than 50 years, in particular, there was a sense of pride in their ritualistic approaches to drinking alcohol, coffee, and tea, and they saw the rituals as pleasurable in and of themselves."[22] Middle-aged drinkers think of alcohol as an accouterment to otherwise pleasurable activities. Younger English drinkers find more pleasure in alcohol's sensations and report more pleasure from drinking while partying, so that youthful drinkers in the United Kingdom, like those in the United States, frequently binge.

WHAT DO CULTURAL DIFFERENCES IN DRINKING STYLES HAVE TO DO WITH YOU?

You hope your children will lead rich and productive lives. You want them to taste the pleasures life has to offer as well. If you visualize an ideal life for your children, you may imagine them working hard and making positive contributions to society, maintaining intimate relationships and good friendships, and enjoying a range of physical, intellectual, and aesthetic activities. They should enjoy life's sensual pleasures moderately, including alcohol. This is certainly not the goal that American alcohol education is pursuing, so you're going to have to teach your children how to do this yourself.

> EXERCISE. What image of alcohol do you convey to your children? What image do you have of alcohol? Answer this true-or-false quiz:
>
> _____ I believe that if I drink too much I can get completely out of control.
> _____ I don't believe adolescents can be expected to control their drinking.
> _____ I am comfortable offering alcohol to a young child; _____an adolescent.
> _____ Drinking is a pleasure that I believe only adults can appreciate.

It may be that your attitudes are restrictive because drinking makes you apprehensive. But you could consider stretching your own concept of appropriate drinking.

The United States is the only Western country that restricts drinking until people become twenty-one. In much of Europe the legal drinking age is considerably lower, and lower still when adolescents drink publicly with their parents. Moderate-drinking cultures—primarily southern European—teach children how to drink at home at an early age. A researcher involved with a major cross-cultural study in Europe noted this difference:

> In the northern countries, alcohol is described as a psychotropic agent. It helps one to perform, maintains a Bacchic and heroic approach, and elates the self. It is used as an instrument to overcome obstacles, or to prove one's manliness. It has to do with the issue of control and with its opposite—"discontrol" or transgression.
>
> In the southern countries, alcoholic beverages—mainly wine— are drunk for their taste and smell, and are perceived as intimately related to food, thus as an integral part of meals and family life. . . . [Alcohol] is traditionally consumed daily, at meals, in the family and other social contexts.[23]

How Did My Daughter Become a Continental Drinker?

Sam took his daughter on a trip to Europe the summer of her sophomore year in high school, when she was sixteen. Ann had always been interested in art, and they had a special time together visiting the Louvre and other great French museums and institutions.

But Sam was shocked to discover that Ann was offered wine regularly at restaurants, and that Ann just as regularly accepted a glass. She then drank the wine demurely, almost studiously. Clearly, she was viewing this as part of the French cultural experience.

Sam himself had never had a drink until college—not exactly twenty-one, but three years older than Ann was. Sam respected his daughter—she was a good student and a good kid—but seeing her lift a wineglass was finally too much for him. "Ann," he said accusingly, "where did you learn to drink like this?"

Ann's answer was a non sequitur: "When you and Mom had people over, I used to sneak a sip from the wineglasses." Of course, this was not the normal way of drinking wine—this was surreptitious tippling, like an alcoholic might do.

But Sam let Ann have a glass of wine with dinner (she never asked for a second) without saying anything more. They even shared a bottle of wine (but no more than a glass and a half for Ann) at a special dinner.

Sam's reaction was admirable, overcoming his initial shock to realize that his teen daughter was able to drink alcohol sensibly. When they returned home, he decided to allow Ann to continue to drink wine at dinner, and to introduce his twelve-year-old son to social, ritualized drinking.

LEARNING TO DRINK ISN'T JUST ABOUT DRINKING

Of course, the ability to drink moderately depends on more than how children are taught to drink. It also derives from how you—and your child—approach life in its entirety. The Chinese and Jewish communities are very helpful in this regard.

Along with disapproving of excessive or destructive intoxication, the Chinese, other Asian, and Jewish cultures admire and reward achievement, hard work, and academic success. Not only are adolescents in these groups more likely to avoid intoxication, but they are also more likely to pursue positive, achievement-oriented goals. Parents in these cultures often support these goals by making personal sacrifices to help their children go to college.

As these groups become a part of the American mainstream, will they continue to confer distinctive cultural values on their children? The answer is a cautious yes. Research finds continuing low rates of alcohol problems among Jewish and Chinese adolescents in succeeding generations as these cultures continue to exert a strong hold over children born into them.

But there is nothing to stop any family or group in the United States from emulating the values frequently found in Chinese and Jewish families. You can certainly show that you value and support achievement and responsibility. Academic success comes from such basic family habits as reading to children, discussing ideas, devoting family resources to worthwhile educational programs, and—most importantly—instilling high standards.

SOMETIMES PEOPLE CHOOSE TO BECOME INTOXICATED

Over half of U.S. high school seniors have consumed an illegal drug, and nearly 60 percent have been drunk. And they have not started partying in college yet! The experience of intoxication has a particular allure for young people—even many who will lose interest in that experience as they mature.

So part of the role of a parent is to recognize and to manage the fact that your children may become intoxicated. Even religious and ethnic groups noted for their sobriety, such as the Jews, make allowances for intoxication. The Virtual Jerusalem Web site tells us that "to get drunk is 'not Jewish' at all, and is condemned strongly by the sages." Yet Purim is a holiday in which "everyone gets drunk, eats a bunch of food and walks around in crazy costumes while making a lot of noise and beating an effigy."[24]

Perhaps you have had experiences like this seventy-one-year-old woman quoted in the Mass-Observation Archive in the United Kingdom:

> Yes, I drank too much when I was young. I remember, as a student consuming gallons of some beer, and having terrible hangovers. Oh, the wickedness and excitement of it all![25]

You may even choose to get drunk on some special occasions: New Year's Eve, reunions with old buddies, a quiet night at home as you look over old photo albums. Sometimes being drunk seems right. Just don't drive to the reunion or Purim party. Similar precautions make sense for your children, as we discuss in the last section of this book.

WHAT ARE THE CONSEQUENCES OF OUR SOCIETY'S BELIEF THAT ADDICTION IS A DISEASE?

Recall that low-alcoholism groups—such as Jews, Italians, and Chinese—insist that their members control their drinking and offer children chances to practice moderation. They also hold people accountable for excessive drinking and drunken misbehavior. As a society, we seem to be aiming to eliminate personal responsibility for substance abuse. When show business or political figures who have been drinking or using drugs run into legal problems, their first stop is the treatment center. Like a free pass out of jail in Monopoly, this enables them to carry on as though they had done nothing wrong. They declare they have a disease that means they should never drink or take drugs. Of course, since they have a disease, they don't know if they'll remain sober.

A RECIPE FOR MODERATION

Ancient and contemporary cultures, as well as individual families, have developed rules and recipes for moderation. Skill at moderation—of appetites and habits—is a primary ability that children acquire through practice. Training your children in moderation begins from the moment they start to eat. Since abstaining from food is not a possibility, you obviously need to teach your children how to eat sensibly. This lesson will serve your children when it comes to managing other appetites, including shopping, gambling, sex, and everything else people may do to self-destructive excess.

Cultural recipes for moderation include the following elements:

1. DON'T MAKE THE ACTIVITY SEEM MAGICAL. Societies in which alcohol is used dangerously often make the experience seem like a genie, as having the power to transform people's experience, but at the same time causing them to lose control. You should instead communicate to children that they can control their drinking, eating, drug use, or anything else they do. Education programs that claim that drinking and drug taking cannot be controlled set up their students for excess and addiction when they do try these experiences. Nor should parents use food as a reward so that it becomes a source of comfort and children eat in order to feel good about themselves.

2. MAKE CLEAR WHAT IS MOST IMPORTANT IN LIFE. Children need to learn that first things are first—there are certain obligations that can't be ignored or shunted off. Your children need to know that family obligations, studying and working, and being a reliable friend trump drinking and partying. You teach them this by demonstrating this kind of trustworthiness in your own life. That is, you don't brush off obligations when you have a chance to do something that is more fun.

3. MODEL MODERATE CONSUMPTION AND MAKE IT A PART OF FAMILY RITUALS. Practice moderation in your own habits as best you can. Cultures and families that foster moderate drinking allow their children to learn to drink in a gradual way. They do so in ceremonial circumstances—such as holidays or other special occasions—or at other family rituals. Think of a Catholic Mass, a Jewish Passover or Sabbath ceremony, or a family toasting one of its members on a special occasion, such as a graduation or a wedding.

Likewise, you may teach children that cakes and sweets are special, occasional treats—like a good dessert after a Sunday dinner, or chocolates on Easter. Even activities such as gambling can be made a special social occasion—a wager with a child over a Super Bowl, or a poker game with friends, or even a visit to a racetrack or casino. Constantly examining odds on games and races on the Internet or spending days at a time at a gambling casino, on the other hand, is inconsistent with a value-driven life.

The French Paradox and the Ritual of Eating

Baby boomers are often surprised on school visits to see that children are now permitted to eat during classes. Americans' eating has fewer time and place limits than ever. The French take a different approach. They view dining as a special occasion, as something worth taking time and investing effort in, of savoring and appreciating.

The French diet is of great interest to Americans since sumptuous French meals typically include full-fat cheeses, creamy sauces, bread, heavy desserts, wine, and after-dinner liqueurs. Yet whereas almost a third of Americans are obese (and two-thirds either obese or overweight), the 2006 *Health Profile of England* reported that less than 10 percent of the French are obese.

According to Mireille Guiliano, "You owe it to your loved ones as well as yourself to know and pursue your pleasures." She codified the French dietary approach for American readers in her book *French Women Don't Get Fat*. The subtitle of Guiliano's book is *The Secret of Eating for Pleasure.*

Guiliano learned the difference between American and French styles of eating when she lived in the United States as a youth and quickly gained twenty pounds. She recommends that Americans learn to concentrate on eating, select good foods and enjoy them, and emphasize quality rather than quantity. Dessert is fine, so long as you leave room for it by eating smaller portions.

Guiliano also recommends wine with meals. Recall that the comparison of the health of the English and Americans in the last chapter found that the English were healthier, were less obese, and drank more. As the

English are to Americans, the French are to the English: 9 percent of
French people are obese compared with 23 percent of the English; the
French drink 14.6 liters of alcohol (pure alcohol, not drinks) annually per
capita and the English 11.4.[26]

The French approach to food illustrates that people do not
become addicted to pleasure—pleasure seeking is the opposite of
compulsive, careless addictive behavior. To adopt the French approach to food, set time aside for meals and take time to eat and
enjoy them, select and cook good food and educate your children
about these things, and make your children mindful of what and
how they eat. I know this is hard to do in present-day America. The
lack of time to prepare and savor food contributes to addictive eating. But make an effort to look for healthier options that are still
convenient—for instance, there are many frozen and prepared
foods that can be healthy and delicious.

4. DON'T PERMIT YOUR CHILD TO USE INTOXICATION AS AN
EXCUSE. Moderate-drinking cultures prescribe not only how to
consume but how people ought to behave when drinking. This
extends even to intoxication. These cultures do not accept that
people get in fights, have casual sex, or disturb or disrespect others
when they are imbibing. People are chastised or punished for their
misbehavior, just as if they had done the same thing when sober.

5. MAKE CLEAR THAT DRINKING MUST BE PART OF A PRO-
DUCTIVE AND POSITIVE LIFE. You and your child should never
lose sight of the fact that control of intoxicant use is not only necessary for achieving goals but a *result* of succeeding at school and
work, maintaining family relationships, and being a good citizen
and a positive member of the community. Children should understand that neither drinking nor any other habit takes place in isolation. You cannot successfully substitute alcohol, drugs, eating,
shopping, or anything else for basic satisfaction with your life and
being a good person.

6. MAKE THE LESSONS EXPLICIT. Reinforce the message of
moderate drinking and other substance use to your children. When

visiting friends and relatives, when observing people on the street and in restaurants, point out people who use alcohol in pleasurable, responsible ways in contrast to those who drink in ugly, abusive, or dangerous ways. Show by your approval and disapproval the kind of people your kids should emulate and the kind they should avoid.

We Don't Do That Here

Jim was so proud when his father brought him along to a large get-together of the men in his Italian American family. Jim was sixteen. Although he had been allowed to drink at home since he was a child, this was the first time he was drinking with adults in public.

Jim noticed that a few non-family members were at the party, including one man he didn't recognize with his uncle. As the evening progressed, this man became intoxicated and harassed the waitress.

Jim watched as his father tapped his uncle on the shoulder. Without another word, Jim's uncle took his friend aside. Jim overheard his uncle say to the man, "We don't do that here—you have to leave."

As long as Jim lived, he remembered those words. Whenever he saw someone visibly drunk or disruptive, the words, "We don't do that here" flashed through his mind.

WHAT ABOUT DRUGS?

How do these guidelines apply to drugs? If your children take drugs—as perhaps you yourself did—you nonetheless expect them to keep their lives on course.

To Every Thing There Is a Season,
and a Time to Every Purpose Under the Sun

Joanne was a single, working mother. As a result, her daughter, Rachel, had to shoulder many chores that her schoolmates did not.

Joanne had a new boyfriend. He was well-off, and asked Joanne to accompany him on a European trip. But the trip was scheduled to coincide with Rachel's appearance in the school play.

"We'll have to go some other time," Joanne reluctantly told her lover. So when Joanne asked Rachel to get home early to do her share of chores, Rachel knew her mother was giving as good as she was getting.

Rachel told Joanne about a schoolmate who got stoned every day before attending school. Joanne reacted sharply: "The school and her parents should make sure that she shows up straight in the morning."

Rachel gave a kid's response: "But you smoked pot when you were in college."

Joanne blurted out: "Yes, but I never smoked before class!"

You may tolerate use that the authorities do not so long as it does not lead to public offenses, health and safety risks, neglecting responsibilities, or other conduct of which you disapprove. Joanne revealed that she had smoked marijuana, that she knew her daughter did, but that drug use that interfered with schoolwork was unacceptable.

WHAT ABOUT YOUR DRUG USE?

If you feel your drug history is reasonable, or perhaps even healthy, then why should your children hear about drug use only from those ex-addicts trooped into schools? Maybe you should help those you love the most in this area, as you do in so many others.

We know you're out there. The 2004 National Survey of Drug Use and Health revealed that among those ages forty to forty-four, almost two-thirds (65 percent) have used an illicit drug at some time, and 14 percent did so in the last year. And these percentages are higher for those with a college education. Although you may be reluctant to share with your children your past or present drug use, your use does give you an advantage in helping your kids learn how to avoid problems if they themselves use drugs.

One college student wrote me about what she had learned from adults who used drugs moderately in the Czech Republic, where she was raised:

> I know quite a few parents who smoke marijuana or do occasional lines of coke, keeping such use secret from their children. But is it better that, given their moderate use, they proffer their own drug-related behaviors as models, in case their children ever do drugs also? This is of course a controversial suggestion, connoting parental encouragement of criminal behavior by their children. Still, having lived in a country where some drugs were decriminalized, I believe that seeing adults use marijuana or Ecstasy occasionally while maintaining their jobs, families, and hobbies was a decisive factor in my own liberation from the idea that drugs are inevitably addictive and in my faith in moderation.

I can't recommend that any parents share marijuana with their children, or even let their children know that they use marijuana or other drugs. As my correspondent points out, to do so might be criminal. In the United States, it even raises the specter that children are asked to inform authorities if they know their parents use drugs. But in places where drug use is not criminalized, it can make sense. And keep in mind that some forms of currently illicit drug use are likely to be legal and permissible someday. Remember that 110 million Americans have used illicit drugs. Are we going to continue regarding all of them as criminals and addicts?

In any case, you already are modeling drug use for children. As we see in the next chapter, how you use painkillers and antidepressants influences how your children view and use drugs. If you feel it is normal and right regularly to turn to mood-altering prescription drugs to allow you to function, your children will also be likely to rely on these and other drugs.

MODERATION AND RISK REDUCTION

In this chapter, we saw that moderation is actually a more sustainable, less risky practice—at least in terms of not swerving off into extremes—than trying to eliminate a behavior entirely. America favors individual rights and freedoms, so prohibitionism always sits uneasily atop American culture. It didn't work with alcohol, and it has many drawbacks with drugs. I discuss the possibility that parents who recognize the possibility of using drugs moderately can help young people to do so in Chapter 9, which deals with minimizing the risk of potentially dangerous behaviors.

SO, WHO'S PERFECT?

No family is perfect, but some are less perfect than others. If you're struggling with family problems or your own personal issues, such as a history of substance abuse, or if your children display emotional disturbances such as depression, ADHD, oppositional defiant disorders, or conduct disorder, then the next chapter considers what you're up against. But there's no reason for you to throw in the towel rather than try to help your children pursue moderation and overall self-control in their lives.

Part Three

AVOIDING HARM: PREVENTION, TREATMENT, AND POLICY

Eight

PREVENTING ADOLESCENT AND FAMILY PROBLEMS FROM CAUSING ADDICTION

This chapter is about the extra challenges that some parents face in avoiding addiction for their kids. These challenges fall into two broad categories—a family history of addiction and emotional problems that kids themselves are dealing with.

AVOIDING SELF-FULFILLING PROPHECIES

If you are worried about your own—or your spouse's or your family of origin's—problems with drugs or alcohol, then you may start out planning that your children *never* should drink.

Never, Never Drink!

Ralph had struggled to quit his alcoholic drinking for much of his adult life. He went to AA several times before finally, at age forty-four, he joined and stayed.

Ralph learned at AA that alcoholism was a "family disease."* His sister was also alcoholic, and Ralph was convinced that alcoholism was a problem he had inherited (although neither of his parents had a drinking problem).

Ralph had three children; at the time he quit drinking, his son was fifteen and his two girls thirteen and ten. To all of them, he drove home the message "never drink." Years later, his son, Chuck, recalled his father taking out

---

* The popular idea that alcoholism is genetically inherited is promoted by, among other books, James Milam and Katherine Ketcham's *Under the Influence*.

a can of beer, shaking it in front of Chuck's face, and shouting, "Never, never touch this. I wasn't much older than you when I started, and alcohol had a hold on me for thirty years."

Nonetheless, Chuck and his sister Clarise, the middle child, were drinking by the time they were in high school. They didn't drink well, and both had numerous problems due to their drinking. Clarise sobered up by the time she left college. Chuck didn't do so until a number of years after college. Clarise still drank occasionally, Chuck not at all. Their younger sister, Evelyn, never started.

So by their twenties, none of Ralph's three kids had a drinking problem—although none had gone to AA. Ralph considered his anti-alcohol preaching to his kids a big success. Chuck and Clarise disagreed. They sometimes reminisced together, "Our family burden was our dad, God bless him."

Oddly, Chuck and Clarise were most concerned about Evelyn. They felt Evelyn, a dreamy and quiet girl who dropped out of college, was the most emotionally vulnerable of all of them. Thus they regarded the child to whom Ralph actually had succeeded in conveying the abstinence message to be the one at greatest risk, although both regretted their own drinking trials by fire.

As Chuck put it, "We got no help in dealing with alcohol." Instead, their father's warnings always seemed to them a looming sword of Damocles hanging over their heads.

As many parents have learned, it is easier to tell kids to abstain than to make abstinence real for them. Even if you convince them to abstain when they are younger (which didn't happen for Chuck and Clarise), odds are that your children won't follow this recommendation their whole lives. Sooner or later, most will violate this proscription.

When they do, the chances are greater that they will drink excessively. This could be due to their suspicion that they are predisposed to addiction—in other words, you have created a self-fulfilling prophecy. Or else they may simply drink more because they fear your disapproval, rebel against your rules, or lack experience at drinking. Billy Sunday, the American model of a fire-and-brimstone preacher, is illustrative. Sunday stumped the country in favor of pro-hibition. Sunday himself had been a moderate drinker as a baseball player, in an era where ballplayers were known for drunkenness, before he preached the gospel of abstinence. Yet both of Sunday's sons predeceased him due to alcoholism.

WHAT CAN—SHOULD—YOU DO?

Not all parents who worry about alcoholism in their family take Ralph's prohibitionist tack. Still, they are bound to worry about their children's drinking.

What Will Become of My Daughter?

Louise's mother and sister were alcoholics, so she constantly worried about her children's drinking. She was particularly concerned about her daughter, Susan, when she went away to college. Said Louise, "My daughter was head of the 'bottle cappers' in high school—this was an anti-alcohol group. She gave lectures to younger students about the dangers of alcohol. She took her position extremely seriously—the kids joked that she was the only one in the group who never drank!

"I was very glad that Susan took this route because of my mother's and my sister's alcoholism. The problem was when Susan went to college. It was really a conservative school. But I found out that quite a bit of drinking went on there anyhow.

"During Susan's second year in college, I got a call that she had been hospitalized after blacking out from drinking. I was horrified, both because of the medical consequences and because of other things that could have happened when she was blacked out.

"Susan tried to reassure me that it wasn't as bad as it sounded. She said she had been exercising and hadn't eaten—that she hadn't had that many drinks.

"I researched the blood alcohol level she registered—which was quite high—and went over its consequences with her. She had given this lecture many times to fellow students, but she acted like it was news to her!

"The counselor at the college was very good. She didn't label my daughter an alcoholic. Instead, Susan was placed on probation and she would have been suspended if she was reported drinking again.

"But she continued to drink. She was very cautious. You have to understand, my daughter is extremely straight—she goes to church and has never had a real boyfriend.

"Now that she is twenty-one she drinks. She tells me she has only one or two drinks at a time. I am somewhat relieved. When I think she will be drinking on a weekend, however, I lie awake worrying. I think, 'Is she becoming like my mother and sister?' Then I worry, 'Am I putting these thoughts in her mind, and making her more likely to become like them?'"

Louise and Susan are actually doing well. It might have been possible to avoid Susan's awkward—and dangerous—introduction to drinking. Louise and her husband (who were light drinkers themselves) might have shared some wine with Susan during special celebrations or holiday meals, as described in the last chapter.

Nothing guarantees children will avoid excessive drinking throughout their lives. But Louise and her husband had created a stable home for their two children, and Susan and her brother were positive, productive people. Susan's older brother also drank regularly with his friends. Both these young adults were good bets to be moderate drinkers despite the alcoholism in their mother's family.

YOU CAN COUNTERACT THE IMPACT OF AN ALCOHOLIC OR ADDICT IN THE HOME

Louise did not face the difficulty of raising children with alcoholism in her home. Yet the large majority (three-quarters) of children of alcoholics do not themselves become alcoholics.[1] In fact, having a parent who is a problem drinker in some cases works to forestall alcoholism in the next generation. A daughter whose father has a drinking problem is less likely than average to have one herself.[2]

Think about it—who knows the difficulties created by parents' alcoholism (or drug abuse) better than their children? Who is more likely to be careful drinking? Children who learn the consequences of excessive drinking often decide they will have no part of that destructive lifestyle. Whether you have alcoholism in your family or not, your children need to develop this kind of mindfulness about their drinking.[3]

Linda Bennett, a medical anthropologist, discovered that families that ate dinner together despite a parent's alcoholism were less likely to pass along alcoholism from parent to child.[4] Such meals—involving either one or both parents—create a sense of structure and belonging and that the kids are being taken care of.

As in many other instances, what works for families with alcoholism turns out to be general principles. A study by the National Center on Addiction and Substance Abuse found that regularly having family meals was the best protection against kids' substance abuse.[5] In one long-term study that looked at factors that determine whether the children of alcoholics become alcoholics themselves, the primary variable that prevented this was that their mothers were warm and supportive.[6]

My Husband May Be an Alcoholic, But . . .

Frances was a traditional woman devoted to her family. But she married an alcoholic. Mike continued to get drunk after the couple married and had children. He sometimes had dark periods when he stayed in the basement drinking several nights in a row, refusing to interact with the rest of the family.

Frances prepared meals for the family every night. When Mike was on a drinking jag, everyone in the family practiced what might be called denial. They would just have a nice meal—discussing the day's activities, television programs, the news—as if nothing was amiss.

Despite his excessive drinking, Mike was a good provider and a faithful spouse. Altogether, the children felt secure. They were expected to do their homework and chores, they had curfews, and in every fundamental way they acted like an ordinary family.

Frances demonstrates how a non-alcoholic parent can provide emotional security and prevent children from imitating their alcoholic parent. Her task was made easier by the fact that her husband never got obstreperously drunk in front of their children. If he had, she would have had to make it clear to her husband that she would not tolerate his acting out at home. She might have needed to ban her husband from the house during his drinking bouts, or else she might have had to leave the house with her kids whenever he was drinking. Many people (usually women) consult me about this kind of difficult—though not impossible—situation.

HIGH-RISK CHILDREN AND THEIR OPPOSITES

A research team measured personality traits that influenced which sons of alcoholics became alcohol abusers. Those boys who were highly likely to disregard the risk of harm, to seek novelty, and to ignore others' opinions were at a tremendously elevated risk to abuse alcohol—97 percent did so at some point. Those low in novelty seeking and at least moderately concerned about avoiding harm almost never did so—only 1 percent abused alcohol. But unusually sensitive boys, those who were very avoidant of harm and sensitive to others' opinions, also had an elevated risk for alcoholism.[7]

The point here is that other factors, besides just being the child of an alcoholic, need to be present for a young person to develop alcoholism. These are the same personality and social factors that (as we saw in Chapter 2) predispose children and adolescents without an alcoholic parent to abuse substances. As one long-term study of children of alcoholics (COAs) found, "many of the factors that predispose to personality disorder have little to do with parental alcoholism per se."[8] The same study found that COAs who became alcoholics themselves were likely to have a lower socioeconomic status and to have had behavior and truancy problems in school.

In other words, the route out of an alcoholic destiny is to deal directly with family and economic problems besides one parent's alcoholism. This is not to underestimate the burden of having an alcoholic parent or spouse. Alcoholic families frequently have more conflict and more than their share of financial problems as well.[9] As a parent in such a family, you (like Frances) do the best for your children by providing them with a stable home, values, and a model for responsible behavior.

IF YOUR CHILDREN HAVE EMOTIONAL PROBLEMS

Children with emotional problems are more likely to abuse substances. Yet the diagnosis of emotional and behavioral disorders among children and adolescents has skyrocketed.[10] The principal disorders diagnosed in children are attention deficit hyperactivity disorder (ADHD) and depression, followed by extreme behavioral problems, bipolar disorder, and schizophrenia and other psychoses.[11]

You certainly will want to help your children get better if they have any of these conditions. Typically, professionals will advise you to put your child on a course of medication. Yet a number of therapeutic drugs, such as anti-depressants and Ritalin, can be addictive, sometimes highly so. Many parents are then faced with the difficult decision of whether to let a severe emotional problem go untreated, or else expose a potentially at-risk child to highly addictive substances.

CHILDHOOD EMOTIONAL DISORDERS AND MEDICATIONS

Childhood and adolescent psychiatric disorders are treated with drugs in the United States: Prozac, Paxil, Zoloft, and others for depression; Ritalin, Adderall, and Concerta to treat ADHD; Zyprexa and Risperdal for psychoses and bipolar disorder. The anti-psychotics Zyprexa and Risperdal are also prescribed for children whose behavior is out of control (a condition called oppositional defiant disorder or conduct disorder).

The psychiatric diagnosis and medication of children and adolescents continues to rise astronomically. It tripled between 1987 and 1996,[12] then tripled from the early 1990s to the mid 2000s.[13] The rate of treatment for ADHD, almost always with medication, almost quadrupled from 1987 to 1997 and has increased since then.[14] Prescription of anti-psychotic drugs for youths *quintupled* from 1993 to 2002.[15] The diagnosis and treatment of bipolar disorder is also rising dramatically,[16] and bipolar is now the fastest-growing mood disorder diagnosed in children.[17]

There seems to be no limit to the growth of the medication of children. These drugs often haven't been studied for the conditions for which they are prescribed.[18] No anti-psychotic, for instance, is approved by the FDA for use in children. Typically, several drugs are combined in therapy, and these combinations have never been tested. In a way, we are experimenting on American children on a massive scale.

Some American experts are troubled by these prescribing practices. Dr. Julie Magno Zito, who has documented the rise in psychiatric medication of children, notes that it is difficult to separate each drug's impact on symptoms and identify all of their side effects.[19] But overall there is surprisingly little resistance to this state of affairs here in the United States. In Britain, in contrast, such medication of children has been checked by medical debate, government restriction, and public opinion.

For example, Britain's medicine regulatory agency has warned against the use of anti-depressants (such as Paxil) for children. A panel of experts concluded that in the case of the most widely prescribed anti-depressants (called SSRIs, selective serotonin reuptake inhibitors) the cure in essence is worse than the disease.[20] An accompanying editorial in Britain's leading medical journal, *The Lancet,* called the story of research into SSRI use in childhood depression "one of confusion, manipulation, and institutional failure" and noted that "use of SSRIs to treat childhood depression has been encouraged by pharmaceutical companies and clinicians worldwide."

SHOULD YOU MEDICATE YOUR CHILD?
WHAT ROLE REMAINS FOR YOU?

The first question is simply whether the drugs are needed. Is your child really suffering from depression, ADHD, bipolar disorder, or whatever has been diagnosed? At one time, for example, it was thought to be impossible to diagnose children or adolescents with bipolar disorder, since their personalities are as yet so malleable and young people are so emotionally labile.[21] In addition, you can ask, are the drugs effective? And are the drugs necessary—that is, will the child outgrow the problem on his own? And, finally, can the drugs themselves be harmful?

One major concern is that some drugs may increase the danger of suicide. In the face of evidence of this, in 2004 the U.S. Food and Drug Administration (FDA) ordered that SSRIs carry warnings that they "increase the risk of suicidal thinking and behavior" in children. Where does that leave parents? Under certain circumstances, you may feel anti-depressants may help—may even be crucial—for your child. But you can't turn your child's fate over to the pharmacist. You need to continue monitoring his or her behavior; if anything, your role in your child's life becomes even more crucial.

Anti-depressants and a Kid's Life

Glen was brought up by two caring parents. Ellen, in particular, was a very involved mother. Nonetheless, by his middle school years, Glen was doing badly at school. He had practically no friends and he seemed to droop as he walked through life. Although Glen was an excellent athlete, Ellen hated watching him play hockey goalie. When Glen allowed a goal, she could see him sag, and she knew he was dying inside.

Ellen consulted a psychiatrist, who prescribed Prozac for Glen. (Prozac is the only anti-depressant approved by the FDA as safe and effective for adolescents.) Ellen was ambivalent about her son's taking the drug—was it really necessary? Would he outgrow this phase on his own? After a game in which the opponent scored several goals, however, she heard him mutter, "My teammates really let me down." Ellen decided then that Prozac was right for Glen.

But Prozac did not solve all Glen's problems. Socially and academically he lagged. Ellen worried that Glen would end up in an outsiders' group in the local high school, and she knew that could mean a lot of drug use. Glen's father made an excellent salary, and Ellen began to search for a private school for her son.

She settled on a small boarding school, close enough for Glen to come home on weekends, that was extremely student-centered. It was not specifically geared to children with emotional problems, which was important for Ellen. At first, her husband resisted. But after he took Glen for a campus visit, he warmed to the idea. Indeed, he started telling people he picked the school!

Glen blossomed there. His grades were excellent. Not only did he have friends—and girlfriends—at school, he started making friends at home, where he'd previously had almost none. Glen was elected captain of his hockey team. He began seeing himself as a leader.

Driving Glen home one weekend, Ellen reminded her son just how much his life had changed. As she did, she realized that *she* had a hard time fully grasping how much Glen's emotional state had improved.

At this point, Ellen's husband complained about Glen's continued use of anti-depressants. "Isn't he normal enough now? Can't he take life on its own terms from here on? It bothers me that when family members tell him how much he's blossomed, he replies, 'I owe it to the Prozac.'"

But Ellen's reaction was, "Just think of it like his needing glasses. It's simply a part of his life."

Ellen had done a remarkable thing, helping her son to progress from depression and an outsider's position to become a well-adjusted and successful high school student. She and her son had built on the improved mood the drug gave him to accomplish real and substantial life changes. What remained to be seen was whether he needed continued medication—perhaps for his entire life—in order to maintain his new self, or whether he could now manage his life on his own.

Glen's diagnosis and treatment worked because his coping skills and social development improved while he was being medicated. But there are consequences for an adolescent's believing his mind is disordered and taking a mood-altering drug during his formative years, some of which are impossible to calculate. The drug benefited

Glen, but his continued use of it could be limiting or even harmful. Thus, you must be cautious when someone (a school counselor, a doctor, staff at a treatment facility) says your child has an emotional disorder. And even if you decide to treat the condition with drugs, you need to periodically reevaluate your child's need for a medication.

A SPEEDY NATION

The broad prescription of medications to treat ADHD—Ritalin, Concerta, and Adderall—has also caused many observers concern. The drugs are all stimulants; Adderall is an amphetamine. All these drugs have effects similar to street amphetamines such as Dexedrine, Ecstasy, and methamphetamine ("crystal meth"), illicit drugs whose use is increasingly popular. Crushing the drugs and snorting or injecting them produces an experience comparable to a cocaine high, and street use of these prescription drugs is widespread.

In fact, Ritalin, Concerta, and Adderall are highly controlled Schedule II drugs because *most* people find the drugs improve their mood and concentration. The issue parents face is whether the present value of using one of these outweighs labeling their children and perhaps making them dependent on the drugs. Dependence on amphetamines—just like on cocaine, alcohol, and opiates—is a diagnosis in the *Diagnostic and Statistical Manual of Mental Disorders, Fourth Edition* (DSM-IV), the American psychiatric manual, and with good reason.

ADHD is often diagnosed in children who are fidgety and unable to concentrate on their studies. Sometimes this distractibility is part of more serious behavior problems. Stimulant drugs do help kids focus. But there are other ways to accomplish this.

Not for My Daughter, Thanks

Connie was told by middle school administrators that her daughter was restless and would benefit from taking Concerta. Connie, a social worker, knew the drug and decided she didn't want her daughter to take it. Instead, she encouraged her daughter, who was physically active and a good athlete, to join the softball and soccer teams, which she thoroughly enjoyed.

At night, Connie sat her child down to make sure she spent the time she needed on homework. Connie saw her daughter as a robust, active child, not as a child with an emotional disorder. Exercise helped her to curb her restlessness without the downside of making her feel she was abnormal.

But other caring parents make different choices. In those cases, children can have complex reactions to being medicated, both feeling that they require the drug and resenting and resisting their diagnosis and medication.

The Child's-Eye View

Eugene had been taking Ritalin since he was a child. He had always been rambunctious and overactive—difficult for his parents to control and inattentive at school. Eugene's parents were extremely concerned; they were themselves highly productive and successful people (his father as a businessman and his mother as a teacher).

Eugene calmed down considerably as he progressed through adolescence. He did well in practical subjects, which he called "real," and not so well in purely academic ones. In Eugene's senior year, he was accepted at a small college to study environmental science.

Eugene had developed a different attitude toward his medications than his parents: "I only take the Ritalin when I need to study. I don't think I will take it throughout college. I need it less and less."

His mother, who witnessed Ritalin being used widely in the school at which she taught, said, "I've been informed that ADHD is a lifetime disorder—it's a problem with Eugene's brain. It alarms me when he says he is planning to get off Ritalin."

But Eugene did not want to be ADHD forever. He didn't want to be singled out that way. "I think everyone can be ADHD—everyone becomes fidgety in a situation where they don't do well or they're bored."

What happens when parents and children see these things differently? Ironically, Eugene's independence of judgment and his wish to scale down his medication use were indications of the success of his treatment. In any case, *you* need to consider your child's views on medication, especially as he or she gets older.

FIVE QUESTIONS TO ASK A CHILD TAKING PSYCHIATRIC MEDICATIONS

1. How do you think you've changed since you've been taking this drug?
2. Do you think you have a condition that most kids don't have?
3. Will you always have it?
4. What causes you to have this condition?
5. Do you have any concerns about taking this drug?

There are no right or wrong answers, of course, but you need to know your child's thinking as you decide with him or her about continuing treatment. The answers to these questions could surprise you. If young people don't accept and take charge of their own medication, then their use of the drugs can be alienating and oppressive.

ADOLESCENT MEDICATIONS AND ADDICTION

Clearly there are basic questions about the impact of these drugs and others commonly prescribed in our society for children and adolescents.

Ritalin as a Drug of Abuse

Jocelyn was given Ritalin starting in junior high school. She resented being diagnosed and labeled as different from other children. She shared her prescription medication with other kids who wanted to try the drug, and she tried the drugs they had—some illicit (such as marijuana), some prescriptions of their own.

Jocelyn developed a substantial drug habit. Although she did graduate from a nursing program, she often fought off periods when she abused drugs and was unable to work, or sometimes to function at all. Her friends and boyfriends were all involved with drugs. The prescription she received in junior high had been her introduction into the world of drugs, populated by other adolescents who relied on drugs to feel good.

I don't endorse the gateway theory of drugs—that youthful drug use inevitably or even frequently progresses to more serious use. Prescribed Ritalin use does not make adolescents into drug abusers.[22] Many kids benefit from ADHD medications, as they do from anti-depressants. But youthful reliance on prescribed drugs *can* become a pattern that extends into adulthood.

We also can't ignore that young people become dependent on anti-depressants and Ritalin-type drugs. There is a rebound effect with both that leaves users with a greater need for the medications the longer they take them. As a result, long-term users undergo withdrawal when weaned from either. It is also striking to think that so many young people's personalities and identities have become tied up with these drugs. "How do you even know who the kid is anymore?" asks drug researcher Julie Magno Zito.[23]

Just as illicit drug users do, people take prescription drugs in order to regulate unpleasant feelings. They depend on the drugs to make them feel "right." Forming legal drug dependencies in place of illicit ones raises difficult questions about addiction. If, as we have seen, addiction occurs when people can feel normal and worthwhile only when they are using a substance, then many young people are forming addictions to legal, prescribed drugs.* Is it possible that a generation of children in the United States—and American society at large—is being socialized into addiction?[24]

---

* The directors of the government drug and alcohol research agencies recommend that psychiatric diagnosis revert to use of the term *addiction,* rather than *dependence,* because they don't want people who are dependent on psychiatric medications to be regarded in the same light as drug addicts. See Charles O'Brien, Nora Volkow, and Ting-Kai Li, "What's in a Word? Addiction Versus Dependence in DSM-V," *American Journal of Psychiatry* 163 (2006): 764–65. This change in nomenclature, however, does not solve the problem identified here.

At the same time, young people's illegal use of prescription drugs is rising precipitously. The Partnership for a Drug-Free America calls the current group of teenagers "Generation Rx" after a survey finding one in five teenagers used Vicodin to get high and one in ten used Ritalin or Adderall illicitly.[25] The National Survey on Drug Use and Health revealed that between 2002 and 2004, people initiated illicit drug use with a pharmaceutical drug more often than with marijuana or any other illicit drug.[26] Many adolescents in drug treatment now report they primarily abuse prescription drugs.

The situation is most acute on college campuses, where surveys find that a fifth of students use Ritalin or Adderall to study, and students actively trade these and other prescription drugs.[27] Dr. Robert A. Winfield, director of the University Health Service at the University of Michigan, notes that "a growing number of students . . . falsely claim to be ADHD so they can get a prescription."

OTHER WAYS TO TREAT EMOTIONAL PROBLEMS

If your child is having problems at school, suffers from emotional problems such as depression, or acts out, then you should explore appropriate treatments. But you must guard against the therapy becoming as limiting as the condition for which you sought treatment.

Two therapies are used to help kids with depression: antidepressant medications and cognitive behavioral therapy (CBT), separately or in combination.[28] (CBT has also been shown to be effective for childhood anxiety.)[29] CBT teaches people how to recognize and revise their depressed thinking. Ideally it gives them a permanent way of avoiding the thinking and behavior patterns that create depression.

One study found that adults with moderate to severe depression improve equally well upon receiving either an SSRI (Paxil) or CBT.[30] However, of those who succeeded initially with one or the other therapy, those who no longer received the CBT were less than half as likely to relapse (31 percent) as those who ceased the drug treatment (76 percent). In fact, they were also less likely to relapse than were those who continued to take Paxil (47 percent).[31]

Cognitive behavioral therapy trains people to think more constructively about themselves—for example, to avoid thinking that they are likely to fail at challenges. Instead they are taught to believe they stand a good chance of succeeding in a new situation. Since the worst outcomes usually don't occur, this is actually realistic thinking. And anticipating success makes it more likely to occur.

At the same time, therapists encourage clients to rouse themselves from their lethargy to engage in positive activities: "Call a friend. Exercise. Do some work that is enjoyable."[32] Developing positive thought pathways and behavior patterns makes particular sense for children as they form strategies for coping with life. The goal is that people ultimately will be able to be their own therapists.[33]

Ted Strikes Back

Ted was captain of his tennis team. But he would have puzzling losses to players who weren't as good as he was. His defeats often came when he got down on himself after he missed a shot. His teammates and coach watched in horror as he melted down, McEnroe-like.

One day an English teacher was watching the team play when Ted had such a meltdown. Seeing Ted in school the next day, he asked Ted to come to his office.

"Ted, I saw you lose to that guy who wasn't as good as you. What was going through your mind when you blew up?"

"Oh, I just started thinking 'What a stupid play. Here I go again. I'm going to lose.'"

"Is there any way you can clear your mind when you make a mistake? You know, just say to yourself, 'It's a fresh point, I'm going to start playing better here.'"

"I don't know, my mind just goes off."

"Have you ever tried? Here, visualize being out on the court after you missed a shot. Say to yourself, 'It's a new point. I'm going to get this one.'"

"Okay, I'll try it: 'I'm going to get this point!'"

The teacher, without any training, was performing cognitive behavioral therapy. Use of such mental gymnastics may seem too simple to be true. But research repeatedly demonstrates CBT works—in fact, as we have seen, some research finds it superior to drug treatments. So although your child may have genuine emotional or behavioral problems, it is worth exploring alternatives before resigning yourself to your child's long-term psychiatric medication.

WHY ARE MORE PEOPLE IN OUR SOCIETY DEPRESSED AND ADDICTED?

Why are we not becoming a happier—or at least a less depressed—society? Given the advances in the treatment of depression in this country, we might expect this mood disorder to be declining. It isn't. Likewise, how do we explain why addiction is increasing with each new generation?

We have seen that substance abuse peaks in adolescence and young adulthood. Although most substance abusers do still "mature out," in recent years a disturbing trend shows that more youthful substance abusers continue the pattern later into life.[34] The same phenomenon is occurring with depression. According to the most thoroughgoing national survey yet conducted, more than thirteen million Americans (about 7 percent) suffer a major depression each year.[35] These depressions are severe: on average, sufferers were unable to work or carry out normal activities during thirty-five days in the year. More than 16 percent of Americans—about thirty-five million people—now suffer from depression at some point in their lives. We are a deeply depressed nation.

The rate of depression among children and adolescents rose radically in the 1980s and 1990s, for reasons that are hard to pinpoint (it is possible both that more children are becoming depressed and that children are being more aggressively diagnosed with depression). Depression is still most likely to begin for those in the twelve-to-sixteen-year-old age bracket. However, many more middle-aged people in twenty-first-century America now show symptoms of depression.[36] Apparently, many who were diagnosed in childhood and adolescence continue to be depressed when they mature.

Labeling children as depressed (or bipolar or ADHD) or chemically dependent (or alcoholic or addicted) is not a life solution. This is most obviously true when children are reacting to specific life traumas, such as their parents' divorce or a family member's death. But whether under these circumstances or for more long-lasting problems, such labeling can become a lifelong problem in itself.

DIVERSITY IS NOT ONLY ABOUT RACE AND ETHNICITY

At the same time that more children and adolescents are diagnosed with significant emotional and addictive problems, our society has become less tolerant of children's differences and idiosyncrasies. Parents increasingly expect their children to have an ideal mix of academic and personality traits.

When your children fall short of this ideal, you may prematurely decide they have a problem. But many children with offbeat personalities right themselves if you give them a chance and support them. Remember, if you don't accept and believe in your children, they will have trouble accepting themselves. Often the best thing that you can do for your children is to appreciate their unique gifts, especially nonacademic ones.

Our Son Wasn't a Disappointment. We Were.

Max and Rhoda would sometimes commiserate that they hadn't been blessed with two talented, well-behaved children. Their son David, unlike his brother, Rob, or either of the parents, didn't get good grades, and he often had to be punished for misbehaving.

Still, they were reluctant to put David in special programs or to medicate him. Instead, they carefully nurtured as well as disciplined him. At the age of fourteen, David discovered that determinedly applying himself to music was a satisfying outlet for his self-expression.

His parents forever felt guilty that they hadn't simply realized that David would find his own niche eventually. But they shouldn't have been too hard on themselves. They found a balance between limit setting and stifling that gave David's musical ability a chance to ripen, while helping him to develop the discipline that was also key to his ultimate fulfillment.

Nonetheless, they would say to each other, "Thank God we lifted the blinders from our eyes so we could see that our children were equally blessed, although each has a different gift."*

WHETHER OR NOT YOUR CHILDREN ENTER TREATMENT, YOU ARE CRUCIAL

Ignoring pain and trauma is not helpful. But neither is labeling temporary problems and misbehavior, no matter how disturbing, as lifelong diseases. Your first response should not always be to send children to a treatment center. As a parent, you should accept that children have different personalities and skills. Don't rush to label such differences as disorders, even when they disadvantage children. Remember, American psychiatry once regarded homosexuality as a disease. If you do decide on therapy, you need to be aware that medication is not the only route. And in any course of therapy, you need to remain involved, as we see in Chapter 10.

---

* A resource for different types of intelligence or giftedness—musical, athletic, verbal, mathematical, interpersonal, emotional, visual, environmental—is the work of Howard Gardner. His 1983 book *Frames of Mind* is the seminal reference for the idea of multiple intelligences.

Nine

KEEPING YOUR CHILD SAFE

Jennifer Moore was murdered during a night of clubbing in New York City. After her car was towed, she and her friend showed up at the car impound lot intoxicated, and the friend passed out. While the attendants called the cops, Jennifer bolted from the lot, which was located in a deserted part of the city. She was followed and abducted by a man who took her to a motel in New Jersey, where he raped and strangled her.

The eighteen-year-old had gone to New York from her suburban home without informing her family. When interviewed, Jennifer's father said that he knew exactly what he would have told his daughter if she had called him from the impound lot: "Stay with your friend and face the consequences of getting drunk and violating your curfew. You may get a penalty. You may get a lecture. You may get grounded. But at least you get to come back home."[1]

It is common for children to mislead their parents around drugs and alcohol. Sneaking around without their parents' knowledge adds to the risks they incur. Ideally you may prefer your children not drink, at least outside the home, but most crucially you want them to be safe. Balancing these two goals in a way that makes safety a clear priority is called risk reduction.

RISK REDUCTION FOR YOUR CHILDREN

Sometimes we are so preoccupied with preventing children from misbehaving altogether that we fail to take simple precautions to prevent their behavior from hurting them forever. Consider the many bad things that can befall young people using, or abusing, drugs or alcohol. Among the potential ways in which they can come to harm while drinking are driving drunk, perhaps getting in an accident; getting into a brawl; having sex while impaired; throwing up and choking on the vomit; suffering alcohol poisoning; blacking out and perhaps being raped or otherwise hurt.

Getting drunk doesn't have to be dangerous if it occurs in a controlled setting. Frequently the problem is not the drinking so much as the environment—which kids choose because it is outside the realm of parental supervision. But if they drink in a protected environment, a hangover is often the worst that can occur. So long as their health and safety (and that of those around them) are protected, they will have time to do better down the road. An example of risk reduction is a safe-driver program, which provides adolescents with rides when they've been drinking.

An important message to your children is that they can tell you anything at moments of real danger. Had Jennifer's father successfully coached her to call him if she ever got herself into a difficult situation, she might be alive today. But it is difficult to expect your kids to turn to you for help if they know they will be punished. You don't want to make it easy for them to violate rules you have set up for them. However, you must still let them know that when they face life-threatening circumstances, your only concern is their safety.

For your kids to protect themselves from risks, they need to be armed with real information about the dangers to guard against. I hope this book has already taught you a lot about separating drug and alcohol facts from fictions. In this chapter I'll focus on the specific dangers youngsters—and you—need to be aware of.

PRACTICING RISK REDUCTION WITH YOUR KIDS

Let's return to Betsy from Chapter 6, a religious woman who asked me for help with her daughter Leslie's binge drinking, which had left Leslie drunk and alone in a stadium parking lot. In that chapter, we considered how to question children in order to clarify their values. Now we turn to the steps Betsy needs to take to protect her daughter.

What's the Worst That Can Happen? Let's Avoid That.

Betsy said she wouldn't do anything that might encourage her daughter's sexual activity or drinking. "I can't support those behaviors—they violate my religious beliefs," she told me.

We discussed Leslie's recent, frightening experience. "What do you think would be the worst thing that could have happened to Leslie in that situation?"

"She could have been raped and really hurt."

"Would you rather that happened than that she call you and ask for a ride?"

After a pause, Betsy said, "Not really."

"What if she were raped and was infected with HIV?"

"No, I wouldn't want that either."

"Or became pregnant?"

"Okay, what are you recommending?"

"What steps can you take to prevent these things from happening until Leslie becomes the person you and she want her to be?"

Among the solutions we considered—which Betsy and her daughter would have to accept as reasonable in terms of their basic values—are the following:

- Birth control pills
- Safe-sex materials (such as prophylactics)

- Arranged rides following concerts and parties, or permission to call without penalty when Leslie and her friends were incapable of driving
- Instructions not to mix multiple drugs and alcohol

These ideas initially upset Betsy. But they disturbed her less than the possibility her daughter would be seriously injured or drop out of school because she became pregnant. Betsy saw that by doing nothing she was increasing her daughter's risks. When Betsy realized that preventing her daughter from being permanently harmed was her major concern, she was able to reach out to Leslie. And her daughter was better able to respond. As Leslie told her, "Mom, I thought you loved God and goodness more than you loved me."

Like Betsy, you need to go beyond your knee-jerk reactions in order to plan for real dangers and worst-case scenarios. You have to have those difficult conversations with your children in which you promise not to punish them in situations where they need to be rescued from serious danger. In Chapter 3, we saw that even the high school substance abuse counselor promised her own children amnesty if they called her before driving when they were drinking.

At the same time, as discussed in Chapter 5, you need to be clear with your kids about your values. Even if you don't punish your children at that moment, you can use the incident to build an understanding about future behavior. To do so, you will have to steer between protecting your children and giving them a blank check to do whatever they feel like without facing consequences. Questioning them in a way that clarifies their own values, as I instructed Betsy in Chapter 6, is a good way to begin.

Say It Ain't So, Dwight

Raquel was a highly involved mother, even after her children entered college. Her son, Dwight, was a good boy and got good grades.

So Raquel was surprised when she received a statement from her insurance company showing that Dwight had been treated in the emergency room of the hospital at the university he attended. Dwight had fallen and suffered a concussion.

Raquel waited for an opportune moment, then brought the matter up. "Dwight, why did you go to the hospital?" Her son explained that he had blacked out while drinking, fallen, and hit his head.

Dwight had had occasional episodes of petit mal seizures as a child— short periods during which he became unfocused and unaware of his surroundings. For this reason Dwight was worried that he might be susceptible to epilepsy. Although Raquel doubted this was a danger, she built on her son's concern when talking with him about avoiding a recurrence.

Dwight was as worried as his mother about injuring himself. He and Raquel agreed that drinking until unconsciousness was a particularly bad idea for him given his medical history. They could then move on to a wider-ranging discussion, such as how Dwight could interact with his college buddies but not repeat his frightening blackout.

HERE'S WHAT TO TELL YOUR KIDS ABOUT DRUGS, AND HOW TO TELL THEM

Actually, the best way to find out what risks your kids are exposed to is to ask them. Remember, most parents are in the dark about how involved their children are with drugs and alcohol, and particularly with the most dangerous substances. Only half know their kids drink or take drugs, while only a quarter of parents realize their adolescent kids have been drunk, that their children have an abuse or dependence problem with alcohol, or that their kids have a marijuana problem.[2]

There's no guarantee that your children will answer your questions, but if you can maintain a neutral and reasonable manner, you may be surprised by their honesty. There are "teachable moments"— such as the one that occurred for Dwight—when a need to deal with an instant situation makes a young person more receptive. Don't blow those moments by overwhelming your children with your anxieties and barraging them with familiar messages that they already ignore.

Your first questions for your children in high school or college should be about their drinking and drug-taking environments, both at school and in their private lives. In order to encourage open communication, withhold judgmental statements—and grimaces. Along with the facts, you need to ascertain your children's views. Talk through with them their feelings about drinking and drug use decisions. This serves two functions—to elicit their values and to find out what they're up to.

Among your questions are:

- Do you have friends who you think have a drinking or drug use problem? (Make it clear that you are concerned about the situations and the behaviors, not about exposing particular individuals to their parents or school authorities.)
- What makes you say they have a problem?
- Have you ever had a problem with drinking or drug use?
- Why did that happen?

You can then switch to risk-reduction mode to come up with ways for your children to protect themselves in their social milieu. All questions focus on your children's own lives, their values, and their actions. Expand from the specific to the general.

- What do you need to do to avoid this happening again?
- Can you manage to do that (the risk-reducing behavior) with your friends? How will you go about it? (Talk through in detail the situations that may arise and how they propose to handle them.)
- Are you spending your spare time in the way that you feel is best for you?
- Do you need to rethink what you're doing at school and with your life?

By listening and encouraging dialogue with your children you may find out that they are actually very aware of substance abuse around them—and how to steer clear of it. Even though they may not abstain, their answers may be reassuring nonetheless:

> "Some kids' idea of a good time, or party, is to get drunk. My friends like to talk and joke and listen to music. We can have a good time without drugs or drinking."
>
> "I've smoked marijuana, but I don't particularly like it."
>
> "I smoke marijuana. I enjoy it. But I know when to quit, and when I need to do my schoolwork."
>
> "I got drunk one time—it was horrible! I threw up, and felt lousy for days. I'll never do that again."
>
> "I usually drink with my friends on weekends. But I never drive, or drink with strangers. I make sure to take care of myself."

Or they may be uneasy about their own use of substances. *They* may be worried that they have a problem.

> "Lately, when I've had a bad day at school, I smoke marijuana. Or I get some drugs from my friends, like Ativan, to take the edge off."
>
> "When I start the evening, I only want to have a few drinks, but I usually end up drinking until I pass out."
>
> "When I've had a tough week at school, all I can look forward to is going out to start the party on Friday. Sometimes I start on Thursday."
>
> "After partying, I have been feeling depressed and having trouble sleeping."

Note that even these behaviors, which might strike us as repugnant or dangerous, are fairly common on college campuses, some even in high school. Adolescents and young adults often use and trade information about illicit and prescription drugs fairly routinely. Most do so successfully, although some are failing, some badly, as we will discuss in the next chapter.

Young people are using what is available to figure out how to live their lives and feel good around their peers. Building on your child's inherent desire to remain healthy, a parental risk-reduction interview ought to include the following elements:

A RISK-REDUCTION INTERVIEW WITH YOUR CHILDREN

1. Ask open-ended questions about their own and their friends' substance use. Do not express judgments, but elicit information carefully. Listen.
2. Review what your children think about the behavior of those around them, and about their own behavior.
3. Review the worst dangers that they and people they know are exposed to.
4. Ask children to brainstorm ways to prevent these outcomes.
5. Make clear that by coming up with these risk-reduction techniques, you are not endorsing or encouraging drug or alcohol use or abuse.
6. The first risk-reduction technique is refusal or avoidance—not drinking or using drugs at all or in specific situations.
7. The second is learning how to avoid dangerous use, such as drinking until they black out, or placing themselves in harm's way when they have been drinking. Along with this, you can review with them what to do, whom to call, and where to go if they or one of their friends has a serious negative reaction to drugs or alcohol.
8. After coming up with prevention and risk-reduction techniques, ask your children to visualize using them, then practice or role-play the kinds of conversations they would have to engage in.
9. Help your children clarify their own values, goals, and self-image so as to strengthen their resolution not to take unacceptable risks. (Remember we are talking about your child's values and not a parroted version of your own.) These might include plans for their future, their relationships with friends they respect and who care about them, or their religious values.
10. Put aside your child's discomfort and your own and let them know that the two of you will revisit these questions from time to time.

THE WORST THING THAT CAN HAPPEN TO KIDS

The worst that can happen to your children from using drugs and alcohol is that they will die. Fortunately, death due solely to drinking or ingesting drugs is extremely rare. When fatalities do occur, they usually involve automobile crashes or other types of accidents where drinking is a contributing factor. Very rarely someone dies in a college binge-drinking incident, or an adolescent or young person dies directly from drug use. When this does happen it gets an enormous amount of media attention that magnifies our sense of the risk involved. But you can reduce greatly even the small chance that your child will be a drug fatality.

The drugs that inspire the most fear are opiates—including oxycodone (OxyContin), hydrocodone (Vicodin), and methadone, in addition to heroin. Yet the real risk of dying from them is small. The government's Drug Abuse Warning Network (DAWN) studied deaths due to opiates in six representative states.[3] The study found the average annual rate of death for all opiates is about 1/100 of 1 percent, or one person per ten thousand. Considering that large numbers of people use prescription painkillers, the odds of narcotic use being fatal are fairly low.

We usually think about deaths resulting from drug use as being due to overdoses. This represents a serious oversimplification, often encouraged by the media, that actually increases the danger of such fatalities.* The perpetuation of the overdose myth offers a window into why we can't deal with all kinds of drug and alcohol risks with kids. In order to do our best to prevent deaths from drug use, we need to open our minds and become better informed.

---

* A spike in heroin deaths in several U.S. cities in 2006, for example, was attributed to a new, pure blend of heroin on the streets. In fact, it occurred because the heroin supply was cut with another painkiller. K. Johnson, "Officials Seeking Source of Lethal Heroin Mixture," *New York Times*, June 15, 2006.

Drug deaths for young people do not occur because they take too much of one drug; people nearly always die due to mixing several drugs. When Strathclyde, Scotland, had a youthful "overdose" epidemic in the late 1990s, the Greater Glasgow Health Board spread the word: "It is actually rare to find someone has died from taking heroin alone—it has almost inevitably been taken as part of a cocktail with [tranquilizers] temazepam or Valium." The DAWN report likewise found that by far most opiate-related drug deaths involved multiple drugs. Most fatalities are due to asphyxiation.

Parents' Worst Nightmare

Kendra lived in a well-off suburb of a major American city. Her parents gave her a great deal of freedom. By the time she was in high school, Kendra was seriously into drugs.

One evening Kendra and her boyfriend took ketamine, an animal tranquilizer that has a hypnotic and psychedelic effect and is physically debilitating. After lying motionless and incapacitated for some time, her boyfriend injected them both with coke in order to "bring them back to life," he later recalled. They then had several vodka drinks. In order to finally get to sleep, they took Valium.

The next morning, Kendra's boyfriend awoke to find Kendra's body cold beside him. He tried to rouse her but was unable to do so. Then he called the police. Kendra was dead when they got her to the hospital.

The police called the death a cocaine overdose, which was widely reported in the media. In fact, the combination of alcohol and the depressant drugs ketamine and Valium was probably the cause.

Kendra would not take heroin, considering it too dangerous. But she often took several drugs and drank. Had Kendra felt able to discuss her drinking and drug use with someone who could have informed her that combining drugs with alcohol presented the greatest danger, her death perhaps could have been avoided. Of course, underlying all this drug use, Kendra's parents were deeply out of touch with their daughter's life, and it had horrible consequences.

SHOULD I TELL MY KIDS THAT DRUGS KILL?

Young people need to hear more than the simplistic message that drugs such as heroin, OxyContin, and Ecstasy are so dangerous that they should never take them. Your children also need to be aware of the following:

- Don't take powerful depressant drugs by yourself. If you use them, do so with friends you can count on to help you if you get in trouble.
- Go immediately to an emergency room (or take your friend or ask to be taken to one) if you become sick or have a negative reaction to a drug.
- Don't take multiple drugs that depress the nervous system (such as tranquilizers, sedatives, and painkillers), or any of these while drinking.
- A person who uses heroin or a painkiller such as OxyContin is better off taking the drug by itself, however "pure" or powerful it may be, than drinking or using other drugs to boost the first drug's effects.
- If you have stopped taking a drug for a while and use it again, you won't tolerate as well the same dose you used before.[4]

There are comparable precautions for avoiding serious harm when using amphetamines such as Ecstasy. For example, heat exhaustion can result from frenetic drug-induced dancing, so hydration and taking time-outs are critical. Very occasionally, worse reactions can occur. Although this is rare, Ecstasy users ought to agree on a plan with their friends to seek medical care if someone has a bad reaction.

A scientific review of Ecstasy use noted that warnings about the drug's deleterious effects on the brain are wildly overdrawn: "Whatever Ecstasy's cognitive effects may be, they are subtle. . . . If people think the health warnings are exaggerated or at odds with their own experience of the drug, the authorities risk losing credibility, and with it their chance to educate anyone about drugs."[5] The lethality of Ecstasy is promoted in drug education. But since deaths due to Ecstasy use are rare, young people may ignore all safety warnings about the drug.[6]

Making cold, hard sense about the dangers of drugs is the best policy. But kids aren't going to hear such warnings and advice in their drug education classes, as we saw in Chapter 3. You can inform yourself about facts such as these and pass them along to your children to fill this vacuum. But this can be tough information for you to share with an adolescent. You may prefer to tell them they need to inform themselves about the dangers of drug use. Some well-informed Web sites offer sound information of this kind.[7]

I PUT MY KID IN TREATMENT—DOESN'T THAT PROTECT HIM?

No, it doesn't. In the next chapter, we see that no external agency—not even treatment—can rescue your children. In some respects treatment may damage your kids' ability to handle alcohol and drugs. The treatment dictate never to drink or use drugs again will usually be violated by young people. Everyone knows this, but no one is allowed to take it into account.

My Son Died Because He Was in Drug Treatment: More Kids Should Get Such Treatment

Robert Shapiro, the well-known defense attorney for O. J. Simpson, suffered a terrible blow when his twenty-four-year-old son, Brent, a student at the University of Southern California, died after taking Ecstasy. Shapiro announced the creation of the Brent Shapiro Foundation, "trying to use Brent's death as a means to let people know that there is an epidemic of a drug disease, not only in this city, not only in this state, but in this country and perhaps in the world with kids starting at age 15."[8]

Brent's death was classified as an overdose by the coroner.[9] But Brent had taken only a half tablet of the drug. He had also been drinking. (Brent

additionally suffered from a heart murmur, caused by mitral valve pro-
lapse, though it is uncertain whether it was a factor in his death.) When
Brent became ill and began vomiting, his fiancée and friends carried him
from the party. They did not seek medical care. Later that night Brent
turned blue and stopped breathing.

Shapiro wants to educate people about the "epidemic of drug disease,"
a disease for which his son had been in treatment. Having been in the best
drug programs that Southern California had to offer, Brent hadn't used
drugs at all for eighteen months at the time of his death. According to
Shapiro, Brent had decided he was not an alcoholic and that he could
drink, but should avoid drugs.

Shapiro also discussed the fact that Brent had taken Ritalin from the
age of five until he was fifteen. According to Shapiro, Brent started smoking marijuana and drinking when he stopped taking Ritalin.

Although recommending that young people enter treatment, as his son
did, Shapiro wasn't that hopeful about how helpful such treatment is. "AA,
which is the best of the best that we have, has in one year an 88 percent
failure rate."

Shapiro's desire to prevent other families from suffering the way
his has is laudable. But continuing to insist that drug use is a disease will not produce better results. In fact, Brent's treatment may
actually have interfered with his taking reasonable precautions or
contributed to his friends' perhaps fatal decision not to take him to
an emergency room.

Brent Shapiro had probably been told hundreds of times in
treatment never to use drugs. Instead, someone as likely to use
drugs as Brent, especially since he hadn't used drugs in a long time,
should have been strongly advised to avoid combining alcohol
and drugs. Furthermore, he and his fiancée and friends should
have been prepared to get medical help when he encountered
problems—particularly given his heart murmur. Instead, it seems
his fiancée's and friends' worries about revealing to either his parents or his drug counselors that Brent had used drugs prevented
them from acting.

PROTECTING YOUNG PEOPLE FROM DRUG REACTIONS
WITHOUT OKAYING THEIR DRUG USE

Brent Shapiro had depended on drugs—first pharmaceuticals, then illicit drugs—throughout his life. But Brent had an extremely good prognosis for overcoming substance abuse: he was a successful student at a good university, enjoyed many friendships, had a supportive family, and was involved in a close relationship with a woman he wanted to marry. Even so, and despite all the reasons he had for remaining clean and every warning he had received, the statistical odds were in favor of Brent's returning to drugs at some point.

So the crucial question for Brent and others like him becomes how someone—a professional, a friend, or a family member—can communicate realistically to lay the groundwork so that their drug use isn't deadly. A conversation acknowledging the possibility of drug use without encouraging or condoning it might have saved Brent's life. Let's imagine such a dialogue with a young person whom we'll call "Sal."

HELPER: Sal, what's your plan around drug use?

SAL: Well, I realize that I've had issues with drugs all my life. After all, I started using them as a child for my hyperactivity. I can really get in a hole with them, where I get sidetracked from the good things in my life—school, my future career, my family, my girlfriend.

HELPER: Do you think you might ever take drugs again?

SAL: I plan not to. That's been driven home to me at the drug rehab I've been through, by AA, by everyone.

HELPER: What do you usually do on weekends? Whom do you spend your free time with?

SAL: Well, I like to go to parties with my girlfriend and other friends.

HELPER: Do people use drugs at these parties?

SAL: Sometimes they do.

HELPER: How do you feel when you see friends using drugs?

SAL: I regret not being able to join them. [Hesitantly] I need to confess that I began drinking again recently.

HELPER: Oh, what did they say about that in rehab?

SAL: They'd be so shocked—they'd scream at me if they knew. But I just don't feel I've ever had a problem with alcohol. It's drugs that get me in trouble.

HELPER: What makes you say you don't have a problem with alcohol?

SAL: Because with alcohol I can take it or leave it. I don't sit around thinking that I need to have a drink.

HELPER: Okay, you seem to have your head screwed on around drinking. Can you imagine yourself ever using drugs again?

SAL: It's funny you should ask that. At the party I was at last week, I did take a toke of marijuana.

HELPER: Speaking of alcohol, do you have any feelings about drinking along with using drugs?

SAL: You know, I've heard that can be really bad for you.

HELPER: Is there any way you can avoid drinking while using drugs?

SAL: I never thought about that. Of course, one toke of weed— excuse me, marijuana—isn't going to cause much trouble.

HELPER: But if you were to use a more serious drug, and you had been drinking?

SAL: Maybe I should think of a way to prevent that.

HELPER: Let's talk about that. By the way, is anything I'm telling you likely to encourage you to use drugs again? If so, I want to state strongly that's not my intention—I hope you won't take drugs at a party, or any other time.

SAL: I know that.

HELPER: What are your girlfriend's views on that matter?

SAL: She's confused about it. She likes to indulge herself sometimes [laughs], but she worries that it will encourage me to use. But she also thinks I'm doing so well in my life that maybe it could be okay [laughs again]. She's never been to Betty Ford.

HELPER: I think your girlfriend is very sensible. I agree that it is how you're doing in your life that matters most. But for you— maybe not for her—drug use presents real risks that call for care and prudence. You know, the fact that your life is going so well makes it doubly important that you don't throw away through a careless mistake all the great gains you've made. I worry that a situation might arise where you will feel like using drugs.

SAL: Yes.

HELPER: So I need to emphasize that, whatever you do, I want the best for you. And that especially concerns bad drug reactions. As soon as you feel you are having any kind of trouble—even while you're in the middle of using the drug—I want you to contact me or someone else who cares for you. And seek medical care—go to the Mt. Sinai emergency room or wherever is closest.

SAL: Okay, I understand.

HELPER: Will you do that?

SAL: Yes, I promise.

HELPER: What about your girlfriend?

SAL: What do you mean?

HELPER: What would she do if you encounter any trouble with drugs?

SAL: Well, she's a little iffy—she knows that people who care for me, and my AA sponsor and my drug counselor, would kill me if they found out I was drinking and drugging.

HELPER: Do you think you could share what we've been discussing with her? Actually, perhaps you could bring her in for one session. Will you make an appointment with her?

SAL: Yes, I will.

HELPER: One last thing. I understand that you have a heart condition?

SAL: Yes. I have an irregular heartbeat.

HELPER: Are you receiving treatment for that?

SAL: I see a cardiologist from time to time. In fact, I got a postcard from his office that I should schedule an appointment.

HELPER: Have you ever discussed your past drug use with him?

SAL: I never brought it up. I'm sure he would have disapproved. And I already know drugs are bad for me.

HELPER: I wonder if there are some drugs he would particularly want you to avoid.

SAL: How could I ask him that?

HELPER: How about something like this: "Doctor, I know you would advise me to avoid all illicit drugs. But are there some drugs that are especially bad for me, given my condition?"

SAL: Hey, that's good—mind if I jot that down?

HELPER: Go right ahead. So you'll discuss this with him?

SAL: Absolutely.

HELPER: I should say, although I'm not a doctor, that I believe cocaine and other stimulant drugs, such as amphetamines and Ecstasy, can cause heart arrhythmias. Whether you are especially susceptible to these is something you ought to discuss with your cardiologist.

SAL: Yes, I will.

HELPER: That's great. I look forward to continuing our conversation.

HARM REDUCTION TREATMENT—AT LEAST AT YOUR HOUSE

Young people and others who have been treated nearly always use again. What are the prospects that, say, an eighteen-year-old will abstain for sixty years? Even George Vaillant, a board member of AA and one of its greatest advocates, found that only 5 percent of patients in an AA-based treatment program he administered did not relapse within a few years.[10]

The question is, "What will this return to drinking or using entail and how bad will it be?" The only option allowed by AA or its drug equivalent, Narcotics Anonymous, is total, permanent, irrevocable abstinence. Thus, when those in such groups or in treatment do use again, they are told they will inevitably head straight back to drug addiction or alcoholism. There is no plan to limit the amount of drinking or drug use or to protect them from damaging themselves. Given the data on relapsing, this is a huge omission.

If your child has been in treatment, what level of return to use should you tolerate? In Chapter 1, we met John, a child from a privileged background who was a heroin addict. His father, Frank, kicked John out of the house. Frank later consulted me.

Let Me In

John's father, Frank, anguished over his decision to expel John from the family home. "If he can't succeed here," Frank worried, "what chance does he have in the outside world?" Still, Frank felt he owed it to his wife, his daughter, and himself to make sure that John didn't disrupt their household any more than he already had.

But he wanted to discuss the issue with me. "John was in a halfway house in another state, and he left. I'm sure he did that so he could party. But when I visited him, I could tell he was keeping himself reasonably clean. At least he wasn't using heroin. But can I trust him enough to let him back into our home?"

"What are your goals for him?"

"Definitely not to use heroin. And I want him to go to community college—and to get good-enough grades to stay there."

"Can you set those as the conditions for his returning home, and stand by them?"

"Yes. But what about smoking marijuana and drinking? Should I permit that? In treatment they said he couldn't touch anything like that without relapsing."

"But you said you thought he was using them, and he hadn't relapsed to heroin."

"That's what I think."

Frank went on to create a set of rules for his son. When John returned, Frank was upset that he went out drinking and smoking marijuana with some of his friends. But Frank saw that John didn't return to his heroin-using group. He also passed all of his courses. "I didn't know that this arrangement was a possibility," Frank said. "But, so far, I give it a cautious stamp of approval. And I do feel good having my son back in my home and trying to fix our family."

There are no guarantees that John will stay off heroin, just as there are no guarantees that anyone returning from treatment will stay clean. But rejecting the insistence on total abstinence gave Frank a wider range of ways to try to help John and bring their family together again.

DEALING WITH A HARM REDUCTION THERAPIST

Not all parents react so positively to harm reduction therapy. As a result, it can be hard for you to find a therapist who admits to practicing harm reduction. Should you find such a therapist, it may be hard for you to accept what that therapist is doing.

An Irate Father

Kristen was referred to me by a college counselor for self-esteem issues, as well as drug and alcohol abuse. Kristen was a senior—at twenty-one, she had the legal rights of an adult.

Along with full-time school attendance, Kristen worked weekends at a chain restaurant. After work, she and friends went on cocaine and alcohol binges, and she often, in her words, hooked up with inappropriate part-ners. Relying on her own values, Kristen had decided to quit drugs and to limit her drinking to one weekend night.

But when she presented the therapy to her father (Kristen's parents were divorced) in order to get him to pay for our sessions, he objected to my approach. Kristen's father called to let me know his feelings: "My daughter tells me that you didn't insist that she stop using drugs [Kristen relapsed and snorted cocaine one night] or quit drinking. What kind of therapy do you practice?"

I didn't criticize Kristen for her cocaine relapse because she already felt bad about it, as people usually do. Rather, I used the episode as a way to help her plan to avoid future relapses by explor-ing the conditions when it occurred, including the setting, her feel-ings, and her companions. My priority was making sure she didn't go on a binge—as AA predicts—or abandon all hope of recovery, and so I didn't overreact to her very typical slip. If Kristen had gone to the Betty Ford Center, they could have simply readmitted her to reiterate the same abstinence lesson at which she had failed.

Planning on getting drunk once a week didn't strike me as ideal—I wouldn't want my daughter doing it. But this planning marked improvement for Kristen. It was the beginning of her taking charge of her social life, rather than just letting it happen to her. Thinking about and planning her recreational time would also help her avoid unwanted sex. As I told her, "You'll know that you're in a solid relationship, one that you feel good about, when you use a contraceptive other than the morning-after pill."

I think that the principles I was encouraging for Kristen—taking control of her life, limiting her intoxicated episodes and their negative consequences, bringing her behavior in line with her own values, finding positive friends and intimate relationships—were ones her father would approve of. But it was uncomfortable for him to confront his daughter's use of intoxicants (I assume she hadn't told him about the sex, which would have been even more difficult for him to deal with).

But this simply put him in the large group of parents who ignore or deny that their children are doing these things. Obviously, her father's disapproval hadn't prevented the problems Kristen came to me with. But if I wasn't going to disapprove of Kristen, I couldn't disapprove of her father. I also had an obligation of confidentiality to Kristen. So I simply told this deeply concerned parent: "We all want the same thing. Please give us time—I think Kristen is learning to act in her own best interests."

Her father was appeased, although his call certainly put pressure on Kristen (and me). We proceeded to work to create a life for Kristen in which, as I said in therapy, "you don't have to come to therapy to express regret." As we progressed in this goal, I imagined her father was also pleased—but my client was Kristen. By the end of our sessions, Kristen said, "I really knew I needed to create a new social life for myself. The old one wasn't working. I think I've reached that point."

RISK REDUCTION AT A DISTANCE

Kristen lived in the same state as her parents, but she didn't live at home. Preparing your child for exposure to new worlds outside the home involves a process of inoculation. Based on the principles of harm reduction and motivational questioning, this preparation includes eliciting values and clarifying goals, formulating and then rehearsing strategies, developing fallback positions (including emergency procedures), and other commonsense principles.

Step 1: Set aside time for a discussion whenever children enter any new peer environment.

Step 2: Ask your children to visualize this new environment, and themselves in it. Ask specifically about drugs, alcohol, and cigarettes. As much as possible, have them imagine and calculate potential risks.

Step 3: Talk through with them their feelings about drinking and drug use decisions in terms of their own plans for college and life.

Step 4: Discuss the kinds of activities and events they will encounter where excessive drinking and drug use are likely to take place. Perhaps they want to join a fraternity and look forward to attending football games. Discuss with them how activities such as these fit in with their overall values and goals—*their* values and goals, not yours.

Step 5: Imagine and explore with them alternative ways of making friends and enjoying a full social life.

Step 6: Rehearse refusal strategies to avoid or limit consumption, such as saying, "I always stop at two" or "I can't have more than two drinks without getting sick."

Step 7: Let your kids know that they can call you at any time to help deal with an emergency, and review with them emergency procedures on their campus.

Your discussion with your children may leave you troubled. If you believe they are abusing drugs or alcohol, what do you do? I turn to remedial options in the next chapter.

RISK REDUCTION AND SMOKING

We reviewed in Chapter 2 the happy information that smoking has declined significantly among American youth. Nonetheless, it is still by far the most common drug habit. According to the 2004 National Survey on Drug Use and Health, almost 40 percent of Americans twelve years and older have smoked cigarettes daily at some point in their lives, and a quarter of Americans have smoked in the last month. Like virtually all other drug-related behaviors, smoking peaks between the ages of eighteen and twenty-five, when about 40 percent of American youth currently smoke.

Adolescents and college students will be exposed to cigarettes. Although you certainly don't like this, young people may be quite adept at harm reduction. The Monitoring the Future study found that between 1980 and 2004, just as many college students had smoked in the past year (36 percent in 1980; 37 percent in 2004) and just slightly more had done so in the previous month (24 percent in 1980, 26 percent in 2004) compared with a quarter century ago.[11]

But contemporary college students who do smoke do so less intensively—only 14 percent smoke daily, compared with 18 percent in 1980. And, most remarkably, about half as many (7 percent) smoke a half pack or more of cigarettes daily today as did so in 1980 (13 percent).[12] Most smoke less. Of course, smoking any number of cigarettes regularly is harmful, but smoking fewer cigarettes is less harmful—and potentially lifesaving over time.[13] A milder habit is also easier to quit. That young people often seem to be able to smoke casually instead of addictively is good.[14]

I Confess—I Gave My Daughter a Cigarette!

On a trip to visit college campuses with his daughter, Alan came across a tobacco shop that sold a foreign brand of cigarettes that he had smoked many years ago. Alan bought a pack.

His daughter noticed the cigarettes and asked for one—which Alan gave her, and which she smoked.

Alan worried about that decision. He questioned his daughter about it several months later.

"Dad, I already was a smoker. But I quit a couple of months before you gave me that cigarette."

"Have you smoked since?"

"No, I don't want to get cancer!"

"How much did you smoke?"

"One cigarette a day," she answered.

Alan wanted to avoid the "forbidden fruit" syndrome that, as we saw in Chapter 7, often occurs with drugs and alcohol. However, his daughter was already on to what he wanted to convey to her—and he could be reassured that she had discovered it herself.

Ten

MAKING TREATMENT WORK: DECIDING ON, MONITORING, AND PARTICIPATING IN TREATMENT

Even if your child has a substance abuse problem, you may opt not to seek treatment. The purpose of this chapter is to show you how to detect substance abuse problems, help you decide if you want treatment for your child, and outline the treatment options. If you do decide on treatment, your role will continue to be crucial—both in selecting an appropriate treatment and in monitoring your child's care. Treatment can succeed for your child only if you are actively involved in it.

THE CRITERIA FOR SUBSTANCE ABUSE PROBLEMS

What tells you that a young person has a substance abuse problem that requires treatment? What if a young man missed work because he smoked marijuana? What if he skipped classes and was doing poorly at school? What if he drove after he smoked pot? Then he qualifies for a substance abuse diagnosis.

What if he smoked every day and panicked when he couldn't get his drug? What if he couldn't go to sleep without smoking? What if he kept saying that he was cutting back his drug use but so far hadn't been able to? Then he would be dependent.

These criteria are set out in the *Diagnostic and Statistical Manual of Mental Disorders, Fourth Edition* (DSM-IV). DSM-IV divides alcohol and drug problems into abuse or the more severe diagnosis, dependence. Abuse entails failing to fulfill work, school, and home obligations, having repeated social or legal problems due to the substance use, or drinking or using drugs in a way that endangers the user's health and safety.

Criteria for the dependence diagnosis include that people regularly imbibe more than they intend to and continue to do so despite incurring psychological and health problems. They are preoccupied by their substance use, which interferes with other important activities. Sometimes they escalate their use in order to achieve the same desired effect (developing tolerance). Or they may experience acute discomfort when they stop use (withdrawal).

Although abuse and dependence seem like extremely serious conditions, they are in fact quite common among young people. Remember that more than a fifth of young people eighteen to twenty-five years old—and a quarter of twenty-one-year-olds— meet the criteria for one or the other condition. But even having a diagnosable problem still doesn't mean that young people should be in substance abuse treatment. We've seen that the majority of people recover even from dependence without treatment.[1]

THE ALCOHOLISM AND ADDICTION TRAP

Treatment programs almost never reject people who are referred to them. Such referrals invariably are diagnosed as "chemically dependent" (alcoholic or drug-addicted). Periodic scandals have rocked the adolescent drug and mental health treatment industry. One notable case, featured on *60 Minutes*, involved Fred Collins. Collins was involuntarily committed to Straight, a treatment program supported by Nancy Reagan, after he admitted he had smoked marijuana one time. "Counselors at Straight were told that all drug users are 'druggies' (addicts) who suffer from 'denial.' "[2] Although Straight no longer exists, the same pattern of misdiagnosis is typical today.

AA—and virtually all other substance abuse treatment in the United States—is built on the concept of the twelve steps. The first step says: "We admitted we were powerless over alcohol," which translates into people beginning the treatment process by admitting they are alcoholics. Telling young people they are alcoholics or addicts is self-defeating. If it convinces them that they are addicts for life, this can become a self-fulfilling prophecy. On the other hand, if they don't accept the label, they are going to turn off to everything they hear in treatment. And they will be attacked for maintaining their beliefs.

Maybe You're an Alcoholic, But I'm Not

Haley was fifteen when the police caught her drinking at a party. The court ordered her into an outpatient twelve-step program.

Her mother and father, though they lived in the same house, were estranged. Haley didn't feel close to either of them. Her father was distant and her mother was immersed in church life. Secretly, Haley yearned for counseling. Maybe she would get that now, she thought.

Haley's group treatment sessions were supervised by a woman in her forties who was, as is typically the case, a recovering alcoholic. At the first session, every participant, all of them much older than Haley, announced that they were alcoholics.

Haley raised her hand. "I was picked up for underage drinking. I don't think that I am an alcoholic." Immediately, several group members set her straight: "That's the alcoholism talking"; "You're in denial, girlie."

Afterward, the counselor spoke to Haley. "I was just like you when I entered treatment—in denial. You wouldn't be here if your drinking wasn't ruining your life. The kids who tell me, 'My drinking isn't that bad' are the ones who end up dead."

Haley turned off to the program right there. She went through it by rote, and celebrated her graduation by going out drinking with friends.

In a famous experiment conducted by David Rosenhan at Stanford in the early 1970s, called "On Being Sane in Insane Places," volunteers had themselves admitted into psychiatric hospitals in order to understand the experiences of mentally ill people.[3] None of the fakes was detected by the hospital staff. All of their behavior—such as taking notes—was instead taken as signs of their mental illness, including when they claimed they were normal. In the same catch-22, people admitted for alcohol treatment who claim they aren't alcoholics are told that their denial proves they *are* alcoholics.

INAPPROPRIATE TREATMENT IS COMMON

Treatment is often mandated by schools, courts, or other institutions. Courts require young drunk drivers and underage drinkers to be treated so that they don't enter the criminal justice system (which nobody wants) but also don't get off scot-free.

Disorderly Doesn't = Alcoholic

At seventeen, Robert was arrested for drinking and driving and fought with the arresting officers. The judge ordered him to undergo alcoholism treatment and to attend meetings of Alcoholics Anonymous.

His mother, Liz, contacted me. "Robert has a problem, but it's not a drinking problem. Robert does have an anger problem. He gets tremendously frustrated when he is thwarted and then he lashes out. Robert's anger is really getting him into trouble."

Liz was able to arrange with the court for Bob to see me—and to attend an anger management program. (Courts are legally required to permit someone who objects to AA to devise an alternative program that isn't based on the twelve steps.)[4]

Bob was a good client. He wanted to change, and he worked seriously on his problems. I saw Bob and his mother again six months and then a year later. Bob was graduating from high school, was headed for college, and hadn't been arrested again or gotten into any fights. He had learned to calmly reflect on situations when he became frustrated, to put his complaints or needs into words, and to try to understand other people's points of view.

WHEN TO SEEK TREATMENT FOR SUBSTANCE ABUSE

What kind of problems must your children have and how severe do they have to be to require treatment?

My Successful Son Is a Stoner

Merle contacted me about her son, George, who was home from college for the summer. "He goes out with his friends every night to smoke marijuana, comes home in the wee hours, and sleeps until the afternoon."

"Does he work?"

"Yes," Merle replied. "He has a job in the afternoons. He's actually a hard worker."

"How's he doing at school?"

"He's a good student, although he certainly could study harder."

"Do you know how much marijuana he smokes?"

"It used to be several times a day. But I told him he couldn't smoke in the house. And he's trying to cut back. Now he only smokes when he's partying with his friends. But that's every night!"

"How do the two of you get along?"

"We have a good relationship—except for the pot.

"Do you think he should go into treatment?" Merle continued. "I got him to go to AA once, but he refused to go again. He said the AA people were 'sanctimonious' and he thought the idea that you are 'powerless' was crazy."

I responded: "Why do you want him to go into treatment?"

"Because he's driving me crazy. He leaves his stuff all over the place. Aside from partying, sleeping, and working, he does nothing. He hasn't read a book or helped me around the house since he's been home."

I said, "Let's review George's situation. He has a job and does well at school. He's popular, gets along well with his mother, and has recently reduced his drug use."

"When you put it that way, it doesn't seem like he needs treatment. But what should I do about his lack of cooperation and motivation?"

"What control do you have over George?"

"I used to give him money, but now I don't. I don't give him the car anymore, but that doesn't bother him, because all his friends drive. I guess the only thing I have left over him is that he lives with me—I could tell him he has to move out if he doesn't follow my rules."

"That's a drastic step, but it is one way to go. It depends on how much his behavior bothers you. On the other hand, perhaps you could improve your communication with him. You say George wants to cut back his smoking or quit?"

"We can't talk about that. I'm too judgmental. He reacts as though I'm attacking him. But this session makes me think I should—and maybe I could—ratchet back my criticism in order to talk with him. He is a good boy."

Even though he had a substance problem, my judgment was that it wasn't beneficial for George to enter treatment. Because his chronic drug use was disturbing his home life, George was a substance abuser. He doesn't qualify as drug (or chemically) dependent, a condition in which people use drugs or drink compulsively. Given George's problem, his mother might have insisted that he enroll in a drug treatment program—where he would certainly be accepted, and moreover be labeled as addicted or drug-dependent. But it was far more useful for Merle to consider how to modify her relationship and communications with George, which we then worked on.

ADOLESCENTS HAVE PROBLEMS OTHER THAN— OR IN ADDITION TO—SUBSTANCE ABUSE

It may seem logical to put adolescents who have problems and are using drugs into drug treatment. However, their substance use is often a symptom of other problems—a struggle for independence, anger, or more general life problems. Bob, the seventeen-year-old we met who was arrested for drunk driving and fighting with the police, had to learn self-management skills. Putting kids into drug treatment when they have behavioral or psychological problems is a mistake. Even those who, like George, do meet the criteria for substance abuse or dependence are well served by being taught the life skills that will allow them to find alternatives to drug use.

They won't learn such skills in treatment. James Frey's bestseller, *A Million Little Pieces,* regales readers with war stories about his crack addiction and alcoholism. Although Frey fabricated many of these tales, he often accurately described the Hazelden treatment program he participated in. I know this because I have reviewed the case records of patients at Hazelden who, like Frey, objected to being force-fed the twelve steps. As Frey complained bitterly, "People like you keep saying it's the only way, so I'm thinking that I might as well just put myself out of my misery now and save myself and my family the pain of the future."

Placing people in treatment they dislike or that violates their sense of themselves is a bad idea. Therapies that attack people's self-concepts undercut their egos just when they are most vulnerable. If young people refuse to accept the chemical dependence diagnosis and label (as they are often wise to do), therapy then becomes a struggle between them and their counselors.

I nonetheless thought George could benefit from treatment that didn't require that he label himself. Even if young people do not have a bona fide substance abuse diagnosis, they may benefit from therapy or help with life problems, as Bob did and Haley could have. But they will not find such help in standard treatment programs, even the most prestigious, such as Hazelden. Frey noted the lost opportunities to help people with these critical issues: "When someone needs help most, you deny it to them because they . . . need a different kind of help than what you think is right."

Parents regularly ask me to rescue their children from addictions. They view addiction as something like a stray infection, one that has nothing to do with the parents or even with the children's own lives.

Help, My Daughter Is Being Kidnapped!

Priscilla consulted me because her previously obedient daughter, Sandy, had given up on school and was spending all of her time on the Internet.

Sandy's father lived in another state, and Priscilla was very close to her child. She often joined Sandy and her friends in their activities.

But Sandy had begun to reject all her school friends. Instead, she e-mailed other boys and girls, most of whom were older than she and out of school, on the Internet. Their talk wasn't explicitly sexual, but more like giggly girl talk.

Priscilla sought my advice when a boy several years older than Sandy showed up to take her on a date. Shocked, Priscilla sent the boy home.

"I want you to cure Sandy's Internet addiction," Priscilla told me.

Priscilla was blind to how she reinforced Sandy's immaturity and how Sandy was now desperately trying to assert her independence. Priscilla was justifiably upset that her daughter would date someone off the Internet. But ordering her daughter's date to leave was typical of their relationship. And telling a rebellious child not to date someone can provoke much worse rebellion.

Priscilla needed to answer the question "How can I be a positive part of my daughter's life while allowing her to become a mature person?" My treatment with Priscilla focused on how her relationship with Sandy led to her daughter's acting out and how to change this.

If you are considering treatment for your child, evaluate whether the problem is solely or primarily drugs, alcohol, or another addiction. Only when other, deeper problems aren't driving serious misuse of substances should you consider conventional rehab programs. Even then, however, you need to guard your child.

THE DOWNSIDES TO AA AND TWELVE-STEP TREATMENT

If your child is referred to substance abuse treatment in the United States, it will use the twelve steps. The twelve steps are a one-size-fits-all approach. Unless children find themselves in the hands of a sensitive counselor, they all undergo the same treatment. When educators and psychologists now understand so much about individuals and their different learning styles, it is distressing that only one alcoholism treatment is used for all ages and kinds of people—including all kinds and severity of substance abuse—in the United States.

For some, this treatment leads out of addiction. It is not generally effective, however. Research does "not demonstrate the effectiveness of AA or other 12-step approaches in reducing alcohol use and achieving abstinence compared with other treatments."[5]

In fact, other treatments that are more effective than the twelve steps, treatments we will review in this chapter, are rarely utilized.[6]

But there can be additional problems when young people, in particular, subscribe to and rely on the twelve steps. Many adolescents and young adults try to follow the twelve steps. We met Wanda in Chapter 4. A girl overdirected by her parents, Wanda engaged in mindless drinking, drug taking, and sex in college in order to follow her peer group. She was suspended from college for dealing drugs with her boyfriend and returned home in disgrace.

Am I Really an Alcoholic, Like I've Been Saying for a Decade?

Wanda's parents quickly enrolled her in a treatment program, which she welcomed as a respite from a life gone out of control. Wanda likewise found that attending AA following treatment calmed her and provided much-needed emotional support.

Wanda was still not twenty-one. Although she had regularly used drugs and alcohol as a part of her social life, she now had no difficulty remaining abstinent—as long as the people around her didn't drink or use.

Although she never admitted it to the group, Wanda wasn't sure that she had a real problem with alcohol. When she was in college, she frequently had to be encouraged to drink more by her friends. Later, Wanda decided, "I was addicted to my friends and my boyfriend."

Nonetheless, Wanda married another AA member and continued attending meetings for the next decade. When she had a daughter, Wanda joined a play group with other mothers in the neighborhood. They served wine and chatted while the kids played.

Wanda always declined the wine, although the other women seemed to be enjoying themselves, sipping as they talked. But she started to think, "I'm not really an alcoholic like I say I am at my AA meetings."

Wanda contacted me. She needed someone to affirm what she now believed—that although treatment had served a function in her life, she was not an alcoholic. People like Wanda, buried under years of an alcoholic and AA group identity, worry what will happen when they reject AA as the bulwark for their existence. After carefully evaluating her drinking when she was younger and reviewing her current life, I agreed that Wanda could try social drinking. But this decision—and the motivation—had to come strictly from her. I emphasized that she always had the option of resuming abstinence if her experiment faltered.

Wanda accepted a glass of wine at the next play group. She eyed the other mothers and made sure to drink no faster and no more than they did. Finding that nothing terrible happened, she continued to drink at subsequent play sessions. Although she drank cautiously, checking her reactions to the alcohol, she was exhilarated. It felt liberating to be free of an image of herself that had limited her for over a decade.

After her daughter began school, Wanda continued to drink when she went out with friends. She never drank at home, out of respect for her husband, who likewise respected Wanda's choice to drink.

Perhaps Wanda could have gone on forever with the fiction that she was an alcoholic. How would it have hurt her? Her alcoholic identity made her feel like an outsider in her new circle of friends. It limited her activities and—most important—her own view of herself. Wanda decided it was wrong to stereotype herself in a way that she no longer believed was accurate.

Wanda's entire alcoholism diagnosis was questionable; she could have succeeded at either abstinence or controlled drinking had she wanted. Wanda—as well as George, Bob, Sandy, and Haley—were all more or less in the same boat. None was courting death. Others, whether because of the severity of their problem or other limitations, require more decisive interventions. They may not have the luxury of choosing how they will resolve their substance problem.

Sally, in Chapter 2, was one of these people. She overdosed on prescribed and illicit medications. She had been drinking and drugging around the clock for weeks straight.

Life and Death in a Treatment Program

When she arrived at the hospital, Sally was sweating and shaking. Her first nights there were nightmares, literally, as she hallucinated ghostly figures. In the morning she found her knuckles were bloody from swinging at the ghouls and hitting the walls of her room.

Sally was prescribed tranquilizers to alleviate her withdrawal, along with a sedative to sleep and an anti-depressant so that she could handle the daily therapy sessions. She would continue to rely on medications to sleep, stay awake, and feel okay for many years.

In the mornings Sally and her fellow patients would get their meds, have breakfast, then return to their rooms, where they were supposed to read treatment literature. But Sally slept some more or went to a designated area to smoke with other residents until their morning group session.

After she recovered from the DTs, Sally participated honestly in the therapy sessions. She hoped to learn the source of her addictions as she struggled to free herself from them. Many of the residents emphasized the twelve steps and the need to accept their own powerlessness. But Sally couldn't accept that she behaved this way because she had an uncontrollable disease. Repeatedly, she was told that she thought too much and needed to "surrender to her higher power." She interpreted this to mean that she should give up trying to make sense of her life on her own.

When the staff told Sally and fellow residents that they had all inherited a biological destiny to be alcoholics, Sally wondered how they knew this was true. Sometimes Sally wished she did believe that she had been born with a disease that explained how she had screwed up her life. It would relieve her of so much anxiety and guilt!

Sally's counselor met with her parents along with Sally just before she left the hospital. The counselor painted a stark future for Sally if she continued her drinking and drug use. Sally and her parents came away from the meeting with a sense of dread.

Her twenty-eight-day stay had given Sally time away from her drinking buddies and made her feel better about herself. When she left the hospital, she was eager to change, but also anxious. She felt guilt toward her parents and embarrassment among her friends, most of whom drank and used drugs heavily themselves.

Two weeks after she returned home, a group of friends asked Sally to go out. She ended up drunk, asleep on the floor. Afraid to return home, she went on a drug and alcohol binge lasting several days. She eventually came home, but resumed her drinking and drug use.

Finally, at the age of twenty-two, Sally decided she could no longer endure her life. Swearing she would change, she swallowed her distaste for the twelve steps and returned to an AA group she had sporadically attended.

This time, she threw herself into the meetings, staying away from familiar "playmates and playgrounds." Sally loved her sponsor, a woman ten years older than she. But her sponsor cut Sally off whenever she questioned the twelve-step approach and the notion that she had a disease.

As much as AA enabled her to remain sober, Sally was still uncomfortable with the group's philosophy. After a year, she dropped out. Although she no longer attended AA, and even though she questioned the doctrines she had been taught, Sally reckoned she shouldn't drink. She had never demonstrated an ability to moderate her consumption.

Sally resolved to find her own path, living a sober life without AA. But, at twenty-three, she faced a daunting challenge—how was she going to create a social life that didn't center around drinking? She didn't know anybody outside of AA who didn't drink.

For two years, Sally struggled to find a social and existential niche for herself. She no longer attended meetings of Alcoholics Anonymous, but she had not found an alternative universe. She got a job as a photographer's assistant—she was a college graduate and had good technical and people skills. But she had nobody to play with. For Sally, being sober meant being alone.

Sally didn't know how to live a full life without alcohol and drugs. It seemed as though her entire adolescence and young adulthood had been mediated by an alcohol buzz. And Sally continued to rely on prescribed sedatives and stimulants to sleep and to work. She continued the smoking habit she had developed in college, which AA had done nothing to discourage.

At twenty-five, Sally began seeking a psychologist who would help her fight her addictions without the dogmatism of AA. When she consulted me, we decided to work on three key areas: developing a social life that didn't center on alcohol, quitting smoking and prescribed mood medications, and creating a meaningful career.

Together, we identified places and activities where she could find people who did not rely on alcohol as their primary social prop. Sally took computer graphics classes and began doing computer graphics in the photography studio and also taking freelance jobs. In part to fill the time previously occupied with partying, Sally began to exercise regularly. As she felt more confident in her abilities and found her life more rewarding, she was able to quit smoking and her array of mood medications.

Still, Sally didn't really know how to deal with people at a personal level—outside of her parents—without drinking. Alcohol made Sally feel smart, worldly, and socially bold. Without alcohol, she didn't believe she was appealing to others. Sally was attractive and men wanted to date her. But single urban men in their twenties assumed that a good time involved drinking.

Sally met a client through her work who noticed her creativity and intelligence, as well as her good looks, and asked her out. When she declined any wine at dinner, he asked her if she was in recovery. "I don't go to AA," Sally answered. "But I choose not to drink. I hope that doesn't bother you."

Sally was engaged in creating a substance-free existence for herself, even in such fundamental areas as going to sleep and waking. Essential to this task was Sally's emerging belief that she was capable of leading a meaningful abstinent lifestyle. Her goal as she saw it was: "Instead of getting drunk to feel wild and crazy or excited about life, I want to actually do something wild and crazy or exciting in life. Instead of drawing attention to myself by self-destructing in order to avoid genuinely trying, I want to try to do things that matter to me."

In order to permanently escape addiction, Sally had embarked on a transformation. Her case illustrates the problems young people have when they spend most of their spare time intoxicated. It also lays out the limits of conventional treatment. To become real, fully functioning adults your children need to be motivated, to develop skills, and to form adult relationships. Don't lose sight of these goals.

Learning to assume adult responsibilities does not mesh well with admitting powerlessness. If you decide as an adult that your own life will be best served by submission to a higher power, God bless you. But that is a tough decision to allow, let alone force on, adolescents and young adults. AA's belief that sobriety only occurs "one day at a time" takes on ominous overtones—that at any moment, a slight aberration can totally derail a young person's life. Having a slip after AA and treatment often means going haywire, as Sally did.

Alcoholics Anonymous meetings provided Sally with a place to meet with people who didn't drink.[7] There are other places where people don't drink, or where they drink moderately, but Sally wasn't familiar with them. When she stopped going to AA, Sally was rejected by all of her AA associates, including her sponsor.

Sally didn't learn any skills during her hospital stay, since she was experiencing withdrawal and was heavily medicated. Besides, her treatment wasn't geared that way. Her counselors didn't know about skills training; they were RNs and recovering people who had picked up a specialized degree in alcohol counseling based entirely on the twelve steps.

Sally did occasionally discuss in groups how to express emotions in a healthy way and to recognize when relapse is most likely (when she was hungry, angry, lonely, or tired—factors easily remembered as the acronym HALT). But she and her fellow patients didn't learn specific skills to cope with these feelings. Everything always came back to the single dominant principle of treatment: they had a disease that meant they could never drink or use drugs again, or they would die.

As we learned in Chapter 5, one of the values that allows children to avoid addiction is being able to think about themselves and their environments. Relying on AA principles in place of thinking may work in the short term, but ultimately the "fake it until you make it" strategy promoted in AA is not a satisfactory life principle. Developing an ability to manage their own lives, called self-efficacy, is critical to young people's mental health. In the end, AA may have saved Sally's life, but AA couldn't teach her how to rebuild it.

Sally's parents were uninformed about addiction and treatment, which is typical. They stood at arm's length from Sally's therapy, much as they were previously detached from her high school and college shenanigans. When they learned the depth of Sally's problems, they were terribly concerned. Obviously, it would have been better for them to have played an active, constructive role throughout Sally's life. But at that point, the only way they knew to support her was to do what her counselor told them.

MAKING INFORMED USE OF TREATMENT

You may not care whether your children can sip wine decades from now—and certainly not if you are worried about their survival. Your sense of crisis is understandable. Still, it's important to take a long-term developmental perspective. Saddling children with a belief that they are forever different and vulnerable gives them a large burden to carry into adulthood, and is often unhelpful even in the short run.

If you feel it is imperative to find treatment for your child, you must monitor and manage that experience. As we have seen, treatment is most likely to be the twelve-step kind. But twelve-step treatments can vary tremendously and may leave room for your child to learn things other than that he or she is powerless. To see that this occurs, you need to participate in the therapy process.

Think of treatment as a contract you are forming with the provider. This contract identifies realistic and useful goals not only for your child but also for your family and for the therapy. You should interview therapists and programs and work with them on a plan, which you should actively monitor. Asking questions and demanding answers proves both your love and your helpfulness.

Don't be intimidated about making yourself a part of the treatment process, including participating in therapy along with your child.

Your planning around treatment should include the following:

1. GOALS. What does your child need to change or to achieve in therapy? Agree on the problems your child has, and the changes that will benefit your child's life. Be clear and specific, and make sure that the goals go beyond simple abstinence. They may include addressing psychological problems such as depression or low self-esteem, peer groups and activities, performance at school, household responsibilities, family relationships, meaning and purpose, and any other important aspect of your child's life.

2. METHODS. How will the therapist or treatment program accomplish these goals? Attending group meetings to get insights into behavior or learning the twelve steps are not by themselves answers. The therapy should have a sensible, proven way of working with children noncoercively in order to modify their feelings and behavior. Therapy should include ways of integrating these changes into the young person's life at home. You need to understand the methods your child has learned in order to continue to make use of them.

3. TIMETABLE. How long will it take to accomplish these goals? Therapy cannot have an open-ended time frame. Nor can the length of treatment be based on how long insurance payments—or your bank account—hold out. If the therapist or program cannot tell you how long therapy will take, they don't really know how to accomplish what they claim. Treatment often becomes an end in itself—an extreme example of which was one girl's involuntary thirteen-year stay in a New Jersey treatment program.[8]

4. AFTERCARE. Therapy is not about your child doing well in the therapist's office or hospital. As we saw in Sally's case, the challenge is learning to function in the outside world. Meanwhile, you need to learn how to interact constructively with your child and how to create and support a positive arc for your child's life. The admonition to attend a support group is not aftercare. It is your right, your obligation, to demand clear plans for how to continue your child's care after treatment. If the staff refuses to respond to your questions, or

can't, they have some self-serving motive or are incompetent. In either case, they're not concerned with your child's well-being and growth.

5. COST. Treatment for substance abuse, or chemical dependence, is expensive in the United States. "The cost of the tough love treatment is comparable to the tuition at an Ivy League university," noted Maia Szalavitz in *Help at Any Cost*.[9] You have to consider this drain on your resources. Bankrupting your family won't help your children. And the most effective therapies, such as motivational interviewing and brief interventions, are also the cheapest, because they are less intensive and take place in an outpatient or counseling setting.

WHAT TO LOOK FOR IN TREATMENT

Treatment of adolescents and young adults based on the twelve steps and confrontational counseling—the therapies that form the backbone of American treatment—does little good, according to William Miller and his colleagues at the University of New Mexico. This team has examined all available research on outcomes of alcoholism treatment.[10] In fact, they found, some individuals do worse receiving standard treatment than if they got no help. Think of Haley, who didn't get needed family therapy, and who got drunk to celebrate completing her program.

Research has identified treatments that do work; they work because they provide the motivation, tools, and support to produce change. Despite their problems, young people bring many assets to therapy. Standard treatment programs typically ignore these resources—indeed, they actively deny young people's values and strengths. The treatments for Wanda, Sally, and Brent Shapiro all failed to utilize their families as well as their intelligence and other personal assets. In contrast, effective treatments for substance abuse draw upon young people's strengths, motivation, and existing support networks. Helping people to recognize and use the resources at their disposal, in order to make changes they themselves want, is central. As a parent, you are one of your child's chief resources.

Effective treatments for substance abuse include the following:

SOCIAL BEHAVIOR AND NETWORK THERAPY

Network therapy helps clients develop better activities and social networks. Therapy sessions encourage clients to examine how they spend their time, who they associate with, and how they can form new social networks to support desired behavior changes.[11] (See Appendix A for help finding this and other therapies.)

MOTIVATIONAL INTERVIEWING

How do you react when someone harangues you that you're wrong? Young people respond best to therapy which instead draws on their own motivations and goals and respects their emerging sense of themselves.

People overcome addictions when they realize that it is in their own best interest to do so. Motivational interviewing (MI) strives to get people to examine their habits in relation to their own values and goals.[12] In Chapter 6, we demonstrated MI with Betsy and her daughter Leslie. Leslie wanted to make money and to achieve social status. Yet her drinking made attaining these goals unlikely. I showed Betsy how to connect Leslie's aspirations and her actions by encouraging Leslie to notice how the people she admired achieved their success.

Motivational interviewing has the following elements:[13]

1. Express empathy ("I understand what you are experiencing").
2. Explore values and goals ("What do you want for yourself?").
3. Develop discrepancies ("Will your behavior help you reach that goal?").
4. Avoid disagreements ("I see your point").
5. Support self-efficacy ("You can achieve what you want").

MI therapists don't argue with clients. Whenever they sense resistance, they pull back. The key to this approach is to push the ball back to the other person. Clients make headway when they recognize truths on their own and thus take ownership of them.

MI therapists don't define people's conditions for them. They focus instead on specific problems young people identify, such as getting stoned instead of studying, getting along with parents, and finding constructive activities. The therapist and client then tackle these issues together.

BRIEF INTERVENTIONS

Motivational interviewing can take place in a single session, which is called a brief intervention (BI). BIs have been found to motivate substance abusers to reduce their alcohol and drug use more often than any other therapy,[14] and college students specifically have benefited from it.[15]

A standard brief intervention has these elements:

- Identifying likely clients (for example, through a positive urine screen)
- Meeting with a peer counselor for twenty minutes at a routine medical visit
- Developing rapport by asking for permission to discuss substance use
- Discussing the pros and cons of clients' substance use in users' terms
- Eliciting the gap between the actual and the desired state of clients' lives
- Developing an action plan
- Following up with a phone call or subsequent office visit

COMMUNITY REINFORCEMENT APPROACH (CRA)

Brief interventions, motivational interviews, and network therapy all rely on young clients to provide most of the impetus for—and to do the work of—changing. It is easy to see why they are the least expensive forms of treatment, as well as being the most effective. Along with the resources they have, however, some young people face considerable life deficits due to their immersion in drugs and alcohol. They can benefit from more structured treatment, such as the community reinforcement approach (CRA).

CRA begins with clients completing a "happiness scale": rating how content they are with crucial parts of their lives, such as drinking, school, social life, personal habits, family relations, emotional state, and ability to communicate. Another scale, called "goals of counseling," helps clients identify specific improvements they want to make in each area. Together with the client, the therapist then develops a plan for achieving these goals.

CRA focuses on very specific ways for young people to avoid addiction. For example, it helps them identify what triggers their addiction. Whereas conventional treatment simply demands abstinence, CRA instead relies on improving people's ability to cope with their worlds as the route to sobriety. CRA is particularly appropriate for young people who have spent so much time abusing substances that they haven't learned essential life skills. It offers training in skills such as how to spend recreational time, have positive social interactions, resist urges to drink or use, and prevent relapse.

COMMUNITY REINFORCEMENT AND FAMILY TRAINING (CRAFT)

When I worked with Merle to help move George away from his reliance on marijuana, I was showing her how to reinforce George's positive behavior. She could reward him, for example, by allowing him to drive again if he maintained his marijuana sobriety. My main tack was to improve the atmosphere in their home and allow them to communicate effectively. This is an example of community reinforcement and family training (CRAFT), which extends the ideas underlying CRA by assisting those who are concerned about substance abusers, including parents, to create environments that reinforce their children's sobriety.[16]

CRAFT conveys the following techniques to parents and others:

1. Increasing children's motivation to change—for example, by questioning young people about how their lives are hurt by their drug use
2. Enhancing communications skills—training on providing non-antagonistic feedback and encouragement

3. Increasing positive interactions between parents and children
4. Non-reinforcing of drug use—ignoring substance abusers when they are using
5. Initiating activities that compete with and prevent drug use
6. Developing outside activities and reinforcement for the parent
7. Planning escape routes for parents whose own lives can be threatened—for example, if young people are violent
8. Planning to introduce the idea of treatment as needed

MULTISYSTEMIC THERAPY (MST)

Multisystemic therapy helps adolescents who are at extremely high risk for drug and alcohol addiction along with other anti-social behaviors.[17] After identifying what those risk factors are, the therapist becomes involved in all facets of children's lives—for example, spending time in their homes and their schools. Parents are trained to set clear rules, to monitor compliance, and to administer punishments and rewards accordingly. Therapy also addresses parents' problems, such as economic issues and emotional disorders. The therapist tries to move teenagers toward positive friendships and away from destructive relationships. Among populations of young people at high risk for being placed in institutions, MST has increased by half to two-thirds the number who are able to avoid institutionalization.[18]

WHAT MAKES SENSE IN TREATING CHILDREN, ADOLESCENTS, AND YOUNG PEOPLE?

Therapies that work for young people just make sense. Social network therapy, motivational interviewing, the community reinforcement approach, skills training, and multisystemic family therapy all address challenges that bedevil children and adolescents without claiming they are permanently handicapped. All enhance parents' and adolescents' feelings of efficacy, rather than telling them they are powerless. If you are contemplating a particular treatment plan for your youngster, consider if it makes sense in the following ways—and if it doesn't, move on. The therapy should:

- Respect young people's values and identity
- Provide real skills and resources
- Help locate new activities and positive social networks
- Credit the patients, rather than the therapy, for positive changes they make
- Enhance their confidence and sense of efficacy—empower them
- Avoid labeling them or convincing them their problems are lifelong

You will be able to organize reasonable treatment for your children. This may mean going outside of ordinary therapy networks—for example, finding specific skills training (communications, anger management, decision making) or therapeutic groups not organized specifically for the purpose of recovery. But standard treatment programs, particularly if they are in hospitals, may have such resources, even if you must ferret them out and insist your children be allowed access to them.

Appendix A lists books, Web sites, and other ways to access the effective treatments listed here.

Eleven

POLICIES FOR A NON-ADDICTED AMERICA

Contemporary America has a special relationship with addiction. It is both spectacularly vulnerable to addiction in its broadest sense and especially afraid of it.

What creates America's addiction proneness? Among the sources of this cultural addictiveness are the lack of well-established customs for regulating use of alcohol and other intoxicants; the temperance tradition and the moralistic attitudes that, as a result, have arisen toward alcohol, drugs, and intoxication; our historical view of alcoholism as a disease (dating to Benjamin West, a physician and signer of the Declaration of Independence); our faith in medicine to solve personal and social problems; our large appetites; our overprotection of our children. And then there is Alcoholics Anonymous, which has dominated our thinking about addiction for more than half a century.

As we've seen, there's much that individual parents and educators can do to combat these tendencies—but too often, this involves fighting an uphill battle against misguided policy, education, and treatment programs. *It doesn't have to be this way.* In this chapter, I present some ideas of what sensible addiction prevention programs and policies might look like.

THE PRINCIPLES OF CHANGE

The changes I propose in our policies are based on ten underlying goals.

1. PREPARE YOUNG PEOPLE TO MAKE THEIR OWN DECISIONS ABOUT WHETHER AND HOW THEY WILL USE SUBSTANCES. There is no alternative to recognizing the truth, unpleasant as it may be: young people will ultimately face unlimited opportunities to be addicted. The defense against addiction lies not in trying to protect kids from all of these situations or in trying to scare them away from drugs, but in giving them the tools they need to make smart decisions for themselves.

2. MAKE SAFETY THE MAIN GOAL OF DRUG AND ALCOHOL POLICIES FOR YOUNG PEOPLE. We need to acknowledge that there will always be drugs, alcohol, and addiction, and that most young Americans will at some point drink or use drugs illicitly. Recognizing these realities clarifies our mission in relation to young people and substance use. Abstinence should not be presented as the *only* way to avoid addiction or life-threatening experiences. We need to teach more realistic alternatives such as moderation and safe use.

3. DON'T PRESENT ADDICTION AS A LARGER-THAN-LIFE EXPERIENCE. No experience, including addiction, is beyond human beings' control. The very ordinariness of addictive experiences makes clear that nearly everyone confronts them to some degree, and more often than not people resolve addictions on their own. As we've seen, the disease model of addiction is not just wrong, it is positively harmful: people are most likely to escape addiction when their values contradict continued addiction and when they *believe* they can escape it.

4. DON'T DEMONIZE ALCOHOL AND DRUGS. Education that portrays alcohol and other substances as overpowering sets young people up for substance abuse. Cultures where alcohol is seen as a manageable experience, on the other hand, are the ones that deal most successfully with drinking. Moderate social drinking should be presented as a viable option to children from an early age, even before they can legally drink outside the home.

5. PRESENT REALISTIC, SCIENTIFICALLY VALID INFORMATION ABOUT DRUGS AND ALCOHOL AND THEIR BENEFITS AND RISKS. If educators are not confident enough in their positions to

tell the truth, then they should change their positions. Kids know when they're being lied to about drugs, so that this propaganda falls on deaf ears. As a result, adolescents stop paying attention to *anything* the government, police officers, or school authorities tell them about the subject.

6. GIVE CHILDREN MORE CHANCES TO INDEPENDENTLY EXERCISE THEIR PHYSICAL AND MENTAL CAPABILITIES. Addiction springs from young people's lack of independence, self-control, and experience with the outside world. Anything that offers children and adolescents greater freedom of movement and opportunities for self-management reduces their susceptibility to addiction.

7. REDUCE AMERICANS' RELIANCE — AT EARLIER AND EARLIER AGES — ON PSYCHOTROPIC MEDICATIONS. We must begin to reverse the dominant mental health notion of our era—that pharmaceuticals are the best way to resolve personal and life issues.

8. INCREASE THE READY AVAILABILITY OF ALTERNATIVE TREATMENT MODELS BESIDES AA AND THE TWELVE STEPS. Alternative treatments include motivational interviewing, brief interventions, community reinforcement, network therapy, and cognitive behavioral therapy for emotional and other problems. AA will always be a part of the treatment panoply. But AA and twelve-step programs should not be favored by government agencies, schools, or health care providers and insurers. Although this diversification process has begun, it is attacked by entrenched treatment interests. The process should instead be accelerated.

9. ELIMINATE COERCION IN TREATMENT. Most people who enter twelve-step treatment for addiction and alcohol abuse today are forced to do so by criminal and family courts and social welfare agencies. A wide variety of treatments should be offered to people in these systems, but none should be forced on them.

10. DON'T CONFUSE SUBSTANCE USE AND CRIMINALITY, CONCEPTUALLY OR LEGALLY. Drugs, alcohol, and other compulsions do not explain why people commit crimes—it is more accurate to say that faulty values underlie both misuse of substances and criminality. Substance use and other addictions should not be acceptable

defenses for misbehavior or legal defenses. Nor should courts arbitrate which treatment approach is appropriate for any individual.

PUBLIC POLICY AND LAW

Policy should be directed toward giving accurate information about the risks of drug use and the advantages of moderation, toward preserving the safety of teens and young adults first and foremost, and away from treating addiction as either a disease or a crime.

The information in all public service announcements about drugs and alcohol should be checked for accuracy by scientific panels. Public service announcements should not be used solely to describe or denounce (and certainly not to exaggerate) drugs' negative effects. Instead, PSAs should spread the word that people can quit addictions of all sorts *without* treatment. Prevention campaigns for teens should focus on the primary substance abuse danger, binge drinking.

Children of any age should be allowed to drink alcohol in restaurants when accompanied by their parents. Americans should be clearly informed that regular, moderate drinking extends their lives and mental acuity.

Drugs should be decriminalized—no criminal penalties for possession of drugs for personal use. (A special place in the pantheon of stupid drug policies is reserved for the refusal of federal aid to students convicted of drug offenses.) Drugs that are now illegal could be provided therapeutically to addicts in controlled clinical settings (as methadone is). Legislation and government policy should support provision of clean needles to addicts who inject, and clean needles should be readily available wherever needed.

Alcohol or drug intoxication or addiction should never serve as defenses for crimes or excuses for misbehavior. Courts should never force people to undergo substance treatment, although a range of substance abuse and other therapy programs should be offered to probationers as well as to prison inmates.

TREATMENT

We must do away with the misguided fixation on abstinence as the only alternative to addiction and the only treatment goal. Reduced drinking should be the typical goal for young people receiving alcohol treatment on college campuses, and it should be offered as an option to all those in treatment, along with the option of abstinence, which may be preferable for many adult alcoholics.

Rather than getting patients to self-identify as "addicts," treatment should aim to rebuild clients' lives and improve their functioning in work, family, and other spheres.

People should determine their own treatment goals in consultation with professional staff, and everyone seeking treatment should have options for treatment and support groups other than those based on the twelve steps. This is particularly true for young people, for whom twelve-step programs should only be a last resort.

Professional training other than twelve-step experiences should be required for all treatment personnel, and substance counselors must be able and willing to treat people using both abstinence and non-abstinence goals.

Non-pharmaceutical treatment options for emotional disorders in children and adolescents should be presented to parents and encouraged.

EDUCATION AND CHILDHOOD EXPERIENCE

Educational policies and practices should acknowledge reality—that kids *do* experiment with drugs and alcohol—and stop wasting energy on fruitless attempts to eliminate all youthful drug use and drinking. Instead, education should primarily aim to protect young people's safety by presenting a range of ways to avoid risks.

Education on substance use must distinguish between moderation and controlled use, on one hand, and abuse and addiction, on the other. Positive effects of alcohol and moderate drinking practices should be a part of secondary school education curricula, and homes and cultures in which moderate drinking is practiced should be recognized and appreciated. The presentation to young people of the dangers of substance use should focus on the consequences of bingeing and excess.

Drug scare stories should be eliminated from the curricula; in their place, educators should teach kids about *real* negative consequences established by research, along with their actual prevalence.

Prevention instructors should have professional training as educators or otherwise demonstrate skill in interactive teaching.

Recovering people should not be the only presenters in school programs, and alternative approaches should always be presented whenever students hear twelve-step messages. People who have used drugs or who drink without negative consequences should be included to speak about their experiences on panels that present substance use information to secondary school students.

Prevention efforts should especially target the children and adolescents at highest risk and seek to integrate them into the school community.

Universities should provide drinking settings that encourage moderation, including beer and wine service, bright lighting, the availability of food, the presence of students at all levels of schooling as well as of faculty, escorts when returning to student housing, and no service to visibly intoxicated drinkers.

A critical public health and prevention priority should be to battle our food addiction epidemic. Elementary schools should take steps to combat obesity: recess and gym should be required throughout elementary and secondary school, and healthy snacks and drinks should be staples in school cafeterias and vending machines.

Simultaneously, we must think in a broader sense about how to give kids greater opportunities for independence and self-efficacy. For instance, safe, supervised outdoor public play settings should be provided where children may be left without their parents.

WHAT DOES REAL DRUG EDUCATION SOUND LIKE?

Government research describes effective programs that are better than DARE but still limited by a prohibition against allowing adolescents to discuss their actual drug and alcohol experiences.[1] Obviously, we are afraid to hear about these experiences. But doing so is essential, and drug education needs methods for taking them into account.

Let's say we are talking to high school students.

I'm not here to tell you whether or not to take drugs or drink. Actually, I think most of you have already made that decision for yourselves.

What I want to explore with you are your own values about these things and how to recognize when a person's substance use—including your own, if you drink or use drugs—is potentially dangerous. Can anyone tell me some signs of harmful or addictive substance use?

Aside from becoming addicted, what are some of the dangers in using drugs and drinking?

What about mixing drugs, or drugs and alcohol?

Which drugs in particular shouldn't be mixed with one another, or alcohol?

We've discussed the signs of substance abuse and addiction, and the dangers facing young people when they take drugs or drink.

What I'd like to turn to now is how you and kids you know can make sure none of these things happen to you.

The boy in the red shirt—give him the microphone. . . . Say that louder, please. . . . That's right, you can abstain from drugs and alcohol. That's always the number one, the fallback position. It can be your position all the time. Or it can be your choice under certain circumstances.

What kinds of circumstances would make you think it is best to abstain? The girl over there . . . You have two circumstances when you abstain—when you're driving, and when you have a test the next day? Excellent. Any others? . . . That's very good: when you recognize a risk of doing or getting into something you don't want to do, like risky sex.

And what are other ways to avoid the potential dangers of drug use and drinking, if people do those things?

How does each of the following affect your use of drugs and alcohol?
- What your parents do, and what they say
- What your brothers or sisters do
- What the cool kids do
- What you see in movies, on television, in advertisements, in ads from the Partnership for a Drug-Free America

How do peer groups affect kids?

Why do you think some kids engage in dangerous substance use? Is it because they weren't told drugs can hurt them? Why do they disregard that information? Is it because they can't control themselves?

Why, and how, do some kids avoid dangerous or excessive substance use? What enables them to avoid harming themselves in this way?

What do kids feel they gain from using drugs or drinking? Do kids who use and drink more heavily than others get different sorts of feelings?

Do kids really feel better from using drugs and alcohol? You say they do in some situations? These substances can be enjoyable?

You say that for some kids, a drug can actually help their state of mind? Tell me what kinds of kids this is true for, or in what situations.

Are there dangers from using drugs, even ones that make people feel or function better, including prescription drugs?

Why do some kids decide not to use drugs or not to drink? Is there a difference between being afraid of drugs or drinking and having positive things to do that rule out using?

How do kids develop meaningful lives? I know that is a big question. Maybe you can think about it before our next session.

How do cigarettes fit in? What do kids get from smoking cigarettes? Why would kids do this, even though they know smoking is harmful? Why do some kids decide not to smoke? Why has smoking declined in recent years among young people? Why is smoking still quite common for youngsters?

Say you know kids who are in the kinds of situations, or who have the kinds of feelings, that can lead to substance abuse. How can you help them? . . . Okay, so you'd warn them they're headed in a bad direction. Do you think that will deter most kids in those situations? No? What will?

What if you know kids who have already begun to abuse substances? What if you think they are abusing substances or are becoming addicts or alcoholics? What can you do to help them? Or is it impossible to help them?

Would you tell any adults? Which adults? What would you have to know about these adults to give you confidence they would handle the information in the right way?

What about substance abuse treatment? What about Alcoholics Anonymous and Narcotics Anonymous? Do they work for kids you know?

Do different kids respond to different kinds of treatment? What makes treatment work for a kid when it does succeed? How should we offer treatment in this school, and what kinds of treatments should be offered, to be most helpful for students with problems?

If you were designing a prevention program for kids in elementary school, what would it include? Would you discuss drugs? What would you say about them? How about alcohol? Would you tell children that drinking can be healthy?

What kind of people do you think have the best impact on kids like you in terms of discussing drug use and drinking? Where do school authorities or other adults go wrong when they talk to kids about substance use? What about public service announcements and advertisements? What makes them effective or not? What would you tell people giving such messages in order to make their messaging more effective? How would you tell them these things so that they don't become defensive?

Can kids and adults ever agree on how to approach substance use or will there always be conflict between them?

This series of questions is designed to get kids to think about and verbalize their experiences. When young people are encouraged to pool their knowledge and discuss their experiences with alcohol and drugs, it quickly becomes clear that, collectively, they already understand what this book has to say. This collective knowledge is bound to be much more realistic than the propaganda conveyed by DARE, government advertising, and public service announcements.

Good drug education is like effective treatments—such as motivational interviewing and brief interventions—that build on individuals' personal resources and values. The purpose is, after all, not to create new knowledge so much as to stimulate young people to clarify their thinking and act upon their best instincts and what they already know to be true.

A COMMONSENSE APPROACH

You'll have noticed that nothing I teach in this book is particularly complicated. Nor does it pretend to be revolutionary. Instead, my focus is on reminding you of the importance of providing real information, rather than propagandizing; of preserving kids' safety, rather than preaching at them; of developing students' independence and ability to make decisions, rather than wishing they would do what authorities want them to.

It's a shame that in American society today, parents and educators need to be reminded of these things. Yet everything I see in my practice, in the news, and as a parent convinces me that we are in sore need of this wake-up call. All this information that should be straightforward, even obvious, has been obscured by the clouds of misinformation you and your kids constantly receive from the "experts." I hope I have managed to counteract some of that misinformation and helped you to trust your own best instincts when you need them most.

Appendix A

EDUCATION AND TREATMENT RESOURCES
FOR ADOLESCENTS

The Stanton Peele Addiction Web site (SPAWS) is at
http://www. peele.net.

EDUCATION AND RISK REDUCTION RESOURCES

Based on the California Statewide Task Force for Effective Drug
Education, R. Skager's pamphlet *Beyond Zero Tolerance: A Reality-
Based Approach to Drug Education and Student Assistance* (San Francisco: Safety First, 2005) is available at www.beyondzerotolerance
.org. It describes the resources students bring to the development of
drug programs and how they can participate in interactive drug
education. See also M. Rosenbaum, *Safety First: A Reality-Based
Approach to Teens and Drugs* (San Francisco: Drug Policy Alliance,
2007).

The best provider of such education programs in the United States
is Up Front (http://upfrontprograms.com). Its key principles are:

- We respect the rights of all students to make choices regarding
  their lives and drug use.
- We must respect, value, and build upon the knowledge students
  already have.
- We believe youth must feel ownership of the discussions. If we
  are successful at creating open dialogue, students will ask for
  what they need.
- We work to increase understanding of drugs and their effects,
  support responsible behavior, and reduce risk and harm.
- We identify all students as being at risk, as drug use is endemic in
  our culture and world.

There is much more available internationally, even as close as Canada, where school-based curricula are not as preoccupied with abstinence as in the United States. See Alberta Alcohol and Drug Abuse Commission curriculum materials at http://teacher.aadac .com/what_ifs/what_if_curriculum_materials.asp. Australia has particularly well-developed and -evaluated materials, such as the School Health and Alcohol Harm Reduction Program at http://www.ndri .curtin.edu.au/shahrp.

EFFECTIVE THERAPIES

Cultural habits die hard. So although information about effective therapies is widely available, these treatments are honored more in the breach than the observance in the United States. You must examine any therapy you select for your child to see whether it *actually* practices what it says. Ask the therapist or staff, "Exactly how do you perform cognitive behavioral therapy, motivational interviews, community reinforcement?"

COGNITIVE BEHAVIORAL THERAPY
The discrepancy between the kind of treatment that research has shown to be effective and what practitioners actually do is nowhere more evident than in cognitive behavioral therapy. Virtually every therapist—and certainly every psychologist—claims to perform CBT. But often this differs little from the diffuse general conversations that constitute the way psychotherapy has been practiced for decades, and which have been shown to be ineffective in treating depression, anxiety, and substance abuse. Therapy institutes created by two pioneers of CBT, the Albert Ellis Institute (see www.rebt.org), and the Beck Institute (see www.beckinstitute.org), offer treatment for individuals.

NETWORK THERAPY
Marc Galanter offers a network therapy program at New York University's Department of Psychiatry (although it differs from the

approach as it is practiced in the United Kingdom). Galanter is the author of the book *Network Therapy for Alcohol and Drug Abuse* (New York: Guilford, 1999). Galanter's version entails regular meetings with family and friends. Unfortunately, this treatment is fixated on American shibboleths such as abstinence and acknowledging the person has an "addictive illness." But it has the advantage of making friends and family an ongoing part of treatment, which is good.

MOTIVATIONAL INTERVIEWING

Motivational interviewing (or enhancement) has become something of a fad in the United States. As a result, all sorts of programs claim to practice the treatment. You can recognize that this isn't so, however, when the program refuses to let the patient determine his or her own goals (including moderation along with abstinence), which is fundamental to MI. Thus, this valuable technique remains somewhat at arm's length from the average patient. William Miller and Stephen Rollnick's *Motivational Interviewing* (New York: Guilford, 2002) describes the operation of the therapy in detail, but is not consumer-friendly. Their group offers training opportunities for professionals and other resources (for example, MI for pregnant mothers, for marijuana use) at their Web site, www.motivationalinterview.org.

BRIEF INTERVENTIONS

Brief interventions are also popular in government-funded efforts—for example, the NIAAA supports initiatives in this area (see "Brief Interventions," *Alcohol Alert,* July 2005, at http://pubs.niaaa.nih.gov/publications/AA66/AA66.htm). On the other hand, it is just too much to expect the United States to promote a technique that aims for *reduced* alcohol and drug consumption, as BIs do. Since BIs are considered to be an alternative for people who aren't willing to seek treatment (even though its results are *better* than those of standard treatments), this therapy isn't offered to consumers so much as it is taught to health professionals. You should ask your health care provider whether he or she utilizes brief interventions. It should be standard practice for health care providers to screen patients for substance abuse issues to begin the BI process.

COMMUNITY REINFORCEMENT APPROACH

As with other therapies supported by research, government agencies recognize the value of CRA. The National Institute on Drug Abuse (NIDA) provides a manual entitled *A Community Reinforcement Approach: Treating Cocaine Addiction* (available at www .nida.nih.gov/TXManuals/CRA/CRA1.html). The Center on Alcoholism, Substance Abuse, and Addictions of the University of New Mexico, a leading developer of CRA and CRA family training (CRAFT), provides a good road map for the therapy (available at http://casaa.unm.edu/crainfo.html). Once again, unfortunately, it would be hard to direct consumers to CRA programs near them.

FINDING A THERAPIST

There are many very competent individual practitioners out there. The trouble is, there are also many therapists who only pay lip service to the above techniques, or who are totally stuck in the AA mind-set. Your challenge, as a parent, is to separate the wheat from the chaff. You (with your child, if possible) should interview therapists to see if they practice in a way that you can be comfortable with, believe in, and work at.

Ask therapists questions such as: Do they believe that all substance-abuse problems are lifelong diseases? Do they believe that everyone with such problems needs to follow the twelve steps and join groups like AA and NA? Are their methods supported by research findings? Are their treatment approaches tailored to the individual client? How? Are they familiar with and do they make use of my work, the work of Alan Marlatt, or William Miller's research? Do they use motivational interviewing? How? Ask them to describe how they interact with a client, so you can get a sense of whether they respect a client's capacity to understand his or her own experience and make constructive personal choices.

You can ask many of the same questions of treatment programs, but I fear your options are highly limited here. Chapter 10 includes a list of criteria for evaluating such programs. Besides the resources listed above, you can also find a lot of useful information (ideas, publications, resources) at my Web site, http://www.peele.net. If you are facing your own problems with addiction, you can consult my book 7 *Tools to Beat Addiction*.

CHECKING ON STANDARD HOSPITAL PROGRAMS

If you end up considering conventional substance abuse treatment for your child, investigate to see that the program meets the requirements of the Joint Commission on the Accreditation of Healthcare Organizations (JCAHO). JCAHO lists approved addiction and alcoholism facilities under the category "behavioral health" at www.joint commission.org/AccreditationPrograms/BehavioralHealthCare. The organization also publishes the pamphlet "How to Choose a Quality Behavioral Health Care Provider of Services to Youth and Children," available at http://www.jointcommission.org/AccreditationPrograms /BehavioralHealthCare/consumer_brochure_yc.htm.

EFFECTIVE MENTAL HEALTH PROGRAMS FOR
OPPOSITIONAL CHILDREN

Columbia University's Center for the Advancement of Children's Mental Health (see www.kidsmentalhealth.org) organizes courses for mental health practitioners to teach them effective therapies for dealing with children. The center also provides education and resources for parents. Effective treatments include Parent Management Training, developed at Yale University and available at Yale, Washington University, and a few other schools; the Incredible Years, developed by Carolyn Webster-Stratton at the University of Washington; Multisystemic Therapy (MST), developed at the Medical University of South Carolina; and Functional Family Therapy (FFT). MST and FFT are oriented to extremely oppositional adolescents rather than children. Multisystemic Therapy has a Web site listing licensed practitioners of this approach around the United States at www.mstservices.com/text/licensed_agencies.htm. FFT also has a Web site at http://www.fftinc.com.

ACADEMIC ADDICTION TREATMENT CENTERS

If you live in a city with a university with an addiction or alcohol research program, you might seek treatment or a referral through that program. Following are the major programs of this type in the United States.*

University of Colorado School of Medicine
303-372-0000; 800-621-7621

Brown University Center for Alcohol and Addiction Studies
401-444-1800

UCLA Center for Advancing Longitudinal Drug Abuse Research
310-445-0874

The Ernest Gallo Clinic and Research Center
888-805-UCSF

University of California–San Diego Center for Criminality and
    Addiction Research, Training and Application
858-551-2944

University of California–San Francisco
415-476-7500

Columbia University/New York State Psychiatric Institute, Substance
    Treatment and Research Service
212-923-3031

* This section is taken, with permission, from Maia Szalavitz's Web site, Help at Any Cost (www.helpatanycost.com/resources.php).

Division on Addictions, Harvard Medical School
617-384-9030

University of Maryland–College Park, Center for Substance Abuse
    Research (CESAR)
301-405-9770

University of New Mexico, Center on Alcoholism, Substance Abuse
    and Addictions (CASAA)
CASAA is the premier alcohol treatment research center in the
    United States, with special focus on motivational interviewing,
    community reinforcement, and community reinforcement and
    family therapy.
505-925-2300; 505-768-0150

University of Pittsburgh Adolescent Alcohol Research Center
Presently conducting research on teen drinking problems and their
    treatment.
412-624-2615

Also at the University of Pittsburgh:
Center for Education and Drug Abuse Research (CEDAR)
412-624-1060

CEDAR Research Center
412-622-6174

New York University Medical Center
212-263-7961

Rutgers University, Center of Alcohol Studies Consultation and
    Treatment Service (CASCATS)
908-445-0941

Alcohol and Drug Abuse Institute, University of Washington
206-543-0937

Also at the University of Washington:
Addictive Behaviors Research Center
Special concentration on college student drinking
206-685-1200

Research Institute on Addictions, University at Buffalo, State
   University of New York
716-887-2566

Institute of Behavioral Research, Texas Christian University
817-257-7000

Yale University School of Medicine
Connecticut Mental Health Center
203-974-7560; 888-622-CNRU

SUBSTANCE ABUSE SUPPORT GROUPS

Unfortunately, I can't recommend any of the existing substance abuse support groups to adolescents or young adults. Chief of these, of course, is Alcoholics Anonymous (or Narcotics Anonymous). Alateen is organized for youngsters with family members who are alcoholics. As this book explains, a group forcing young people to accept that they are possessed by a lifelong disease is more likely to discourage youngsters, or even worse, to convince them to fulfill the group's prophecy.

The major alternatives to AA and twelve-step groups virtually all only allow abstinence goals, which make less sense for teens and young adults. The chief of these alternative groups is SMART Recovery, which is not as monomaniacal about abstinence as AA and practices a variety of cognitive behavioral therapies. Other support groups with abstinence goals are Women for Sobriety, Secular Organizations for Sobriety, and LifeRing recovery. These groups are available in only a few locations, as is Moderation Management (MM), the only support group with a moderation goal. However, like the other groups, MM generally appeals to long-term adult drinkers.

The American Self-Help Clearinghouse "Self-Help Group Sourcebook Online" at http://mentalhelp.net/selfhelp lists every possible type of support and self-help group, and instructs you how to start a new mutual-aid self-help support group.

Your best advice is to examine any available groups to see if their climate is comfortable for young people and allows them to pursue appropriate goals—or else to see about starting one of your own.

GOVERNMENT RESOURCES

The Substance Abuse and Mental Health Services Administration lists "Model Programs: Effective Substance Abuse and Mental Health Programs for Every Community" at http://modelprograms .samhsa.gov. Of course, all of these must be zero-tolerance.

The National Institute on Drug Abuse has set up a national network for clinical trials, which aims to be similar to the cancer treatment network run by the National Cancer Institute at some of the best hospitals in the country. The main Web site for the Clinical Trials Network is www.nida.nih.gov/CTN/Index.htm. It lists local treatment providers who are participating in research, so these programs should be actively working to move research evidence into practice.

GOVERNMENT WATCHDOG AGENCY REPORT FINDING GOVERNMENT MEDIA PROGRAM INEFFECTIVE UNDERSTATES THE CASE

Government-funded research shows that government prevention policies don't work, and actually do worse than that. From 1998 to 2004, Congress appropriated $1.2 billion to the Office of National Drug Control Policy (ONDCP) for a comprehensive anti-drug media and community education campaign. The appropriation required an independent assessment of the impact of the campaign, which was conducted by a respected research firm and published as *ONDCP Media Campaign: Contractor's National Evaluation Did Not Find That the Youth Anti-Drug Campaign Was Effective in Reducing Youth Drug Use.*

According to the government's own watchdog agency, the U.S. Government Accountability Office (GAO), "The evaluation provides credible evidence that the campaign was *not* effective" (emphasis added). More basically, "it raises questions concerning the understanding of the factors that are most salient to teens' decision-making about drugs and how they can be used to foster anti-drug decisions."[1]

Students and parents exposed to the media campaign had a positive impression of the ads and recalled their messages. But adolescents who saw the ads did not use fewer drugs, quit more often, or became less likely to initiate use. In fact, examining nine subgroups of youths, the evaluation found that "greater specific exposure was associated with higher levels of initiation" for twelve- and thirteen-year-olds, girls, African American youths, and lower-risk youths.

Although adolescents reported positive responses to the ads' negative drug use messages, greater exposure did not lead young people to disapprove more of drug use. Instead, the ads "may have promoted perceptions among exposed youth that others' drug use was normal." Parents exposed to the ads became more negative toward drugs and resolved to speak to their children about them. But changes in parental attitudes and behavior did not change children's drug use and attitudes.

When the evaluation's preliminary results were negative, ONDCP revised its campaign to focus specifically on marijuana. But this modification produced even worse results. Between 2002 and 2004, for the entire group of young people studied, "exposure to the redirected campaign was associated with higher rates of marijuana use initiation."

During some of the years of the campaign, youthful marijuana use declined marginally in the United States. But the evaluation established that any decline was due to external factors, not to the ads. Nonetheless, the ONDCP used the small reduction to attempt to undercut this embarrassing exposure of its incomprehension and ineffectiveness: "In response to the GAO report, drug czar John Walters questioned the accuracy of the Westat survey."[2]

Walters' rejection of the evaluation was predictable but cannot be sustained. The evaluation itself was a major focus of the program and was budgeted at $43 million. "Both Congress and ONDCP recognized the need for a separate evaluation of the campaign." The ONDCP enlisted the services of the government drug research organization (NIDA) in order to conduct the assessment. NIDA selected Westat, which employed the most sophisticated research and statistical methods available. Westat also involved the prestigious Annenberg School of Communications of the University of Pennsylvania.

Nonetheless, as DARE does, Walters discounted the evaluation in order to continue his office's expensive but self-defeating prevention efforts.

HARM REDUCTION FOR DRUG ADDICTS

In the field of drug addiction, harm reduction describes all efforts to prevent people from being hurt by their substance use. A typical harm reduction program is providing clean needles to addicts so that they won't get AIDS or hepatitis. At least then they will survive and stand a chance of getting off their drug.

The risks from chronic heroin use are high: users may develop an abscess or other infection; they can experience an overdose; they may die of exposure or malnutrition; they can be infected with HIV. And just seeking and using illegal drugs on America's streets is a dangerous business. Offering addicts clean needles or a safe injection site (as is done in Vancouver) or even providing them with heroin (as is done in Switzerland and other European countries) prevents them from suffering the worst harms. Everything short of a fatal disease or accident or a long prison term gives drug users a chance to improve their lives. This policy reduces their need to commit crimes as well, which also protects the public.

Many people oppose clean needle and similar programs because they feel it "sends the wrong message" by accepting or tacitly endorsing drug use. Many politicians in the United States are more than willing to get on that bandwagon. But every major public health organization—the Centers for Disease Control and Prevention, the American Public Health Association, the American Medical Association, the Office of the Surgeon General—agrees that addicts in clean-needle programs are more likely to enter drug treatment, to use less harmful drugs (such as methadone), or to quit drug use altogether.[1] Beginning to take care of themselves while establishing a relationship with a helping agency or counselor more often places addicts on a path to recovery.

HARM REDUCTION WEB SITES

The Harm Reduction Coalition lists programs for drug users, including a list of U.S. needle exchanges and information on harm reduction practices and resources for drug users at www.harm reduction.org.

The Drug Policy Alliance also lists harm reduction practices and principles, as well as safe drug use practices, at www.drugpolicy .org/reducingharm.

NOTES

One The Problem Is Addiction, Not Drugs

1. R. Yoder, "Strung Out on Love and Checked In for Treatment," *New York Times,* June 11, 2006.
2. J. Shedler and J. Block, "Adolescent Drug Use and Psychological Health: A Longitudinal Inquiry," *American Psychologist* 45 (1990): 612–30.
3. Institute of Medicine, *Progress in Preventing Childhood Obesity* (Washington, DC: Institute of Medicine, 2006).
4. G. M. Vogel, "Defying Diabesity," *USC Trojan Family Magazine,* autumn 2005.
5. Wikipedia, "Koren Zailckas: Alcoholism," http://en.wikipedia.org/wiki/Koren_Zailckas, accessed September 6, 2006.
6. R. W. Hingson, T. Heeren, and M. R. Winter, "Age of Alcohol-Dependence Onset: Associations with Severity of Dependence and Seeking Treatment," *Pediatrics* 118 (2006): e755–63.

Two Youthful Drug and Alcohol Use

1. S. L. Fisher, K. K. Bucholz, W. Reich, et al., "Teenagers Are Right—Parents Do Not Know Much: An Analysis of Adolescent-Parent Agreement on Reports of Adolescent Substance Use, Abuse, and Dependence," *Alcoholism: Clinical and Experimental Research* 30 (2006): 1699–710.
2. L. D. Johnston, P. M. O'Malley, J. G. Bachman, and J. E. Schulenberg, "Teen Drug Use Down but Progress Halts Among Youngest Teens," press release, University of Michigan News Service, December 19, 2005.
3. M. Sherman, "Drug Use by Teenagers Declines," Associated Press, December 21, 2004.
4. C. R. Bingham, J. T. Shopel, and X. Tang, "Drinking Behavior from High School to Young Adulthood: Differences by College Education," *Alcoholism: Clinical and Experimental Research* 29 (2005): 2170–80.

5. These figures from the 2002–2005 National Survey on Drug Use and Health (NSDUH). Substance Abuse and Mental Health Services Administration, "Underage Alcohol Use Among Full-Time College Students," *NSDUH Report* 31 (2006).

6. Substance Abuse and Mental Health Services Administration, *2004 National Survey on Drug Use & Health* (Washington, DC: U.S. Department of Health and Human Services, 2006). NSDUH provides a comparison of MTF and NSDUH figures at www.drugabusestatistics .samhsa.gov/nsduh/2k5nsduh/2k5Results.htm#Tab9-1.

7. American Psychiatric Association, *Diagnostic and Statistical Manual of Mental Disorders, Fourth Edition, Text Revision* (Washington, DC: American Psychiatric Association, 2000).

8. D. A. Dawson, B. F. Grant, F. S. Stinson, et al., "Recovery from DSM-IV Alcohol Dependence: United States, 2001–2002," *Addiction* 100 (2005): 281–92.

9. Ibid.

10. B. F. Grant, D. A. Dawson, F. S. Stinson, et al., "The 12-month Prevalence and Trends in DSM-IV Alcohol Abuse and Dependence: United States, 1991–1992 and 2001–2002," *Drug and Alcohol Dependence* 74 (2004): 223–34.

11. Bingham, Shopel, and Tang, "Drinking Behavior."

12. *2004 National Survey*, Table 2.56B.

13. K. J. Sher, T. J. Trull, B. D. Bartholow, et al., "Personality and Alcoholism," in K. E. Leonard and H. T. Blane, eds., *Psychological Theories of Drinking and Alcoholism,* 2nd ed. (New York: Guilford, 1999), 85, 87.

14. R. A. Zucker, "Pathways to Alcohol Problems and Alcoholism: A Developmental Account of the Evidence for Multiple Alcoholisms and for Contextual Contributions to Risk," in R. Zucker, G. Boyd, and J. Howard, eds., *The Development of Alcohol Problems: Exploring the Biopsychosocial Matrix of Risk,* Research Monograph 26 (Rockville, MD: National Institute on Alcohol Abuse and Alcoholism, 1994), 255–89.

15. M. Windle and P. T. Davies, "Developmental Theory and Research," in K. E. Leonard and H. T. Blane, eds., *Psychological Theories of Drinking and Alcoholism,* 2nd edition (New York: Guilford, 1999), 178.

16. Ibid., 186.

17. Sher et al., "Personality and Alcoholism," 91.

18. Windle and Davies, "Developmental Theory and Research," 182.

19. This study is called the National Epidemiologic Survey on Alcohol and Related Conditions (NESARC). See D. A. Dawson, B. F. Grant, F. S. Stinson, P. S. Chou, et al., "Recovery from DSM-IV Alcohol Dependence: United States, 2001–2002," *Addiction* 100 (2005): 281–92.

20. T. K. Greenfield, J. Guydish, and M. T. Temple, "Reasons Students Give for Limiting Drinking," *Journal of Studies on Alcohol* 50 (1989): 108–15.

21. J. V. Den Bulk and K. Beullen, "Television and Music Video Exposure and Adolescent Alcohol Use When Going Out," *Alcohol and Alcoholism* 40 (2005): 249–53.

22. J. G. Querido, T. D. Warner, and S. M. Eyberg, "Parenting Styles and Child Behavior in African American Families of Preschool Children," *Alcoholism: Clinical and Experimental Research* 25 (2001): 1284–92.

Three Why Our Drug Education Doesn't Work

1. S. Bacon, "Alcohol Issues and Social Science," *Journal of Drug Issues* 14 (1984): 7–29.

2. L. D. Johnston, P. M. O'Malley, J. G. Bachman, and J. E. Schulenburg, *National Results on Adolescent Drug Use: Overview of Key Findings, 2005* (Bethesda, MD: National Institute on Drug Use, 2006).

3. C. Currie, C. Robert, A. Morgan, et al., eds., *Young People's Health in Context* (Copenhagen: World Health Organization, 2004), Table 3.14.

4. Substance Abuse and Mental Health Services Administration, "Federal Report Shows New Nonmedical Users of Prescription Pain Relievers Outnumbered New Marijuana Users Between 2002 and 2004," *SAMHSA Advisory*, October 27, 2006.

5. Partnership for a Drug-Free America, *Generation Rx: National Study Confirms Abuse of Prescription and Over-the-Counter Drugs* (Washington, DC: Partnership for a Drug-Free America, May 2006).

6. Substance Abuse and Mental Health Services Administration, *2004 National Survey on Drug Use & Health* (Washington, DC: U.S. Department of Health and Human Services, 2006).

7. Johnston et al., *National Results*, Table 10.

8. K. Butler, "The Grim Neurology of Teenage Drinking," *New York Times*, July 4, 2006. This *Times* article does not make clear that it is heavy and binge drinking that produces such damage. See J. M. Townshend and T. Duka, "Binge Drinking, Cognitive Performance and Mood in a Population of Young Social Drinkers," *Alcoholism: Clinical and Experimental Research* 29 (2005): 317–25.

9. Substance Abuse and Mental Health Services Administration, *1997 National Household Survey on Drug Abuse* (Washington, DC: U.S. Department of Health and Human Services, 1997/2005), Table 7.7; *2004 National Survey*, Table 2.3B.

10. H. Wechsler and B. Wuethrich, *Dying to Drink* (New York: St. Martin's, 2002).

11. Substance Abuse and Mental Health Services Administration, "Under-age Alcohol Use Among Full-Time College Students," *NSDUH Report* 31 (2006).

12. A. M. White, C. L. Kraus, and H. S. Swartzwelder, "Many College Freshmen Drink at Levels Far Beyond the Binge Threshold," *Alcoholism: Clinical and Experimental Research* 30 (2006): 1006–10.

13. *2004 National Survey,* Table 5.25B.

14. R. Hingson, T. Heeren, M. Winter, and H. Wechsler, "Magnitude of Alcohol-Related Mortality and Morbidity Among U.S. College Students Ages 18–24: Changes from 1998 to 2001," *Annual Review of Public Health* 26 (2005): 259–79.

15. Teens Today, *2006 Survey Results* (Boston, MA: Liberty Mutual and Students Against Destructive Decisions, September 2006).

16. T. Lewin, "Does It Work? Substance-Free Dorms," *New York Times,* November 6, 2005.

17. M. Jameson, "Anti-drug Overdose? Many School Prevention Programs Don't Help, Scientists Say, and May Even Do Harm," *Los Angeles Times,* May 15, 2006.

18. DARE, "About D.A.R.E.," www.dare.com/home/about_dare.asp.

19. S. L. West and K. K. O'Neal, "Project D.A.R.E. Outcome Effectiveness Revisited," *American Journal of Public Health* 94 (2004): 1027–29.

20. D. P. Rosenbaum and G. S. Hanson, "Assessing the Effects of School-Based Education: A Six-Year Multilevel Analysis of Project D.A.R.E.," *Journal of Research in Crime and Delinquency* 35, 4 (1998): 381–412.

21. Jameson, "Anti-drug Overdose?"

22. Substance Abuse and Mental Health Services Administration, U.S. Department of Health and Human Services, "Model Programs: Effective Substance Abuse and Mental Health Programs for Every Community," March 7, 2005, http://modelprograms.samhsa.gov/template_cf.cfm?page=effective_list.

23. K. Foley, D. Altman, R. Durant, and M. Wolfson, "Adults' Approval and Adolescents' Alcohol Use," *Journal of Adolescent Health* 35, 4 (2004): 294.

24. B. Hibell, B. Andersson, T. Bjarnason, et al. *The ESPAD Report 2003: Alcohol and Other Drug Use Among Students in 35 European Countries* (Stockholm: Swedish Council for Information on Alcohol and Other Drugs, 2004).

25. S. L. Fisher, K. K. Bucholz, W. Reich, et al., "Teenagers Are Right—Parents Do Not Know Much: An Analysis of Adolescent-Parent Agreement on Reports of Adolescent Substance Use, Abuse, and Dependence," *Alcoholism: Clinical and Experimental Research* 30 (2006): 1699–710.

26. J. Baskin, L. Newman, S. Pollitt-Cohen, and C. Toombs, *The Notebook Girls* (New York: Warner, 2006).

27. S. Lehman, "Sex, Drugs, and Enticing Jew-Fros," *New York,* April 10, 2006.

Four You Can Raise a Non-Addicted Child

1. J. Brockman, "Children Don't Do Things Half Way: A Talk with Judith Rich Harris," *Edge,* June 29, 1999, www.edge.org/3rd_culture/harris_children/harris_p1.html.
2. J. Kagan, *Three Seductive Ideas* (Cambridge, MA: Harvard University Press, 1998).
3. www.TheAntiDrug.com/advice/advice_monitor.asp?id=banner.
4. B. Denizet-Lewis, "An Anti-Addiction Pill?" *New York Times Magazine,* June 25, 2006.
5. J. Kagan, J. S. Reznick, and J. Gibbons, "Inhibited and Uninhibited Types of Children," *Child Development* 60 (1989): 838–45.
6. R. Fredrick, "Wash. U. Study Looking into Alcoholism," *KWMU News,* June 25, 2006, http://publicbroadcasting.net/kwmu/news.news main?action=article&ARTICLE_ID=933259&sectionID=6.
7. C. Johnson et al., "Pooled Association Genome Scanning for Alcohol Dependence Using 104,268 SNPs: Validation and Use to Identify Alcoholism Vulnerability Loci in Unrelated Individuals from the Collaborative Study on the Genetics of Alcoholism," *American Journal of Medical Genetics* (B) 2006; DOI 10.1002/ajmg.b.30346.
8. Denizet-Lewis, "An Anti-Addiction Pill?"
9. Femalefirst, *Osbourne's Family Addiction,* November 17, 2005, www.femalefirst.co.uk/celebrity/72312004.htm.
10. R. A. Chambers, J. R. Taylor, and M. N. Potenza, "Developmental Neurocircuitry of Motivation in Adolescence: A Critical Period of Addiction Vulnerability," *American Journal of Psychiatry* 160 (2003): 1041–52.
11. A. M. White, J. G. Bae, M. C. Truesdale, et al., "Chronic-Intermittent Ethanol Exposure During Adolescence Prevents Normal Developmental Changes in Sensitivity to Ethanol-Induced Motor Impairments," *Alcoholism: Clinical and Experimental Research* 26 (2002): 960–68.
12. A. Heinz, "Staying Sober," *Scientific American Mind,* April/May 2006, 57–61.
13. D. A. Dawson, B. F. Grant, F. S. Stinson, et al., "Recovery from DSM-IV Alcohol Dependence: United States, 2001–2002," *Addiction* 100 (2005): 281–92.
14. Wikipedia, "Koren Zailckas: Alcoholism," http://en.wikipedia.org/wiki/Koren_Zailckas, accessed September 6, 2006.
15. J. Shreeve, "Beyond the Brain," *National Geographic,* March 2005, 2–29.
16. A. W. Flaherty, *The Midnight Disease: The Drive to Write, Writer's Block, and the Creative Brain* (Boston: Mariner Books, 2005).

17. See K. A. Ericsson, ed., *The Road to Excellence: The Acquisition of Expert Performance in the Arts and Sciences, Sports, and Games* (Mahwah, NJ: Erlbaum, 2006).

18. S. J. Dubner and S. D. Levitt, "A Star Is Made," *New York Times Magazine,* May 7, 2006.

19. K. Makimoto, "Drinking Patterns and Drinking Problems Among Asian-Americans and Pacific Islanders," *Alcohol Health & Research World* 22 (1998): 270–75.

20. F. Butterfield, "Why Asians Are Going to the Head of the Class," *New York Times,* August 3, 1986.

21. C. S. Dweck, *Mindset—The New Psychology of Success* (New York: Random House, 2006).

22. W. R. Miller, V. S. Westerberg, R. J. Harris, et al., "What Predicts Relapse? Prospective Testing of Antecedent Models," *Addiction* 91 (supp. 1996): S155–71.

Five Discipline and Values

1. M. Weissbluth, *Healthy Sleep Habits, Happy Child* (New York: Fawcett, 1999).

2. Ferber first described his approach in his 1985 book *Solve Your Child's Sleep Problems.* Twenty years later, Ferber revised his book, *Solve Your Child's Sleep Problems: New, Revised, and Expanded Edition* (New York: Fireside, 2006). Ferber indicated that if parents are uncomfortable with hearing a baby cry—or if the child has special emotional needs—they can try alternatives. News reports and talk shows declared that Ferber had changed his mind. But Ferber still doesn't accept children staying up until they decide to go to bed. Instead, as long as children do not have separation issues, Ferber continues to recommend short periods of crying so that children can learn to go to sleep alone.

3. J. O. Finckenauer, *Scared Straight and the Panacea Phenomenon* (Englewood Cliffs, NJ: Prentice Hall, 1982).

4. W. Mischel, Y. Shoda, and M. I. Rodriguez, "Delay of Gratification in Children," *Science* 244 (1989): 933–38.

5. CBS, *60 Minutes,* "The Echo Boomers," aired December 26, 2004.

Six Independence and Control

1. Although the overwhelming majority of adolescent and young adult substance abusers outgrow this behavior, research over the last two decades also indicates that many young people are slower to achieve sobriety. D. A. Dawson, B. F. Grant, F. S. Stinson, et al., "Recovery from DSM-IV Alcohol Dependence: United States, 2001–2002," *Addiction* 100 (2005): 281–92. In other words, more adolescents are extending their

harmful drinking and drug use into early adulthood and beyond. As a result, a national survey found that between 1992 and 2002, the prevalence of alcohol abusers increased over 50 percent in the United States. B. F. Grant, D. A. Dawson, F. S. Stinson, et al., "The 12-Month Prevalence and Trends in DSM-IV Alcohol Abuse and Dependence: United States, 1991–1992 and 2001–2002," *Drug and Alcohol Dependence* 74 (2004): 223–34.

2. Institute of Medicine, *Progress in Preventing Childhood Obesity* (Washington, DC: Institute of Medicine, 2006).

3. C. Mulvihill, Á. Németh, and C. Vereecken, "Body Image, Weight Control and Body Weight," in C. Currie et al., eds., *Young People's Health in Context* (Copenhagen: World Health Organization, 2004), 120–29.

4. Ibid., Table 3.1.

5. J. Banks, M. Marmot, Z. Oldfield, and J. P. Smith, "Disease and Disadvantage in the United States and in England," *Journal of the American Medical Association* 295 (2006): 2037–45.

6. (UK) Department of Health, *Health Profile of England* (London: Department of Health, 2006).

7. CBS, *60 Minutes*, "The Echo Boomers," aired December 26, 2004.

8. A. H. Mokdad, J. S. Marks, D. F. Stroup, and J. L. Gerberding, "Actual Causes of Death in the United States, 2000," *Journal of the American Medical Association* 291 (2004): 1238–41.

9. M. Szalavitz, *Help at Any Cost* (New York: Riverhead, 2006), 10.

10. Ibid.

11. Diana Baumrind, a psychologist at the Institute of Human Development at the University of California, Berkeley, originated this typology.

12. S. M. Bianchi, J. P. Robinson, and M. A. Milkie, *Changing Rhythms of American Family Life* (Washington, DC: American Sociological Association, 2006).

13. D. E. Bednar and T. D. Fisher, "Peer Referencing in Adolescent Decision Making as a Function of Perceived Parenting Style," *Journal of Clinical Child and Adolescent Psychology* 31 (2002): 272–77.

14. B. Seaman, *Binge: What Your College Student Won't Tell You: Campus Life in an Age of Disconnection and Excess* (New York: Wiley, 2005) describes the epidemic bingeing on alcohol, accompanied by casual sex, on college campuses, while Tom Wolfe's *I Am Charlotte Simmons* does the same in novel form.

Seven **The Moderating Household**

1. K. Foley, D. Altman, R. Durant, and M. Wolfson, "Adults' Approval and Adolescents' Alcohol Use," *Journal of Adolescent Health* 35, 4 (2004): 345–46.

2. L. D. Johnston, P. M. O'Malley, J. G. Bachman, and J. E. Schulenburg, *National Results on Adolescent Drug Use: Overview of Key Findings, 2005* (Bethesda, MD: National Institute on Drug Use, 2006).

3. J. M. Townshend and T. Duka, "Binge Drinking, Cognitive Performance and Mood in a Population of Young Social Drinkers," *Alcoholism: Clinical and Experimental Research* 29 (2005): 317–25.

4. "Parental Involvement Can Help Prevent Underage Drinking," *Medical News Today,* September 30, 2004, http://www.eurekalert.org/pub_releases/2004-09/wfub-pic093004.php.

5. C. Kutter and D. S. McDermott, "The Role of Church in Adolescent Drug Education," *Journal of Drug Education* 27 (1997): 293–305.

6. S. Weiss, "Religious Influences on Drinking: Influences from Select Groups," in E. Houghton and A. M. Roche, eds., *Learning About Drinking* (Philadelphia: Brunner-Routledge, 2001), 116.

7. M. Ramstedt and A. Hope, *The Irish Drinking Culture: Drinking and Drinking-Related Harm, a European Comparison* (Dublin: Report for the Health Promotion Unit, Ministry of Health and Children, 2003), http://www.healthpromotion.ie/uploaded_docs/Irish_Drinking_Culture .PDF. Binge drinking was defined as "at least one bottle of wine, 25 centilitres of spirits [about 8.5 ounces], or four pints of beer, or more, during one drinking occasion."

8. M. Plant and P. Miller, "Young People and Alcohol: An International Insight," *Alcohol and Alcoholism* 36 (2001): 513–15.

9. G. E. Vaillant, *The Natural History of Alcoholism,* rev. ed. (Cambridge, MA: Harvard University Press, 1995), 289.

10. C. Currie, C. Roberts, A. Morgan, et al., eds., *Young People's Health in Context* (Copenhagen: World Health Organization, 2004), Table 3.12.

11. J. Scott and D. Leonhardt, "Class in America: Shadowy Lines That Still Divide," *New York Times,* May 15, 2005.

12. Substance Abuse and Mental Health Services Administration, *2004 National Survey on Drug Use & Health* (Washington, DC: U.S. Department of Health and Human Services, 2006), Table 2.56B.

13. Virtual Jerusalem, http://www.virtualjerusalem.com/jewish_holidays/purim/drinking.htm.

14. B. Glassner and B. Berg, "How Jews Avoid Alcohol Problems," *American Sociological Review* 45 (1980): 647–64.

15. M. G. Monteiro and M. A. Schuckit, "Alcohol, Drug and Mental Health Problems Among Jewish and Christian Men at a University," *American Journal of Drug and Alcohol Abuse* 15 (1989): 403–12.

16. M. L. Barnett, "Alcoholism in the Cantonese of New York City: An Anthropological Study," in O. Diethelm, ed., *Etiology of Chronic Alcoholism* (Springfield, IL: Thomas, 1955), 186–87.

17. Between 1992 and 2002, the national survey of drinking in America found alcohol dependence doubled among Asian males—nearly all among the young—from 1.6 to 3.2 percent. This suggests young Asian men are starting to party with their non-Asian friends. However, the alcohol dependence rate for all American men in 2002 was 5.4 percent. B. F. Grant, D. A. Dawson, F. S. Stinson, et al., "The 12-Month Prevalence and Trends in DSM-IV Alcohol Abuse and Dependence: United States, 1991–1992 and 2001–2002," *Drug and Alcohol Dependence* 74 (2004): 223–34.

18. K. Makimoto, "Drinking Patterns and Drinking Problems Among Asian-Americans and Pacific Islanders," *Alcohol Health & Research World* 22 (1998): 270–75.

19. S. Peele and A. Brodsky, "Exploring Psychological Benefits Associated with Moderate Alcohol Use," *Drug and Alcohol Dependence* 60 (2000): 221–47.

20. G. Lowe, "Drinking Behavior and Pleasure Across the Life Span," in S. Peele and M. Grant, eds., *Alcohol and Pleasure: A Health Perspective* (Philadelphia: Brunner/Mazel, 1999), 249–63.

21. Ibid., 258.

22. Ibid., 259.

23. A. Allamani, "Policy Implications of the ECAS Results: A Southern European Perspective," in T. Norström, ed., *Alcohol in Postwar Europe: Consumption, Drinking Patterns, Consequences and Policy Responses in 15 European Countries* (Stockholm: National Institute of Public Health, 2002), 197.

24. Virtual Jerusalem, www.virtualjerusalem.com/jewish_holidays/purim/customs.htm.

25. Lowe, "Drinking Behavior," 258.

26. H. Leifman, "Trends in Population Drinking," in T. Norström, ed., *Alcohol in Postwar Europe: Consumption, Drinking Patterns, Consequences and Policy Responses in 15 European Countries* (Stockholm: National Institute of Public Health, 2002), Table 3.6.

Eight **Preventing Adolescent and Family Problems from Causing Addiction**

1. E. Harburg, W. D. DiFranceisco, L. Webster, et al. "Familial Transmission of Alcohol Use: II. Imitation of and Aversion to Parent Drinking (1960) by Adult Offspring (1977), Tecumseh, Michigan," *Journal of Studies on Alcohol* 51 (1990): 245–56.

2. Ibid.

3. E. G. Langer, *Mindfulness* (Reading, MA: Addison-Wesley, 1989).

4. L. A. Bennett, S. J. Wolin, D. Reiss, and M. A. Teitelbaum, "Couples at Risk for Transmission of Alcoholism: Protective Influences," *Family Process* 26 (1987): 111–29.

5. National Center on Addiction and Substance Abuse, "The Importance of Family Dinners," September 2006, www.casacolumbia.org/support casa/item.asp?cID=12&PID=150.

6. R. E. Drake and G. E. Vaillant, "Predicting Alcoholism and Personality Disorder in a 33-Year Longitudinal Study of Children of Alcoholics," in P. E. Nathan et al., eds., *Annual Review of Addiction Research and Treatment* (New York: Pergamon Press, 1991), 15–23.

7. C. R. Cloninger, S. Sigvardsson, and M. Bohman, "Childhood Personality Predicts Alcohol Abuse in Young Adults," *Alcoholism* 12 (1988): 494–505.

8. Drake and Vaillant, "Predicting Alcoholism," 22.

9. M. El-Sheikh and E. M. Cummings, "Marital Conflict, Emotional Regulation, and the Adjustment of Children of Alcoholics," in K. C. Barnett, ed., *New Directions in Child Development: Emotion and Communication* (San Francisco: Jossey-Bass, 1997), 25–44.

10. B. Carey, "What's Wrong with a Child? Psychiatrists Often Disagree," *New York Times,* November 11, 2006.

11. American Psychiatric Association, *Diagnostic and Statistical Manual of Mental Disorders, Fourth Edition, Text Revision* (Washington, DC: APA, 2000).

12. J. M. Zito, D. J. Safer, S. dosReis, et al., "Psychotropic Practice Patterns for Youth: A 10-Year Perspective," *Archives of Pediatric and Adolescent Medicine* 157 (2003): 17–25.

13. Carey, "What's Wrong."

14. M. Olfson, M. J. Gameroff, S. C. Marcus, and P. S. Jensen, "National Trends in the Treatment of Attention Deficit Hyperactivity Disorder," *American Journal of Psychiatry* 160 (2003): 1071–77.

15. M. Olfson, C. Blanco, L. Liu, C. Moreno, and G. Laje, "National Trends in the Outpatient Treatment of Children and Adolescents with Antipsychotic Drugs," *Archives of General Psychiatry* 63 (2006): 679–85.

16. J. McClellan, "Commentary: Treatment Guidelines for Child and Adolescent Bipolar Disorder," *Journal of the American Academy of Child and Adolescent Psychiatry* 44 (2005): 236–39.

17. Carey, "What's Wrong."

18. B. Carey, "Antipsychotic Drug Use Is Climbing, Study Finds," *New York Times,* June 5, 2006.

19. Ibid.

20. C. J. Whittington, T. Kendall, P. Fonagy, et al., "Selective Serotonin Reuptake Inhibitors in Childhood Depression: Systematic Review of Published Versus Unpublished Data," *Lancet* 363 (2004): 1341–45.

21. J. M. McClellan and J. S. Werry, "Evidence-Based Treatments in Child and Adolescent Psychiatry," *Journal of the American Academy of Child and Adolescent Psychiatry* 42 (2003): 1388–1400.

22. R. A. Russell, M. Fischer, L. Smallish, and K. Fletcher, "Does the Treatment of Attention-Deficit/Hyperactivity Disorder with Stimulants Contribute to Drug Use/Abuse? A 13-Year Prospective Study," *Pediatrics* 111 (2003): 97–109.

23. Carey, "What's Wrong."

24. G. Crister, *Generation Rx: How Prescription Drugs Are Altering American Lives, Minds, and Bodies* (New York: Houghton Mifflin, 2005).

25. Partnership for a Drug-Free America, "Generation Rx: National Study Reveals New Category of Substance Abuse Emerging: Teens Abusing Rx and OTC Medications Intentionally to Get High," press release, April 21, 2005, http://www.drugfree.org/Portal/DrugIssue/Research/PATS%20Teens%202004%20Report/Teens_Abusing_Rx_and_OTC_Medications.

26. Substance Abuse and Mental Health Services Administration, "Federal Report Shows New Nonmedical Users of Prescription Pain Relievers Outnumbered New Marijuana Users between 2002 and 2004," *SAMHSA Advisory,* October 27, 2006.

27. A. Jacobs, "The Adderall Advantage," *New York Times,* July 31, 2005.

28. McClellan and Werry, "Evidence-Based Treatments." J. March, S. Silva, S. Petrycki, et al., "Fluoxetine, Cognitive-Behavioral Therapy, and Their Combination for Adolescents with Depression: Treatment for Adolescents with Depression Study (TADS) Randomized Controlled Trial," *Journal of the American Medical Association* 292 (2004): 807–20.

29. S. N. Compton, J. S. March, D. Brent, et al., "Cognitive-Behavioral Psychotherapy for Anxiety and Depressive Disorders in Children and Adolescents: An Evidence-Based Medicine Review," *Journal of the American Academy of Child and Adolescent Psychiatry* 43 (2004): 930–59.

30. R. J. DeRubeis, S. D. Hollon, J. D. Amsterdam, et al., "Cognitive Therapy vs. Medications in the Treatment of Moderate to Severe Depression," *Archives of General Psychiatry* 62 (2005): 409–16.

31. S. D. Hollon, R. J. DeRubeis, R. C. Shelton, et al., "Prevention of Relapse Following Cognitive Therapy vs. Medications in Moderate to Severe Depression," *Archives of General Psychiatry* 62 (2005): 417–22.

32. S. Burling, "Study on Depression Boosts Talk Therapy," *Philadelphia Inquirer,* April 4, 2005.

33. Ibid.

34. D. A. Dawson, B. F. Grant, F. S. Stinson, et al., "Recovery from DSM-IV Alcohol Dependence: United States, 2001–2002," *Addiction* 100 (2005): 281–92.

35. R. C. Kessler, P. Berglund, O. Demler, et al., "The Epidemiology of Major Depressive Disorder: Results from the National Comorbidity Survey Replication (NCS-R)," *Journal of the American Medical Association* 289 (2003): 3095–105.

36. D. S. Hasin, R. D. Goodwin, F. S. Stinson, and B. F. Grant, "Epidemiology of Major Depressive Disorder: Results from the National Epidemiologic Survey on Alcoholism and Related Conditions," *Archives of General Psychiatry* 62 (2005): 1097–106.

Nine Keeping Your Child Safe

1. J. Wisloski, K. Burke, and R. F. Moore, "Heartbroken Dad Ponders Why He Didn't Get Through," *New York Daily News,* July 29, 2006.

2. S. L. Fisher, K. K. Bucholz, W. Reich, et al., "Teenagers Are Right—Parents Do Not Know Much: An Analysis of Adolescent-Parent Agreement on Reports of Adolescent Substance Use, Abuse, and Dependence," *Alcoholism: Clinical and Experimental Research* 30 (2006): 1699–710.

3. Substance Abuse and Mental Health Services Administration, "Drug Abuse Warning Network: Opiate-Related Drug Misuse Deaths in Six States: 2003," *The New DAWN Report* 19 (2006), http://dawninfo.samhsa.gov/files/TNDR06OpiateMisuse.htm.

4. Australia has also had rashes of youthful "overdose." A study conducted by Australia's National Drug and Alcohol Research Centre discovered that deaths attributed to heroin overdose most often occurred when heroin was taken in combination with either alcohol (40 percent) or tranquilizers (30 percent). The center recommended: "Fatal heroin overdose is potentially preventable. Educating users about the risks of co-administering alcohol and other depressant drugs with heroin, the comparative safety of injecting heroin in the company of others and the need to call for intervention sooner may reduce the frequency of heroin-related deaths." D. Zador, S. Sunjic, and S. Darke, "Heroin-Related Deaths in New South Wales, 1992," *Medical Journal of Australia* 164 (1996): 204.

5. D. Concar, "Ecstasy on the Brain," *New Scientist,* April 20, 2002, http://mdma.net/misc/ecstasy-mdma.html.

6. Deaths due to Ecstasy use are few. In 2002 (the latest year for which data are available), of all hospital emergency room visits due to drugs, only about 1 percent were due to *any* of the following so-called club drugs: GHB, ketamine, LSD, or Ecstasy. Of these 8,100 ER visits nationally in 2002, three-quarters involving any club drug also involved another drug, usually alcohol, marijuana, or cocaine. Substance Abuse and Mental Health Services Administration, "Drug Abuse Warning Network: Club Drugs 2002 Update," *DAWN Report,* July 2004.

7. See the Drug Policy Alliance Web site at www.dpf.org/homepage.cfm.
8. CNN, "Interview with Robert and Grant Shapiro," *Larry King Live,* aired October 21, 2005, http://transcripts.cnn.com/TRANSCRIPTS/0510/21/lkl.01.html.
9. C. Pelisek, "Brent Shapiro's Final Hours," *LA Weekly,* November 25–December 1, 2005.
10. G. E. Vaillant, *The Natural History of Alcoholism,* rev. ed. (Cambridge, MA: Harvard University Press, 1995).
11. L. D. Johnston, P. M. O'Malley, and J. E. Schulenberg, *Monitoring the Future National Survey Results on Drug Use, 1975–2004*: Volume II, College Students and Adults Ages 19–45, NIH Publication No. 04–5508 (Bethesda, MD: National Institute on Drug Abuse, 2005).
12. S. Moran, H. Wechsler, and N. A. Rigotti, "Social Smoking Among US College Students," *Pediatrics* 114 (2004): 1028–34.
13. K. Bjartveit and A. Tverdal, "Health Consequences of Smoking 1–4 Cigarettes a Day," *Tobacco Control* 14 (2005): 315–20.
14. I am indebted to Michael Males for pointing out these and other trends in drug use. See M. Males, "Social Smoking by University of California Students," University of California, Santa Cruz, Sociology Department, draft, December 1, 2005.

Ten **Making Treatment Work**

1. See D. A. Dawson, B. F. Grant, F. S. Stinson, et al., "Recovery from DSM-IV Alcohol Dependence: United States, 2001–2002," *Addiction* 100 (2005): 281–92.
2. M. Szalavitz, *Help at Any Cost* (New York: Riverhead Books, 2006), 33.
3. D. L. Rosenhan, "On Being Sane in Insane Places," *Science* 179 (1973): 250–58.
4. S. Peele, C. Bufe, and A. Brodsky, *Resisting 12-Step Coercion* (Tucson, AZ: See Sharp, 2000).
5. M. Ferri, L. Amato, and M. Davoli, "Review: Alcoholics Anonymous and Other 12-Step Programmes for Alcohol Dependence," *Cochrane Database of Systematic Reviews* 3 (2006), http://www.mrw.interscience.wiley.com/cochrane/clsysrev/articles/CD005032/frame.html.
6. W. R. Miller, P. L. Wilbourne, and J. E. Hettema, "What Works? A Summary of Alcohol Treatment Outcome Research," in R. K. Hester and W. R. Miller, eds., *Handbook of Alcoholism Treatment Approaches: Effective Alternatives,* 3rd ed. (Boston: Allyn and Bacon, 2003), 13–63.
7. L. A. Kaskutas, J. Bond, and K. Humphreys, "Social Networks as Mediators of the Effect of Alcoholics Anonymous," *Addiction* 97 (2002): 891–900.
8. Szalavitz, *Help at Any Cost.*

9. Ibid.

10. Miller, Wilbourne, and Hettema, "What Works?"

11. As far as I am aware, this treatment has been tested only in the UK. UKATT Research Team, "Effectiveness of Treatment for Alcohol Problems: Findings of the Randomised UK Alcohol Treatment Trial (UKATT)," *British Medical Journal* 331 (2005): 541–43.

12. The research and theory in support of motivational interviewing, as well as detailed descriptions of its practice, are presented in W. R. Miller and S. Rollnick, eds., *Motivational Interviewing: Preparing People for Change,* 2nd ed. (New York: Guilford Press, 2002).

13. Modified from W. R. Miller, "Enhancing Motivation for Change," in R. K. Hester and W. R. Miller, eds., *Handbook of Alcoholism Treatment Approaches: Effective Alternatives,* 3rd ed. (Boston: Allyn and Bacon, 2003), 137–38.

14. Miller, Wilbourne, and Hettema, "What Works?" review the evidence for the effectiveness of brief interventions for alcoholism. For use of brief interventions in cocaine and heroin use, see J. Bernstein, E. Bernstein, K. Tassiopoulos, et al., "Brief Motivational Intervention at a Clinic Visit Reduces Cocaine and Heroin Use," *Drug and Alcohol Dependence* 77 (2005): 49–59.

15. N. P. Barnett, T. O. Tevyaw, K. Fromme, et al., "Brief Alcohol Interventions with Mandated or Adjudicated College Students," *Alcoholism: Clinical and Experimental Research* 28 (2004): 966–75.

16. R. J. Meyers and B. L. Wolfe, *Get Your Loved One Sober: Alternatives to Nagging, Pleading, and Threatening* (Center City, MN: Hazelden, 2004).

17. S. W. Hengeller, S. F. Mihalic, L. Rone, et al., *Blueprints for Violence Prevention, Book 6: Multisystemic Therapy* (Boulder, CO: Center for the Study and Prevention of Violence, 1998).

18. Ibid.

Eleven Policies for a Non-Addicted America

1. Substance Abuse and Mental Health Services Administration, U.S. Department of Health and Human Services, "Model Programs: Effective Substance Abuse and Mental Health Programs for Every Community," March 7, 2005, http://modelprograms.samhsa.gov/template_cf.cfm?page =effective_list.

Appendix B Government Watchdog Agency Report Finding Government Media Program Ineffective Understates the Case

1. U.S. Government Accountability Office, *ONDCP Media Campaign: Contractor's National Evaluation Did Not Find That the Youth Anti-Drug Campaign Was Effective in Reducing Youth Drug Use,* Government Publication No. GAO-06-818 (Washington, DC: U.S. Government Printing Office, 2006), www.gao.gov/new.items/d06818.pdf.
2. Join Together, "GAO Calls for ONDCP to Prove $1-Billion Media Campaign Works," August 28, 2006, www.jointogether.org/news/head lines/inthenews/2006/gao-calls-for-ondcp-to-prove.html.

Appendix C Harm Reduction for Drug Addicts

1. J. Normand, D. Vlahov, and L. E. Moses, eds., *Preventing HIV Transmission: The Role of Sterile Needles and Bleach* (Washington, DC: National Academy Press, 1995); R. H. Needle, S. L. Coyle, J. Normand, et al., "HIV Prevention with Drug-Using Populations—Current Status and Future Prospects: Introduction and Overview," *Public Health Reports* 113, suppl. 1 (1998): 4–18.

ACKNOWLEDGMENTS

I am forever indebted to five people who enriched my message and skill in presenting it. Amy McCarley, in addition to providing editorial comments, opened her store of experience to help me understand the people in these pages. Barbara Ensor not only edited significant parts of the manuscript, she altered my entire approach to writing. In addition to suggesting the topic, Archie Brodsky was the glue that held this project together. Julian Pavia, my editor at Random House, went beyond the call of duty in his contributions. And Anna Peele gave me a kid's-eye view of the subject matter, as well as being a gift to everyone in her family.

Ruth Meyler read every chapter in this book, taking the time to dot my "i"s and cross my "t"s. Amy, Barbara, Archie, Anna, Vicki Rowland, and Marie Viljoen made helpful inputs on the title, cover design, and other production matters. My cousin, Rich Fromberg, assisted with comments and emotional support. I also acknowledge with appreciation the support of Ana Kosok, Synn Stern, Charlotte Wallace, Alice Rogers-Pearlman, Rich Dowling, Susan Akers, Anne Smith and her family, and my adult children, Dana and Haley Peele, and their mates.

Nancy Love's role as my agent does not adequately convey her generosity and helpfulness. I am also grateful to Drs. Michele Kinderman and Richard Samuels for the chance to work as a psychologist while having time to write this book. Professors McWelling Todman and Lala Straussner offered me opportunities to sharpen my ideas while teaching at, respectively, New School University's Department of Psychology and New York University's School of Social Work. Ernie Drucker, John Davies, and Douglas Cameron have provided me with the invaluable opportunity to serve as an editor of the journal *Addiction Research and Theory*. Ethan Nadelmann and Mitch Earleywine have always supported my professional efforts and thinking.

Maia Szalavitz generously shared her vast store of knowledge and personal experience in the treatment field. Marsha Rosenbaum, Rod Skager, Charles Reis, Beth Fraster, and Rosie McMahon kept me in touch with the most advanced thinking in interactive drug education, as Andrew Tatarsky, Phil Harris, Allan Clear, Pat Denning, Edith Springer, Alan Marlatt, and Ana Kosok did with harm-reduction treatment. Ona Kondrotas informed me of some European approaches to harm reduction for young people. Michael Males provided information and insights on the changing land-scape of youthful substance use in the United States. Ted McDaniel is one of several readers of my work who pointed me toward criti-cal sources of information.

Last, I appreciate beyond words the struggles and humanity of those depicted in the cases in this book, people who showed me how complex—but reversible—addiction is.

INDEX

INDEX

ABOUT THE AUTHOR

STANTON PEELE is a psychologist and attorney in New Jersey. He has pioneered ideas and treatment for addiction for thirty years, including harm reduction, relationship and other nonsubstance addictions, and motivational and solution-focused therapy. Among his books are *Love and Addiction, The Meaning of Addiction, Diseasing of America, The Truth About Addiction and Recovery*, and *7 Tools to Beat Addiction*. He has published more than 150 professional and popular articles in the field. Dr. Peele has won the Mark Keller Award presented by the Rutgers Center of Alcohol Studies and the Career Achievement Award in Scholarship from the Drug Policy Alliance. He is an adjunct professor in New School University's Psychology Department, where he teaches clinical approaches to substance abuse and adolescent treatment and prevention. Dr. Peele is associate editor of the journal *Addiction Research and Theory*. He maintains a Web site at www.peele.net through which he provides coaching for addiction-related issues.